—— {keys} ——
to
Great Writing

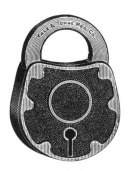

Stephen Wilbers

WRITER'S DIGEST BOOKS
CINCINNATI, OHIO
www.writersdigest.com

Keys to Great Writing. Copyright © 2000 by Stephen Wilbers. Manufactured in the United States of America. All rights reserved. No part of this book may be reproduced in any form or by any electronic or mechanical means including information storage and retrieval systems without permission in writing from the publisher, except by a reviewer, who may quote brief passages in a review. Published by Writer's Digest Books, an imprint of F+W Publications, Inc., 4700 East Galbraith Road, Cincinnati, Ohio 45236. (800) 289-0963. First paperback edition 2007.

Visit our Web site at www.writersdigest.com for information on more resources for writers.

To receive a free weekly e-mail newsletter delivering tips and updates about writing and about Writer's Digest products, send an e-mail with "Subscribe Newsletter" in the body of the message to newsletter-request@writersdigest.com, or register directly at our Web site at www.writersdigest.com.

11   10   09   5   4   3

Library of Congress has catalogued hardcover edition as follows:

Wilbers, Stephen
    Keys to great writing / by Stephen Wilbers.
      p. cm.
    Includes bibliographical references and index.
    ISBN-13: 978-0-89879-932-3 (hc : alk. paper)
    ISBN-10: 0-89879-932-5 (hc : alk. paper)
      1. English language—Rhetoric—Handbooks, manuals, etc. 2. English language—Grammar—Handbooks, manuals, etc. I. Title.

PE1408.W58198   2000
808'.042—dc21   00-042302
                                                                      CIP
    ISBN-13: 978-1-58297-492-7 (pbk. : alk. paper)
    ISBN-10: 1-58297-492-6 (pbk. : alk. paper)

Edited by Jack Heffron and Michelle Howry
Designed by Sandy Conopeotis Kent
Cover designed by Matthew Gaynor
Production coordinated by Sara Dumford

"Harlem" from *Collected Poems* by Langston Hughes. Copyright © 1994 by the Estate of Langston Hughes. Reprinted by permission of Alfred A. Knopf, a Division of Random House.

Portions of this book have been published previously in *The College Board Review*, the *Minneapolis Star and Tribune*, and in two self-published collections of columns: *Writing for Business* (The Good Writing Press, 1993) and *Writing With Wilbers* (The Good Writing Press, 1995).

{Acknowledgments}

Every writer needs a good editor, and I have been fortunate to have the able assistance of Steve Blake, Madeline Hamermesh, Sally Lederer, and Susan Peterson in writing and revising an early draft of this book. I want to express particular appreciation to Steve Blake, who offered encouragement and insight during our many pleasant runs along the Minnehaha Creek and around Lake Harriet, and to Susan Peterson, who edits my column for the *Minneapolis Star Tribune*, whose care and dedication to her craft are an inspiration, and who has never once yelled at me for missing a deadline. I also want to offer special thanks to my wife's mother Dorothy, whose pride I take pride in, and to my wife Debbie and children Eddy and Kate, whose love and support are always with me.

{Dedication}

To my parents, Larry Wilbers and Margaret Stevens

{About the Author}

Stephen Wilbers is a writing consultant, syndicated columnist, and award-winning author. He teaches at the University of Minnesota and at Hamline University, where he won a 1995 Outstanding Faculty Award. Since December 1991, he has written a weekly column on effective writing, which appears in the *Minneapolis Star Tribune* and other newspapers. He has published two collections of his columns, *Writing for Business* (winner of a 1994 Minnesota Book Award) and *Writing by Wilbers.* For his Ph.D. dissertation he wrote a history of the Iowa Writers' Workshop, which was published by the University of Iowa Press.

Steve was born in Cincinnati, Ohio. He earned his B.A. at Vanderbilt University, and his M.A. and Ph.D. at the University of Iowa. He spent his junior year abroad in Aix-en-Provence, where he fell in love with the French language and the Cours Mirabeau. As a 1985 Visiting Fulbright Fellow at the University of Essex, he lived for five months in Wivenhoe, England, accompanied by his wife, Debbie, and two young children, Eddy and Kate. He and his wife now live in Minneapolis, which affords him easy access to the Boundary Waters Canoe Area Wilderness of northern Minnesota, where he and his father—along with various family members and friends—have taken annual canoe trips for the past twenty-two years. At the University of Minnesota, he directed one of the largest student academic support services operations in the country before serving as Associate Director of the Program in Creative and Professional Writing. Since 1990, he has worked full time as a student and teacher of writing.

For sample columns, writing exercises, and links to writing resources on the Internet, visit his Web page at www.wilbers.com.

{Table of Contents}

{PART THREE}

Drafting and Revising

{ Foreword }

What are the keys to great writing?

In my work as a part-time college professor, writing consultant, and newspaper columnist, I am often asked that question. Not always in those words, but in words to that effect. How do I make my writing vivid and memorable? How do I set myself apart from other writers? How do I convey my personality, my point of view, my values? How do I learn to write with style?

Taking the last question first, I suggest that you do three things: read, study, and practice. Read good writers, study specific stylistic techniques, and practice applying those techniques. The first activity, reading, will help you develop your style over time (and offer you other immeasurable benefits and pleasures along the way). The other two activities, study and practice, are more intentional, self-conscious endeavors. They involve analyzing and imitating proven techniques to produce predictable results.

As many authors before me have said, to develop your style, begin with simplicity. The nineteenth-century English critic and essayist Matthew Arnold declared: "People think I can teach them style. What stuff it is. Have something to say and say it as clearly as you can. That is the only secret of style."

Say what you have to say. Say it simply and directly. To improve your style, begin by reducing your writing to its essential elements. Then build. Finally—with caution and at some risk—embellish. Add flourish if it suits you (and if it suits your audience and subject), keeping in mind that flourish is not the same as fluff. Even as you attempt elegance, your principal goal should be clarity.

In *The Elements of Style*, William Strunk and E. B. White warn against "all mannerisms, tricks, adornments." They advise the writer to approach style by way of "plainness, simplicity, orderliness, sincerity." In *On Writing Well*, William Zinsser says, "you have to strip down your writing before you can build it back up," and he offers his own "cardinal goals" of good writing: "humanity, clarity, simplicity, vitality." In *Style: Ten Lessons in Clarity and Grace*, Joseph Williams includes a cluster of techniques for writing concisely as one of his ten lessons. Those three books, read and studied by countless writers, form the foundation for this book, and I want to acknowledge my debt to them, as well as to the many other sources I cite throughout my text.

In this book, I present five keys to great writing: economy, precision, action, music, and personality. Economy involves rejecting the notion that more is necessarily better. As Strunk and White point out, economy doesn't mean that every sentence must be short, but that every word must count.

The second key, precision, has to do with your command of language, your ability to use just the right word to capture your meaning, to say exactly what you mean, and to say it memorably. That's where reading makes a difference. Reading helps you develop a good ear, and you need a good ear to know which word is best. Compare *elderly* with *old* and *ocean* with *sea*, for example, and you'll understand why Hemingway didn't call his tale *The Elderly Man and the Sea* or *The Old Man and the Ocean*.

Action and music are the keys that add energy and vitality to your writing. Action has to do with making your sentences tell stories. It is created by using verbs, rather than nouns, to express your meaning. Compare "The previously undisclosed evidence caused irreparable harm to the prosecutor's case" with "The previously undisclosed evidence destroyed the prosecutor's case." The first sentence is static, the second dynamic.

The fourth key, music, has to do with the rhythm and the sound of language. Sometimes you establish a rhythm, as Samuel Johnson did when he wrote, "What is written without effort is in general read without pleasure." And sometimes you offer variety, as accomplished writers do when they follow a long, complex sentence with a short, snappy one. Like this.

The fifth key, personality, goes beyond language to the reader's sense of the person behind the words. To grasp the importance of personality, think of a novel you read long ago. The one thing that stays with you—even after you have forgotten the characters, the setting, and the plot—is your sense of the writer as a person. Your perception of the author's personality or presence is like a residue that lingers long after everything else has vanished. That residue is style in its most profound sense.

There are, to be sure, other components of effective writing. To be a competent writer, you must understand purpose, point of view, organization, support, and coherence, and you must know how to use them to your advantage. But these elements have more to do with the craft of writing than the art. Working effectively with purpose, point of view, organization, support, and coherence will make you a competent writer, but they won't necessarily make you a great writer. Your style, on the other hand, represents the essence of who you are. It distinguishes you from every other writer on the planet.

Learn the five keys to great writing. Understand the five elements of composition. Practice the techniques relating to both. Do these things, and you'll be on your way.

And don't forget the real reason you write. Behind the language, beyond the techniques, is the greatest gift you have to offer: yourself.

{ Introduction }

What distinguishes writing that is exceptional and well crafted from writing that is nondescript and ordinary? What does it mean to "write with style"?

In *The Elements of Style*, E. B. White acknowledges the difficulty in defining style:

> There is no satisfactory explanation of style, no infallible guide to good writing, no assurance that a person who thinks clearly will be able to write clearly, no key that unlocks the door, no inflexible rule by which the young writer may shape his course.

As White asserts, style defies neat definition. But look more closely at White's sentence. Read it out loud. Listen to its cadence. Even as White acknowledges that style cannot be satisfactorily explained, his writing exemplifies style. He gives his sentence a pleasing sound by using a simple device—the repetition of the word *no*. To appreciate the effect of this device, simply remove it: "There isn't any satisfactory explanation of style, infallible guide to good writing, assurance that a person who thinks clearly will be able to write clearly, key that unlocks the door, or inflexible rule by which the young writer may shape his course." Stripped of its distinguishing feature, the sentence is limp, like a window shade with a broken spring.

On a surface level, style—or at least stylistic technique—is easily described and imitated. You can appropriate any stylistic technique you like and use it for your own purposes. You can study White's style. You can analyze and imitate White's word choice and sentence structure. With practice, you even can incorporate certain features of White's style into your own stylistic repertoire. But, in all likelihood, you cannot write as White writes—at least not consistently and not over time. You cannot be E. B. White.

I am talking now about style on two levels: surface style and deep style. Surface style has to do with technique. It is acquired by deliberate study and practice. It can be put on, like a suit of clothes, to achieve a particular effect. Deep style, on the other hand, has to do with who you are, both as a writer and a person. It results from genuine self-exploration, self-discovery, and self-revelation. It is developed over time, sometimes over a lifetime.

In its deeper meaning, style has as much to do with the reader's perception of the writer as a person as it does with the writer's use of language. Take Kurt Vonnegut as an example. How would you describe his style? Would you say it is lively? Fast-paced? Humorous? Irreverent? Cynical? Now, are you describing your perception of Vonnegut's writing, or your perception of Vonnegut as a person? Are you describing his use of language or his personality? At some point, the distinction blurs. Style and person become one.

Similarly, style and content are inseparable. Consider the power that White gives his sentence by rhythmically repeating the word *no*. The stripped-down version, though unchanged in content, lacks the authority of the original.

Again using White's style as an example, note how he refers to his former college professor, William Strunk, Jr., and how he describes the book they coauthored: "Will himself had hung the tag 'little' on the book." Had White stopped there, he would have made his point clearly and capably. But White continues, "He referred to it sardonically and with secret pride as 'the *little* book,' always giving the word 'little' a special twist, as though he were putting a spin on a ball." And in that elaboration, we hear White's voice. With that special twist and that little spin, we get a sense of E. B. White the man, the writer, the person behind the words.

Later, in acknowledging the difference between his former professor's more prescriptive approach to writing and his own more intuitive approach, White builds on the baseball analogy, again offering a glimpse of his personality and character:

> I suppose I have written *the fact that* a thousand times in the heat of composition, revised it out maybe five hundred times in the cool aftermath. To be batting only .500 this late in the season, to fail half the time to connect with this fat pitch, saddens me, for it seems a betrayal of the man who showed me how to swing at it and made the swinging seem worth while.

What sets White's style apart from that of other skilled writers? Is it his playful use of metaphor, his unhurried pace, his willingness to pause to embellish his point by connecting it with just the right image or experience from everyday life? What stylistic features account for his achieving a reputation not only as one of America's great essayists, but also as the writer of *Charlotte's Web, Stuart Little, The Trumpet of the Swan,* and other delightful children's stories?

We may differ in our appreciation of his particular traits, but we are left with the same general impression: White writes with personality. He conveys intelligence, warmth, lightheartedness. He re-creates himself in, and through, his writing. He makes us enjoy his company and want to be in his presence.

In response to the age-old questions, Can style be learned? Or does it develop naturally? I say, yes and yes.

My intent in writing this book is to help you achieve a higher competence, to help you write more clearly, emphatically, and memorably, whatever your present level of development. The five elements of style, the five elements of composition, the approach to drafting and revising—all apply to you, whether you are young or old, and whether you want to improve your effectiveness in creative writing, on-the-job writing, or college course work.

As you read this book, I invite you to consider your goals and assess your strengths and weaknesses. And as you do, I ask that you not be your own worst enemy. Don't make assumptions about yourself and your skills that are self-limiting. There are four myths in particular that can prevent you from realizing your potential as a writer:

Myth #1: Only people with natural ability can learn to write well. According to "the myth of the chosen few," either you've got talent or you don't. If you've got it, writing comes easily; if you don't, you'll never be more than a duffer.

The reality is that anyone with average intelligence and commitment can become a competent writer. As Marvin Bell, a poet and longtime faculty member in the Iowa Writers' Workshop, is fond of saying, talent is cheap. What counts is determination.

Myth #2: People who are good in math and science are inherently incapable of using language effectively. Equally limiting is the assumption that certain types of skills are mutually exclusive. If you are good with numbers, the thinking goes, you can't be good with words.

But there are too many examples of talented and accomplished technical writers for this to be true. (Charles Darwin, Marie Curie, Stephen Jay Gould, and Lewis Thomas come to mind.) Furthermore, certain traits—such as a penchant for concentrating on specific, concrete detail and the ability to think logically—are characteristic of both science-minded and language-minded people. Like "the myth of the chosen few," the "technically-minded-people-can't-write myth" can serve as a convenient excuse for inattention and lack of effort.

Myth #3: Achieving writing competence is a matter of learning to avoid errors. Avoiding mistakes that interfere with precision or undermine credibility is crucial. If you fail to convey a basic grasp of language in your writing, nothing else really matters. Regrettably, many writers, even college graduates, make so many significant and distracting errors that questions of correctness necessarily take precedence over more interesting issues of viewpoint, persuasive strategy, and style.

At the same time, truly competent writing is more than a matter of correctness. As Joseph Williams reminds us in *Style: Ten Lessons in Clarity and Grace*, "A writer who obsesses on usage can write in ways that are entirely correct but wholly unreadable." According to Williams, we should put good usage "in its place—behind us—before we move on to more important matters."

Myth #4: Learning to write well is easy if you just learn the right tricks. No matter how tempting it is for teachers of writing—me included—to try to make it seem easy, writing is a complicated, challenging endeavor, and acquiring proficiency requires years of careful study and discipline.

This is not to say that there are no simple principles and easy-to-learn techniques. In fact, there are many—a sentence has two natural stress points, a conventionally structured paragraph has three parts, an organizational statement is usually presented as the last sentence in an opening paragraph—but genuine competence involves more than prescription and formula. It also involves a feeling for language that comes from close association and familiarity, like the intimacy that develops between longtime friends.

So I invite you to set aside these myths and ask yourself: What are your expectations of yourself as a writer? How good do you want to be? Are you satisfied if you can get the job done—that is, if you can get your point across without making distracting errors in spelling, grammar, usage, and punctuation? (Nothing to apologize for there.) Or do you expect more of yourself than basic competence?

Here is a self-assessment you can use to place yourself at one of four levels of writing expectations. Check every item that applies to you.

{ Self-Assessment }

My goals are:

Level 1: Basic Competence
- To express my ideas clearly and concisely
- To write correctly (or avoid the most obvious and common errors that might undermine my credibility)
- To have confidence in my writing skills

Level 2: Above-Average Competence
- To write with emphasis and personality
- To produce text that is nearly error-free
- To be comfortable writing in various styles and formats for various audiences
- To look for occasions and seek out opportunities to express my ideas in writing
- To publish an article in a newsletter, newspaper, magazine, or journal

Level 3: Exceptional Competence
- To command language with remarkable precision and nuance
- To be recognized in my company or organization as a knowledgeable and reliable source of information on grammar, punctuation, usage, and style
- To publish articles on a regular basis or to publish a book that is reviewed favorably by critics, or both

Level 4: Extraordinary Competence
- To establish a national or international reputation as an unusually talented and gifted writer
- To write with such extraordinary insight and beauty that people will be reading what I have written one hundred years from now

The fourth category pertains to those writers who aspire to greatness, who long to create an enduring work of art that will live for centuries. For them, I think the desire to write comes from an impulse to preserve, to bring order from chaos, to leave something of themselves behind for posterity, and, in a sense, to achieve immortality. Although few people are willing to devote a significant portion of their lives to creating a literary masterpiece, many dream of doing so, and for them writing will always hold a certain fascination.

Now for the more important question: Do your expectations exceed your performance? If so, what are you currently doing to attain your desired level of competence?

If your answer is "nothing" or "not much," I hope this book will motivate you to start making significant progress toward achieving your goals. I hope it will inspire you to look for opportunities to apply the advice I offer to your daily writing, to start working on a few techniques at a time. As you commit yourself to improving your writing, remember that genuine progress takes time. Don't expect to accomplish everything at once.

Just as you have expectations of yourself, I also have expectations of you. To make significant improvement in your writing, you need to possess—or cultivate—the following attributes:

Confidence. You need to believe that your efforts to improve your writing will make a difference, that the precious time and energy you carve out of your busy schedule and devote to self-improvement will pay off in ways that are observable and significant.

You need to have confidence not so much in your present writing skills as in your ability to learn and develop new skills. You need to believe that writing is a learnable skill and that you possess the intelligence and aptitude to get the job done.

Self-knowledge. You need to have a realistic awareness of your strengths and your weaknesses. You need to know what you do well and what you do poorly as a writer.

You need to go beyond generalities, to assess your performance in specific, definable areas, such as expression (word choice that is appropriate to the purpose, audience, and material), clarity of purpose (an effective central argument), organization (coherent arrangement of material), support (evidence that is relevant, specific, detailed, sufficient, and persuasive), and correctness (conformity to rules of spelling, grammar, usage, and punctuation).

Attention/learning mode. You need to open your mind to learning new information (or perhaps recapturing old information). You need to free yourself of distractions and to place yourself in an attentive, learning mode. You need to become fully absorbed with the task and the material at hand.

Commitment and determination. You need to really want to improve. You need to recognize that nobody can teach you how to write, but with the right guidance and the right materials, you can teach yourself a great deal. You need to commit the necessary time and to protect that time from competing demands.

Practice/follow-through. You need to practice your newly learned skills to keep from losing or forgetting them. You need to drill yourself, to return to each lesson, to work with each technique until it becomes second nature for you. You need to think long term rather than short term. You need to stay with it.

If you possess these attributes, I believe you can learn to write not only with clarity and emphasis, but with personality and style.

{PART ONE}

Keys to Great Writing

CHAPTER 1: ECONOMY

Make Every Word Count
TRY YOUR HAND AT EDITING A POEM.

TRUST A WORD TO DO ITS WORK.

Use Fourteen Techniques to Eliminate Wordiness
EDIT FOR PATTERNS OF WORDINESS.

1. Delete redundant modifiers.
2. Delete redundant categories.
3. Replace redundant word pairs with single words.
4. Replace wordy expressions with single words.
5. Delete "hollow" hedges and meaningless intensifiers.
6. Delete needless repetition.
7. Delete *that* for brevity; retain *that* for clarity.

KNOW HOW TO START; KNOW WHEN TO STOP.

8. Avoid protracted introductions.
9. Use *it*, *there*, and *what* constructions carefully.
10. Trim sentence endings for closing emphasis.

TAKE THE MOST DIRECT ROUTE.

11. Prefer action verbs to nominalizations.
12. Avoid indirect negatives.
13. Avoid needless attribution.
14. Limit personal commentary.

REVIEW THE FOURTEEN TECHNIQUES.

CHAPTER ONE

{Economy}

Make Every Word Count

If I could teach only one key to great writing, it would be this: *Make every word count.*

Use words sparingly, as if you were planting a garden one seed at a time—not throwing out handfuls of seed willy-nilly, hoping a few kernels might land in the right spot and take hold. Get the full value out of every word you write. Recognize the power of a single well-chosen word. Trust it to do its work. As a rule, the more economically you use language, the more powerfully you will deliver your message.

The difference between wastefulness and frugality—and the difference in the reader's perception of you—can be dramatic. Compare, for example, "In the unlikely eventuality that you encounter various and sundry difficulties with the above-referenced project, apprise me of the situation at your earliest convenience" with "Let me know if you have any problems." Sometimes the difference is subtle. Compare "I added three more cities to my itinerary" with "I added three cities to my itinerary."

Economy of language is, of course, only one characteristic of an accomplished style. Other factors, such as colorful word choice and specific detail, also play a part. The sentence "I added three cities to my itinerary" is concise, but it is less engaging than "I added Aix-en-Provence, Cannes, and Nice to the itinerary of my long-delayed tour of southern France."

Try your hand at editing a poem.

The following exercise illustrates the power of making every word count. I have taken a well-crafted, concisely written poem by Langston Hughes and ruined its compact effect by junking it up—or, if you prefer, weighing it down—with unnecessary words. See if you can restore the poem's beauty and power by deleting the words I have added. No words need be added—only deleted—to arrive at the poem as Hughes wrote it. One word must be cut in half.

Listen carefully to each word as you read my corrupted version of the poem out loud. Use your ear. You will probably be able to identify most of the extraneous language, even if you don't know the poem and even if you're not a poet.

What Life Is Like in Harlem
What happens to a dream that has been deferred for a time?

Does it dry up
Like the way a raisin does when it's in the sun for a while?
Or does it fester like the way an ugly sore would—
And then after that does it run and run?
Does it stink like rotten meat would smell to you?
Or does it sort of crust and sugar over—you know—
Like the way a syrupy sweet would?

Maybe though it just sags in a downward motion
Like the way a heavy load would sag.

Or does it on the other hand explode like a bomb would?

The place to begin cutting is the title: "What Life Is Like in Harlem" is easily reduced to "Life in Harlem." But keep going. Be ruthless. Make *every* word count.

The title of the poem as Hughes wrote it is, quite simply, "Harlem." After all, what else would a poem titled "Harlem" be about but "What Life Is Like in Harlem"?

After you have tried your hand at deleting the rest of the unnecessary language in the poem, compare your edited version with the poem as Hughes wrote it. (The words I added to create the exercise are marked with brackets and underlining.)

[What Life Is Like in] Harlem

What happens to a dream [that has been] deferred [for a time]?

Does it dry up
Like [the way] a raisin [does when it's] in the sun [for a while]?
Or does it fester like [the way] a[n ugly] sore [would]—
And then [after that does it run and] run?
Does it stink like rotten meat [would smell to you]?
Or [does it sort of] crust and sugar over[—you know—]
Like [the way] a syrupy sweet [would]?

Maybe [though] it just sags [in a downward motion]
Like [the way] a heavy load [would sag].

Or does it [on the other hand] explode [like a bomb would]?

Removing 59 unnecessary words reduces the text (including the title) from 113 to 54 words and uncovers a great poem. Read the pared-down version out loud and listen for two things: First, it's more concise, more rhythmic. The rhyme is uncovered. The words have a more pleasing sound. Second, and more significant, the leaner version conveys a decidedly different impression of the person behind the words. The poet, who in the first version sounded irresolute, now comes across as decisive, dynamic, emphatic, commanding. Beneath the unnecessary words lay a powerful poem, but its power was obscured by needless language, much as the beauty of an unfinished sculpture is obscured by the remaining stone. (We writers have an advantage over sculptors: If in our zeal to make every word count we inadvertently remove something important, we can easily restore it.)

Trust a word to do its work.

From this simple illustration, we can draw a powerful lesson in style: Whenever we can say in one word what it took us six words to say in our first draft (as we saw in editing the title from "What Life Is Like in Harlem" to "Harlem"), we have probably improved our copy.

Wordy writers tend to be people who don't trust a word to do its work, so they surround it with a few extra words for good measure. Writers who command language with energy and precision, on the other hand, understand the power of a single well-chosen word. It's a question not only of habits of speech but also of orientation toward language. Wordy writers don't fully trust language; concise writers do.

Make every word count. Using words economically is a matter of trusting language. I suspect that E. B. White had this in mind when he wrote, "Style takes its final shape more from attitudes of mind than from principles of composition." If you don't trust each word to do its work, you will use more words than needed. Respect the power of language.

Use Fourteen Techniques to Eliminate Wordiness

Nearly every handbook you pick up extols the virtues of concise writing. Not many handbooks, however, offer detailed advice on *how* to write concisely. What follows are fourteen editing techniques that will help you eliminate wordiness.

Keep in mind that these techniques are meant to guide you in your editing, not in your drafting. (I discuss stages of writing in Part 3.) In fact, when you are creating your text—when you are trying to find the words that capture your thoughts and hoping to build momentum—don't give these principles and techniques a thought. Just let the words flow (or fly, if they will), knowing you will come back later and edit meticulously, even ruthlessly. Trust your ability to decide which words are air-worthy and which should be grounded.

Edit for patterns of wordiness.

Do what experienced editors do: Think in terms of categories of wordiness rather than isolated instances. Train yourself to distinguish between words that convey meaning and words that do not.

Redundancy is a problem for many writers. As Joseph Williams points out in *Style*, there are three common types: redundant modifiers (in which the modifier implies the meaning of the word modified, as in *past memories, personal beliefs, important essentials,* and *consensus of opinion*); redundant categories (in which the category is implied by the word, as in *large in size, pink in color, extreme in degree,* and *honest in character*); and redundant word pairs (in which the second word reiterates the meaning of the first, as in *first and foremost, hopes and desires, full and complete, precious and few,* and—if I may drop the italics—so on and so forth).

1. Delete redundant modifiers.

Both Mark Twain and Ernest Hemingway cautioned writers against the careless use of modifiers. The challenge in eliminating redundant modifiers, however, is that familiarity breeds complacence. The more frequently we hear and read certain word combinations, the more acceptable they begin to sound and the more likely we are to use them unthinkingly—not because they are the best, most natural and concise way to say what we have to say, but simply because they sound familiar.

Isn't that a true fact? (A *true fact?*) The *end result*—a phrase as redundant as a *new initiative*—is wordy writing.

When editing, look closely at your modifiers. Make certain they don't repeat the meanings of the words they modify. (Aren't *facts* always *true?* Don't *results* always occur at the *end?* Aren't *initiatives* always *new?*) If they do, delete them. There is no point in repeating the same idea twice. *(Repeating twice?)*

Here are some commonly used redundant modifiers:

active consideration	new initiatives
basic essentials	past history
basic fundamentals	past memories
climb up	personal beliefs
completely finish	personal opinions
consensus of opinion	present status
descend down	refer back
each individual	repeat twice
end result	sudden crisis
final outcome	terrible tragedy
free gift	true fact
future plan	various different
important essentials	

In any event, it is my personal opinion that one of the important essentials and basic fundamentals of good writing is to avoid wasting the reader's time with needless and otherwise unnecessary words. Don't you agree?

2. Delete redundant categories.

When a word implies its category, don't write both the word and the category. For instance, *round in shape, heavy in weight,* and *pink in color* are redundant because we know that *round* is a *shape, heavy* is a *weight,* and *pink* is a *color.*

Avoid these and other redundant categories:

area of mathematics	odd in appearance
at an early time	period in time
extreme in degree	period of time
heavy in weight	pink in color
honest in character	round/square in shape
in a confused state	shiny in appearance
of a strange type	unusual in nature
of a cheap quality	

Remember: Redundant categories can leave your reader in a confused state of mind that is extreme in degree and perplexing in nature.

3. Replace redundant word pairs with single words.

The third type of redundancy, *redundant pairing,* has a long tradition in English. The habit was given a boost by—of all things—the Norman Conquest, beginning with the battle of Hastings in 1066, when King Harold of England was defeated by Duke William of Normandy. During the subsequent rule by Norman nobles, approximately 10,000 French and Latin-based words were assimilated into the English language. Of these, some 7,500 are still in use today.

As Bill Bryson points out in *The Mother Tongue: English and How It Got That Way,* English speakers are presented with choices that many languages simply do not offer. We operate in a language that is extraordinarily rich, not only in quantity of words (the *American Heritage Dictionary* contains more than 200,000 entries) but also in synonyms, or words and expressions that have the same or nearly the same meaning. We can choose, for example, to offer someone either *a hearty welcome* (using words derived from the old Anglo-Saxon words) or *a cordial reception* (using words that come to us from Latin via French). The wording we choose depends on the tone and nuance we desire.

The problem with having such a plethora of choices is that we tend to pile words on rather than choose one word and stick with it. Availing ourselves of too many of these wonderful possibilities when expressing a simple thought can lead to wordiness—or, if you prefer, prolixity, verbosity, loquaciousness, and grandiloquence. See what I mean?

Redundant pairing became more deeply ingrained in English usage when the disenfranchised Anglo-Saxons began borrowing words from the Norman nobles (just as earlier Anglo-Saxons borrowed from their Roman conquerors and, before that, the ancient Celts borrowed from their Anglo-Saxon conquerors). The Anglo-Saxons thought the borrowed word sounded more learned, and so they got in the habit of pairing it with a familiar native word. And here we are, more than nine centuries later, still pairing our words. (Who said habits of speech were easy to break?)

The following pairings are common in speech, where rhythm plays an especially important role in how we perceive language, but they should be avoided in writing:

any and all	one and only
basic and fundamental	over and done with
each and every	peace and quiet
few and far between	precious and few
first and foremost	true and accurate
full and complete	various and sundry
hope and desire	and so on and so forth

One type of specialized writing, legal writing, has its own idiom of word pairs, such as *free and clear, full and complete, null and void,* and *suffer or permit.* Although some lawyers defend these phrases as traditional terms of art, others avoid them. In *Plain English for Lawyers,* Richard Wydick argues against their use unless "you want your writing to have a musty, formbook smell," in which case "by all means use as many coupled synonyms as you can find." Wydick also notes, however, that according to David Mellinkoff in *Mellinkoff's Dictionary of American Legal Usage,* "[a] few coupled synonyms have become so 'welded by usage' that they act as a single term" and that these pairings "can be tolerated when used in their proper legal context." Mellinkoff's examples include *aid and abet, aid and comfort, cease and desist, full faith and credit, metes and bounds,* and *pain and suffering.*

4. Replace wordy expressions with single words.
Many expressions in everyday use should be avoided in writing. They detract from your style because they take too many words to get the job done. Again, the challenge in guarding against them is that we hear them so often they become familiar.

If a word or phrase doesn't add meaning, either delete or condense it. Delete *in the final analysis,* or change it to *finally* or *ultimately.* Change *during the course of* to *during.* Change *due to the fact that*—a "vile expression" that caused William Strunk to "quiver with revulsion"—to *because.* Change *expect to happen* to *anticipate.*

Here is a longer list of common wordy expressions to watch for when editing:

Change this	To this
on the grounds that	because
for the reason that	because
inasmuch as	because
insofar as	because, so far as
due to the fact that	because
based on the fact that	because
in view of the fact that	because
owing to the fact that	because
in spite of the fact that	although, despite
in the amount of	for
a majority of	most
a number of	some, many
as of this date	today (or specify date)
until such time as	until
in due course	after (or rewrite)

Change this	To this
prior to	before
in advance of	before
subsequent to	after
at the conclusion of	after
on a regular basis	regularly
on a daily (weekly, monthly, yearly) basis	daily (weekly, monthly, yearly, or annually)
in this day and age	now, today
at this point in time	now
at the present time	now
at the present point in time	now
time period	time, period
at an early date	soon
as soon as possible	(specify date)
at your earliest convenience	by (specify date)
during the course of	during
during the time that	during, while
in order to	to
so as to	to
so as to be able to	to
with a view to	to
for the purpose of	for, to
by means of	by
by virtue of	by
through the use of	by, with
both of them are	both are, they are
both of these are	both are, they are
relative to	regarding, about
as regards	regarding, concerning, about
pertaining to	about

Change this	To this
in regard to	regarding, on, about
in respect to	on, about
in connection with	about, concerning
in spite of	despite
in support of	to, for
in the event that	if
in a situation in which	if, when, where
in instances in which	if, when, where
in the region of	near, close to
in the vicinity of	near, close to
in (close) proximity to	near, close to
in the area of	in
in the field of	in
in terms of	by, through (or rewrite the sentence)
together with	with
the question as to whether	whether
he is a man who	he
she is a woman who	she
is indicative of	indicates
make reference to	refer to
have the capability to	can
make a contribution to	contribute
take into consideration	consider
make a connection with	connect
with reference to	of, on, for, about
with regard to	of, on, for, about
with respect to	on, for, about
with the possible exception of	except

Change this	To this
of the understanding that	understand that
of the opinion that	think that
of the belief that	believe that
cannot help feeling	can only feel
cannot help but feel	feel (or delete)

5. Delete "hollow" hedges and meaningless intensifiers.

When should you use hedges such as *perhaps* and *sometimes* to qualify your assertion? When should you use intensifiers such as *very* and *absolutely* to add emphasis to your point? These are questions that must be addressed whenever you make a statement. How you answer them depends on your desired tone and point of view (topics I discuss in Chapter 7).

At times you will want to qualify or limit a claim by using a qualifier. Rather than "Commitment leads to success," for example, you might write, "Commitment *often* leads to success." At other times you will want to add emphasis by using an intensifier: "Commitment *always* leads to success."

Whatever your persuasive strategy, take a close look at your hedges and intensifiers. Be certain they are making a genuine contribution. Like other types of meaningless modifiers, hedges and intensifiers are often totally unnecessary. In the preceding sentence, for example, the qualifier *often* effectively limits my claim and should be retained, whereas the intensifier *totally* serves no purpose and should be deleted. To determine when to use a modifier and when to omit one, try the sentence without the modifier and see if anything important is lost.

Even when a statement needs to be qualified or intensified, be careful not to overdo it. As with all modifiers, you can have too much of a good thing. Compare, for example, "I was *rather* surprised by your *somewhat unexpected* decision to come home" with "I was surprised by your decision to come home." Also, compare "*Never in my entire life* have I *ever* been so *totally and completely* offended by *such grossly* obnoxious behavior" with "*Never* have I been so offended by *such* obnoxious behavior" or, depending on your ear, "*Never* have I been so offended by *such grossly* obnoxious behavior."

6. Delete needless repetition.

When used as an intentional device to create emphasis, repetition can be a powerful tool. It can create emphasis and intensity (as in Martin Luther King, Jr.'s famous speech, "I have a dream that one day. . . . I have a dream that one day . . ."). Careless repetition, however, not only wastes the reader's time, but also diminishes the writer's effectiveness. Compare "An important factor that must be addressed is the age factor" with "An important factor that must be addressed is age." Also, compare "If you compare fly-fishing with ice fishing, you will find that fly-fishing is more exciting than ice fishing" with "If you compare fly-fishing with ice fishing, you will find that fly-fishing is more exciting." Better yet, that sentence can be rewritten using even fewer words by making the comparison more directly: "Fly-fishing is more exciting than ice fishing."

Sometimes you must repeat an idea or thought to convey your meaning and to increase coherence between sentences, but again, watch for needless repetition. Repeating the same words within a sentence or within successive sentences will steal the energy from your style and make your writing sound flat: "There is no substitute for *regular practice*. Every coach insists on *regular practice*." You can avoid this sort of deadening repetition simply by replacing the repeated noun with a pronoun: "There is no substitute for regular practice. Every coach insists on *it*."

Here's a sentence for you to revise: "Although I wrote the draft, Madeline helped me revise the draft."

As a rule, unless you are repeating a word or phrase for stylistic effect (that is, unless your repetition is deliberate and selective), avoid repeating a word or phrase within a sentence or within successive sentences.

7. Delete that for brevity; retain that for clarity.

What about *that?* When should *that* be used, and when should *that* be omitted? That is one of the most frequently asked questions that people ask me.

The challenge in offering a simple answer is that that *that* that that question refers to is an unusually nimble, hard-working word. It can serve as an adverb ("I didn't realize that she was *that* tall"), a demonstrative pronoun ("*That* is my brother"), a conjunction introducing a noun clause that acts as the object of a verb ("I was told *that* you are an experienced accountant"), and a relative pronoun ("The report *that* was approved by the board was written by Susan"), to cite just a few examples.

It is in the latter two uses, as a conjunction and as a relative pronoun, that *that* often may be omitted to good effect ("I was told you are an experienced accountant"; "The report approved by the board was written by Susan").

To set aside the grammatical terms and put it as simply as possible: Delete *that* for brevity; retain *that* for clarity. If deleting *that* would compress the sentence in a way that improves its flow and rhythm, take it out. Compare "I recommend *that* you take my advice" with "I recommend you take my advice." If deleting *that* would create ambiguity or momentarily mislead the reader, leave it in. Compare "The attorney believed her client was guilty" with "The attorney believed *that* her client was guilty."

In the end, however, your use of *that* is a matter of personal preference. As Patricia O'Conner advises in *Woe Is I: The Grammarphobe's Guide to Better English in Plain English,* you may prefer to retain *that* after "thinking" verbs such as *know, believe, decide,* and *realize.* For example, "I know *that* you are correct," "I believe *that* his willingness to work hard was responsible for his success," and "I realize *that,* once again, I am ten minutes late." You also may find it useful to retain *that* when offering an aside at the beginning of a second clause ("He admitted *that,* without her support, he was helpless").

How can you tell when omitting *that* improves the flow and rhythm of a sentence and when *that* is needed for clarity? The best way is to use your ear.

Know how to start; know when to stop.

To write with emphasis, keep in mind a disarmingly simple principle: Beginnings and endings count more than middles. The next three editing techniques will help you manage these two crucial points in your sentences.

8. Avoid protracted introductions.

Sometimes we place undue emphasis on relatively unimportant matters before we get to the heart of what we are saying. As many writers of fiction know, the first few sentences of a draft, or even the first few paragraphs or pages, often turn out to be expendable. The story, they discover when revising, doesn't really begin until later. What at first seemed essential was merely a warm-up for the writer, not something engaging to the reader. By all means, do your warm-up exercises if they help you loosen up and get things under way, but delete them from your final copy.

The following phrases or clauses usually can be eliminated or shortened:

Change this	To this
First of all,	First, (or delete)
The first point I want to make is	First, (or delete)
The first thing that needs to be said is	First, (or delete)
What I want to do next is	Next,
In the final analysis,	Finally, (or delete)
Last of all,	Finally, (or delete)
Last but not least,	Finally, (or delete)
After all is said and done,	(Delete)
In my opinion,	(Consider deleting)
To be honest,	(Consider deleting)
To tell the truth,	(Consider deleting)
In all candor,	(Consider deleting)
Needless to say,	(Delete)
For all intents and purposes,	(Delete)
Obviously,	(Consider deleting)
Of course,	(Consider deleting)
Insofar as . . . is concerned,	Regarding, As for, For
In fact,	(Delete, unless you are elaborating a point)
As a matter of fact,	(Delete)

Mark Twain exposed the lack of substance in the last phrase when he quipped, "*As a matter of fact* precedes many a statement that isn't."

Wordy introductions don't go over well with today's readers, who, for the most part, are hurried and easily distracted. Long-winded, leisurely introductions try their patience. Serve your material straight up. Let it stand (or fall) on its own merits.

Change this	To this
It is important to note that we will open an hour early on Monday.	We will open an hour early on Monday.
The first point that needs to be made in all this is that the swiftest traveler is the one who goes afoot.	The swiftest traveler is the one who goes afoot.
In his novel *The Catcher in the Rye*, J. D. Salinger writes about Holden Caufield, a troubled youth whose secret dream is to protect younger children from harm.	In *The Catcher in the Rye*, J. D. Salinger depicts Holden Caufield as a troubled youth whose secret dream is to protect younger children from harm.

9. Use it, there, and what constructions carefully.

In everyday language, "expletives" refer to vulgar or obscene words, but in reference to grammar they have a more particular meaning. An expletive is a place-holding word such as *it*, *there*, and *what* that fills a vacancy in a sentence without adding to its meaning. In the sentences, "*It* is fun to read" and "*There* are three secrets to writing a great novel," *it* and *there* merely occupy the first positions in the sentences, delaying the meaningful words "fun to read" and "three secrets to writing a great novel" to the right of the verbs.

A common type of wordiness results from beginning sentences with *it is*, when *it* is used as an expletive, as in "*It* takes about fifty hours of in-flight training to acquire a private pilot's license." Compare that sentence with "Acquiring a private pilot's license takes about fifty hours of in-flight training." Note that the problem I am describing has to do with using *it* as an expletive, not as a pronoun referring to an antecedent ("Poverty will always be with us. *It* is an intractable problem.").

Although *it is* constructions generally should be avoided, they have their uses. As I point out when I discuss coherence in Chapter 10, for example, they can be used to increase continuity and flow by moving new information to the right side of a sentence, where it connects naturally to the elaboration or development that follows. *It is* constructions also can be useful in creating a formal tone or in depersonalizing an action or a position. Compare, for example, "*It is* the conclusion of this jury that the defendant's actions constitute wilful negligence" with "We the members of this jury have concluded that the defendant's actions constitute wilful negligence." Nevertheless, more straightforward sentence structures are generally preferable.

Many sentences beginning with *it is* can be recast by using a noun or pronoun as the subject and changing the following adjective or noun to an active verb. Other *it is* constructions can be shortened or simply eliminated.

Change this	To this
It is my (our) understanding that	I (We) understand that (or delete)
It is my opinion that	I think that (or delete)
It is my belief that	I believe that (or delete)
It is my (our) recommendation that	I (We) recommend
It is my suggestion that	I suggest
It is my conclusion that	I have concluded
It is my decision that	I have decided (or delete)
It is my determination that	I have determined (or delete)
It is imperative that you	You must
It is hoped that	I hope that
It is agreed that	We agree that
It is thought that	We think that (or delete)
It is often the case that	Often
It is important to note that	Note that, Note: (or delete)
It should be noted that	Note that, Note: (or delete)
It should be pointed out that	(Consider deleting)
It appears that	(Consider deleting)
It would appear that	(Consider deleting)
It is apparent that	(Consider deleting)
It has been recommended that	(Consider deleting)

Change this	To this
It has been suggested that	(Consider deleting)
It has been determined that	(Consider deleting)

Like *it is* constructions, *there* constructions generally should be avoided because they are indirect and wordy. Compare, for example, "*There* has been a decline in faith in government on the part of U.S. citizens over the past ten years" with "U.S. citizens have less faith in government today than they had ten years ago."

There are at least three instances, however, when *there* constructions can serve a useful purpose. The first of these, as noted by Williams, is when a topic is being introduced for further development, as in the first sentence of a paragraph (as in the first sentence of *this* paragraph). Consider these two sentences: "There is one problem that needs to be solved before we can proceed" and "One problem needs to be solved before we can proceed." When introducing a topic for development, some writers prefer the first version to the second because the extra words slow the progression of thought, thereby directing the reader's attention to the topic to be developed. In this instance, slowing the pace is not a stylistic flaw but a strategic choice.

The second instance when *there* constructions work well is in short, emphatic declarations, as in "*There* is no excuse for sloppy editing," "*There* is never enough time to do everything I want to do," and "*There're* two outs" (though most baseball announcers are more likely to say, "*There's* two outs").

Finally, accomplished writers often use *there* constructions to good effect in descriptive passages. F. Scott Fitzgerald, who wrote exquisite descriptions, opens the third chapter of *The Great Gatsby* with these sentences:

> There was music from my neighbor's house through the summer nights. In his blue gardens men and girls came and went like moths among the whisperings and the champagne and the stars.

There could be eliminated from the first sentence ("Music emanated from my neighbor's house through the summer nights"), but its elimination would be a loss. In the next paragraph, Fitzgerald again uses the construction:

There was a machine in the kitchen which could extract the juice of two hundred oranges in half an hour if a little button was pressed two hundred times by a butler's thumb.

Similarly, in *Boundary Waters: The Grace of the Wild*, Minnesota author Paul Gruchow offers this description of the country along Lake Superior's North Shore after a season of generous rainfall:

The wild raspberries are plump, juicy, and sweet. The leaves have already dropped from the wild rose bushes, and some of the red-orange hips, sizzling with color, are almost as big as crab apples. There are bunchberries and thimbleberries among the brambles, and pin cherries in the taller thickets.

Perhaps *there* constructions work well in description because they provide the writer with a simple, unobtrusive means of serving up objects for the reader's contemplation. Or perhaps the word *there* retains a hint of the adverbial or locating function it has when it is used in constructions such as "*There* [in the drawer] was the missing knife" and "*There* [in the woods] are bunchberries and thimbleberries . . ."

In any event, *there* constructions should be used carefully because, more often than not, they waste the reader's time.

Change this	To this
There are many accomplished writers who use *there* constructions in their descriptions.	Many accomplished writers use *there* constructions in their descriptions.
There are many well-known politicians who are planning to attend.	Many well-known politicians are planning to attend.
There are three supervisors who are causing all the problems.	Three supervisors are causing all the problems.
There is a demand for correct spelling on the part of readers.	Readers demand correct spelling.

Similarly, *what* constructions, so common in speech, should be used sparingly in writing.

Change this	To this
What I want to do next is	Next,
What you will find on your first day is	On your first day you will find
What she really wants is recognition.	Above all, she wants to be recognized.

As always, however, there are exceptions to the rule. Skillful writers know how to use *what* constructions to good effect, as Louise Erdrich does in *The Beet Queen:* "He was a young man with a hard-boned, sad, unshaven face. What I remember most about him was the sadness."

10. Trim sentence endings for closing emphasis.

As I noted above, beginnings and endings count more than middles. Of particular usefulness is the natural stress that occurs at the end of every sentence. Both in poetry and in prose, the words that come last carry the most weight. In poetry, it's no coincidence that the *rhyme* usually comes at the end of each *line*. (Can you hear the natural emphasis in that sentence?) In prose, the function of the period is to *punctuate* the words that precede it. To write with emphasis, take advantage of a sentence's natural stress points by reserving them for your most important words. You may find it helpful to think of these locations as reserved parking. Only "VIP" words can park there.

Because of their special importance, sentence endings should be managed carefully. Unfortunately, in both writing and speaking, we have a tendency to keep going after we have made our point. We seem to have trouble knowing when to stop, knowing when enough is enough. As a result, we fail to conclude with our most important words and we allow our sentences to sprawl on after they have done their work.

To guard against this tendency, look for opportunities to trim sentence endings. If you reduce "Does it stink like rotten meat would smell to you?" to "Does it stink like rotten meat?" you do more than eliminate unnecessary words. You also move the VIP phrase, *rotten meat,* to the end of the sentence, where it receives the prominence it deserves.

As another example, consider this sentence: "Restructuring is not an easy thing to do." The meaning is clear, but the sentence structure is flat and unemphatic. To take advantage of the sentence's naturally stressed position, place the VIP words at the end, and you have: "Restructuring is not easy." Or, if you prefer: "Restructuring is difficult."

When you write a sentence that lacks energy, such as, "We need to do something now about the problems we are experiencing," ask yourself: Have I concluded the sentence with the word or words I want to emphasize? Sometimes you have more than one choice. In that example, you could emphasize *problems:* "We need to do something now about these problems." Or you could emphasize *now:* "We need to do something about these problems now." Can you hear the concluding emphasis in these examples? It's as though every sentence ends in a downbeat.

Certain words needlessly state that something exists. For example, sentences ending in words like *experiencing, existing, happening,* and *occurring* can usually be trimmed. These words are expendable because they state the existence of something that already has been named in the sentence, and once something has been named, the reader can see that the thing exists.

A sentence that rambles on past the word or words deserving emphasis is a missed opportunity. Consider this sentence: "We are continually looking for new markets to get into." Eliminating the needless phrase, *to get into,* moves the VIP phrase, *new markets,* into the naturally stressed position: "We are continually looking for new markets." As Williams and others have pointed out, if you want to control the emphasis of your sentences, trim your sentence endings.

Here are four sentences for you to trim:
- I want to reduce the number of interruptions that are happening.
- We need to plan carefully to prevent these problems from recurring.
- Every employee should respond to complaints that our customers express.
- Your account has been closed because of excessive overdraft activity.

In the last example, you can do more than trim *excessive overdraft activity* to the more economical *excessive overdrafts*. You also can reverse the order of the main clause *(Your account has been closed)* and the phrase that follows it *(because of excessive overdrafts)*. Now the emphasis falls on the word that—one suspects—is most significant to the reader: "Because of excessive overdrafts, your account has been closed."

Another point of natural emphasis occurs at the beginning of a sentence. Compare, for example, "You have asked me twice now to respond to your requests on short notice" with "Twice now you have asked me to respond to your requests on short notice." Likewise, compare "I have never felt more frustrated" with "Never have I felt more frustrated." In both examples, the writer sounds more exasperated in the second version of the sentences.

Again, the concept is simple: Beginnings and endings count more than middles. And like so many principles of effective writing, the principle of natural stress applies broadly. It applies not only to the first and last positions in a sentence, but also to the first and last sentences in a paragraph, and to the first and last paragraphs in a document.

Take the most direct route.

A good part of writing concisely is simply a matter of taking the most direct route to your destination. The last three techniques will help you with your itinerary: Prefer action verbs to nominalizations, avoid indirect negatives, and avoid three types of circumlocution.

11. Prefer action verbs to nominalizations.

Many writers suffer from an overdependence on nouns. Given the choice between a verb and the noun form of a verb (called a "nominalization"), they instinctively choose the noun, perhaps under the mistaken notion that the noun will add authority and weight to their words. Well, it does add weight, but it's the wrong kind of weight, and this tendency results in a noun-heavy style. For example, rather than writing "I need to revise that sentence," they will write, "I need to make a revision in that sentence."

The problem with nominalizations is that they usually require a weak verb (such as *make*, as in *make a revision*, and *conduct*, as in *conduct an investigation*) and a preposition (such as *of,* as in *undertake a study of,* and *under,* as in *take under consideration*). This weak verb/noun combination, sometimes coupled with a preposition, is not only wordier but also less direct, less emphatic, and less energetic than its action verb equivalent *(revise, investigate, study,* and *consider).*

Here's another example of a sentence weighed down by nouns: "My suggestion is that we make a reduction in our overhead." Compare that sentence with "I suggest we reduce our overhead." The verb-energized version is not only more concise (six words rather than eleven), but also more emphatic—and the person standing behind those words sounds more decisive.

If you want your style to be energetic and lively, take the most direct route and use the most energetic and lively part of speech in the English language: verbs. (In Chapter 3 I discuss the power of verbs—and the problems with nominalizations—in more detail.)

12. Avoid indirect negatives.

To be *not* unlike something is to resemble it. To be *not* in agreement is to disagree. To be *not* pleased is to be displeased.

Avoid indirect statements using the word *not*. Not that *not* is not a good word, but as Strunk and White advise, use it to express denial ("I did *not* do it") or to create antithesis ("Do this, *not* that"), not to avoid making definite statements.

Change this	To this
The alterations were *not significant.*	The alterations were *insignificant.*
We did*n't* break any laws.	We broke *no* laws.
She was*n't very nice* to us.	She was *rude* to us.

Likewise, you will write with more emphasis if you replace indefinite expressions such as *not any, not anything, not many, not much,* and *not ever* with more definite words such as *no, nothing, few, little,* and *never.* Rather than "I didn't do anything wrong," for example, write "I did nothing wrong." Rather than "I don't know much about geometry," write "I know little about geometry."

As is often the case, however, emphasis depends as much on the sound of language as on a particular principle of economy. (In certain situations, you might prefer the first version of the sentences above.) Which of the following statements, for example, do you think is more emphatic? "I am not happy about your coming home so late." "I am unhappy about your coming home so late." To my ear, the first statement is more emphatic.

13. Avoid needless attribution.

Get to your point directly and efficiently. Avoid using meaningless phrases such as *it is thought, was found, has been observed,* etc., to attribute your statements and ideas to anonymous sources. A statement by its very existence implies that someone, somewhere, *thought* it, *found* it, or *observed* it. The reader doesn't need to have the obvious made explicit.

Change this	To this
It often has been said that one bird found in the hand is felt to be worth two birds in the bush.	One bird in the hand is worth two in the bush.
Structural integrity has been found to be difficult to measure.	Structural integrity is difficult to measure.

If you are taking an idea or a quotation from an actual source, by all means identify the source ("According to the Secretary of State, . . . "). Otherwise, simply make your statement. Have the courage to present your thoughts as your own ideas and opinions. If your readers demand to know who gave you the authority to speak your own mind, tell them I did.

14. Limit personal commentary.

We live in an I-centered society, and our self-absorption sometimes leads us to inject ourselves into sentences where we don't belong. Guard against a tendency to provide a step-by-step account of your thought process. Limit personal commentary.

Unless you are the true subject of the picture ("As president of this company for the past twenty-five years, I have always emphasized the importance of treating people fairly"), place yourself behind the camera rather than in front of it.

Change this	To this
In reading this essay, I was led to rethink my position on freedom of speech.	This essay caused me to rethink my position on freedom of speech.
I have a problem with your coming in late every morning.	Your coming in late every morning is causing problems.
I seriously doubt that a drop of five hundred points in the stock market means all investors should change their asset allocations.	A drop of five hundred points in the stock market doesn't mean all investors should change their asset allocations.
The first thing I want to say is that whenever I encounter situations like this, I am reminded of Poor Richard, who, as I recall, said, "A fat kitchen makes a lean will."	As Poor Richard said, "A fat kitchen makes a lean will."

So to illustrate my last two points, as has been observed by many writers and readers, if you want to write with emphasis and style it is generally agreed that you should avoid needless attribution and limit personal commentary, two instances of wordiness that seem to me to waste your reader's time.

In other words, if you want to write with emphasis and style, avoid needless attribution and limit personal commentary. Don't waste your reader's time.

Review the fourteen techniques.

To review, here are the fourteen techniques for eliminating wordiness:

Edit for patterns of wordiness.
1. Delete redundant modifiers.
2. Delete redundant categories.
3. Replace redundant word pairs with single words.

4. Replace wordy expressions with single words.
5. Delete "hollow" hedges and intensifiers.
6. Delete needless repetition.
7. Delete *that* for brevity; retain *that* for clarity.

Know how to start; know when to stop.

8. Avoid protracted introductions.
9. Use *it, there,* and *what* constructions carefully.
10. Trim sentence endings for closing emphasis.

Take the most direct route.

11. Prefer action verbs to nominalizations.
12. Avoid indirect negatives.
13. Avoid needless attribution.
14. Limit personal commentary.

CHAPTER 2: PRECISION

Use the Right Word
LISTEN CAREFULLY.

COLLECT GOOD WORDS.

USE A THESAURUS TO REMIND YOU OF WORDS YOU
ALREADY KNOW.

Make a Definite Impression
PREFER THE CONCRETE AND THE PARTICULAR TO THE
ABSTRACT AND THE GENERAL.

APPEAL TO THE FIVE SENSES.

PREFER STRONG ACTION VERBS OVER WEAK ABSTRACT
NOUNS.

Avoid Common Errors in Word Choice
DON'T TRUST YOUR MODIFIERS.

AVOID SEXIST LANGUAGE.

AVOID FANCY WORDS (OR DON'T SUCCUMB TO POMPOUS
DICTION AND ACUTE PROLIXITY).

AVOID LANGUAGE THAT CREATES DISTANCE BETWEEN YOU
AND YOUR READER.

CHAPTER TWO

{Precision}

Use the Right Word

Word choice isn't everything.

Your effectiveness as a writer also depends on the rhythm and flow of your sentences, the organization of your material into paragraphs, and the arrangement of your paragraphs into a coherent whole. It depends on your handling of content, your point of view, and your rhetorical strategies for engaging your audience. It depends on cosmetic features such as correct grammar and punctuation, and on deeper, more enduring qualities such as originality, creativity, and imagination. But if you want to write with style, word choice is a good place to start. Like notes to a musician, words are the writer's medium.

In this chapter I discuss the second key to great writing: how to choose words that will make your writing more vivid, precise, bold, original, and memorable, and how to avoid certain common word-choice errors.

Listen carefully.

In the spring of my daughter's senior year in high school, she, my wife, and I toured the campus of a university in Chicago. As our group was walking through the student recreation center, our student tour guide said he would take us down to the weight room—"Except," he explained, "I'm afraid you might hear some profound language down there."

Well, from college students one would hope to hear "profound language"—especially considering the cost of tuition these days—but I suspect what our congenial host meant was "profane language."

People who write with authority are people who pay attention to language. They are alert to the sound and meaning of words. As a result, they have at their command the vocabulary they need to express their thoughts with precision and nuance.

To write with style, tune your ear to language. Attend to connotation (mood and feelings) as well as denotation (literal meaning). Remember that no two words are exact synonyms. As I pointed out in my foreword, there's a reason Hemingway didn't call his tale *The Elderly Man and the Ocean.*

Collect good words.

Be on the lookout for words that are useful in your everyday writing, for words that suit your style and personality. When you encounter a word you like, make it yours. Consider its meaning and the context in which it is used. Look it up. Write it down. Remember it. Look for occasions to use it well.

Browse a dictionary. The next time you're in the reference area of the library, check out one of the thirteen volumes of the *Oxford English Dictionary,* the definitive source of word derivations. Look for words whose meanings are only vaguely familiar to you and study them. Check their root meanings for information that will help you remember them. Learn how to spell and pronounce them. Move them from your larger comprehensive vocabulary, which you depend on as a listener and reader, into your smaller expressive vocabulary, which you depend on as a speaker and writer. Without good words, you're like a flashlight without good batteries.

Use a thesaurus to remind you of words you already know.

Whether printed or programmed, a thesaurus is an indispensable tool—when used properly. Be wary, however, of using a synonym from a list of suggestions if you are encountering the word for the first time. Use a thesaurus to remind you of words you have some experience with and feeling for.

A thesaurus will help you not only rewrite the familiar—"You can't edify an antiquated canine concerning novel maneuvers"—but find the best, most precise word to convey your meaning. Compare, for example, "His claim to represent the Rolling Stones was *deceptive*" with "His claim to represent the Rolling Stones was *fraudulent.*"

A thesaurus also can help you make your point with less monotony and more precision by suggesting alternatives. Compare "Surrounded by careless word choice, the careful writer must always be careful" with "Besieged by thoughtless word choice, the careful writer must always be on guard."

Make a Definite Impression

Not all words serve a writer's purpose equally well. As you continue to broaden your vocabulary and develop your style, you will find that certain types of words are more useful than others.

Prefer the concrete and the particular to the abstract and the general.

It would be difficult to explore some of the great themes in literature and philosophy without abstract words like *truth, beauty,* and *goodness,* but, as a rule, effective writing draws its energy from specificity, not from abstraction and generality. You are more likely to make a definite impression on your reader if you use specific, rather than abstract, words. Rather than "We were affected by the news," write "We were relieved by the news" or "We were devastated by the news." Use words that convey precisely and vividly what you are thinking or feeling.

Compare "Cutting down all those beautiful old trees really changed the appearance of the landscape" with "In two weeks, the loggers transformed a ten thousand-acre forest of old-growth red and white pine into a field of ruts and stubble."

Appeal to the five senses.

As the novelist Joseph Conrad advised, don't tell the reader; show the reader. The best way to avoid vagueness and to write vividly is to appeal to your reader's senses. You can go beyond merely telling to showing by using "concrete words" or "sense words," words that refer to things that can be seen, smelled, heard, tasted, or touched.

Rather than "She leads a hectic life," write "Her life is so hectic she moved dirty dishes to a new apartment." Rather than "The Cardinal liked to have dinner late in the afternoon, just before the sun began to fade," write, as Willa Cather does in *Death Comes for the Archbishop:*

> The Cardinal had an eccentric preference for beginning his dinner at this time in the late afternoon, when the vehemence of the sun suggested motion. The light was full of action and had a peculiar quality of climax—of splendid finish. It was both intense and soft, with a ruddiness as of much-multiplied candlelight, an aura of red in its flames. It bored into the ilex trees, illuminating their mahogany trunks and blurring their dark foliage; it warmed the bright green of the orange trees and the rose of the oleander blooms to gold; sent congested spiral patterns quivering over the damask and plate and crystal.

When writers think of detail, they tend to think only of visual detail, but detail that appeals to the other senses, especially the sense of smell, can evoke strong feelings within your reader. Rather than "Whenever I go home to Brownsville, I have mixed feelings," write, as Alfred Kazin does in *A Walker in the City:*

> Every time I go back to Brownsville it is as if I had never been away. From the moment I step off the train at Rockaway Avenue and smell the leak out of the men's room, then the pickles from the stand just below the subway steps, an instant rage comes over me, mixed with dread and some unexpected tenderness.

Conversely, to obfuscate or obscure your meaning, use abstract words *(pacification, collateral damage, ethnic cleansing)* that do not evoke an image in the mind of the reader. As George Orwell contends in his famous essay "Politics and the English Language," the aim of political speech and writing often is to defend the indefensible:

People are imprisoned for years without trial, or shot in the back of the neck or sent to die of scurvy in Arctic lumber camps: This is called *elimination of unreliable elements*. Such phraseology is needed if one wants to name things without calling up mental pictures of them.

As Orwell's point is often paraphrased, whenever someone uses language that fails to evoke a mental image, you should be concerned about that person's intent.

Prefer strong action verbs over weak abstract nouns.

As I will discuss in Chapter 3, verbs are the most important part of speech. For a lively, energetic style rather than a noun-heavy, lethargic style, choose strong, action verbs (such as *collide* and *recommend*) rather than weak verbs linked to abstract nouns (such as *have a collision* and *make a recommendation*). Rather than "It is my suggestion that we make a commitment to the solution of this problem," write "I suggest we commit ourselves to solving this problem," or simply, "We need to solve this problem."

Now it's your turn: Make an attempt to make a revision in *this* sentence.

Avoid Common Errors in Word Choice

As I discussed in Chapter 1, meaningless modifiers are a common source of wordiness. Other common word choice errors include sexist or noninclusive language, fancy language, and distance-creating language.

Don't trust your modifiers.

Adjectives and adverbs are the trickiest words to use well. Even when they are meant to intensify, they can diminish. Whenever you use a modifier, follow the advice I offered in discussing the "Harlem" editing exercise: Try the sentence without it. If nothing is lost, leave the word out. Compare "We took *very immediate* action" with "We took *immediate* action." The difference is subtle but significant.

Remember, Mark Twain and Ernest Hemingway didn't tell us not to use modifiers (why would we have them if we weren't supposed to use them?); they said to use them carefully.

Avoid sexist language.

Which of the following sentences do you find least objectionable?
A.   A good manager knows his strengths and weaknesses.
B.   A good manager knows her strengths and weaknesses.
C.   A good manager knows his or her strengths and weaknesses.
D.   A good manager knows their strengths and weaknesses.
E.   Good managers know their strengths and weaknesses.

My guess is you chose E. By making both the noun *managers* and the pronoun *their* plural, you avoid a number of problems: the exclusive use of the masculine pronoun *his*, the exclusive use of the feminine pronoun *hers*, the inclusive but awkward *his or her*, and the distracting shift from the singular *manager* to the plural *their*.

Converting nouns and pronouns from the singular to the plural is perhaps the most graceful way to write inclusively. Here are some other practical methods of avoiding sexist language:

- **Replace the masculine pronoun with an article *(a, an, or the)*.** Change "The accused has a right to confront his accuser" to "The accused has a right to confront the accuser."
- **Use the second person.** Change "If a new associate works hard, he might make partner" to "If you work hard, you might make partner."
- **Eliminate the masculine pronoun.** Change "Ask any feminist and he'll tell you so" to "Any feminist will tell you so."
- **As a last resort, use the inclusive but awkward *he or she* or *his or her*.** Change "Have you ever admired an otherwise inept CEO for his ability to give good speeches?" to "Have you ever admired an otherwise inept CEO for his or her ability to give good speeches?"

Although slashed constructions such as *she/he* and *his/hers* are inclusive, they are awkward, so it is best to avoid them.

Though not an acceptable choice to many readers, sentence D, "A good manager knows their strengths and weaknesses," merits comment. More and more writers are mixing singular nouns and plural pronouns, and according to Casey Miller and Kate Swift in *The Handbook of Nonsexist Writing*, they are doing so on good authority. For centuries, many writers (including Shakespeare) commonly used *they* to refer to both plural and singular nouns.

The third edition of *The American Heritage Dictionary* offers this comment: "Third person plural forms, such as *their*, have a good deal to recommend them: They are admirably brief and entirely colloquial and may be the only sensible choice in informal style." The dictionary goes on to point out, however, that "this solution ignores a persistent intuition that expressions such as *everyone* and *each student* should in fact be treated as grammatically singular," and it recommends that "writers who are concerned about avoiding both grammatical and social problems are best advised to use coordinate forms such as *his or her*." It concludes: "The entire question is unlikely to be resolved in the near future."

Here's my position: Let's declare the singular *they* acceptable when it refers to a noun or another pronoun used in an indefinite sense and be done with it. If either *John or Jane* wants to see me, tell *them* to come right in. I'm ready to see *them*. I'm eager to see *them*. I'm tired of seeing *him or her*. But we should continue to respect singular and plural agreement when a pronoun refers to a noun or another pronoun used in a definite sense. In other words, *everyone* has a right to *their* opinion, and I, for one, am ready to hear it. John or Jane, however, will have to wait a long time for *my receptionist* to finish *their* lunch.

Avoid fancy words (or don't succumb to pompous diction and acute prolixity).

There is a difference between vivid language and unnecessarily fancy language. As you search for the particular, the colorful, and the unusual, be careful not to choose words merely for their sound or appearance rather than for their substance. When it comes to word choice, longer is not always better. As a rule, prefer simple, plain language over fancy language.

Here are some examples of fancy words that are commonly used when simpler, plainer words would suffice. There's nothing inherently wrong with the words on the left, but some writers tend to use them—perhaps out of anxiety or insecurity—when they want to impress their readers with big words rather than solid content. If the fancy word on the left conveys your meaning more accurately and more precisely than the one on the right, by all means use the fancy word. But if the plain word on the right conveys your meaning just as well, don't be afraid to use the plain one.

Fancy word	Plain word
acquire, procure, secure	buy, get
advise	tell, let [someone] know
apprise	inform
ascertain	learn, find out
assist, expedite, facilitate	help
attempt, endeavor, undertake	try
be cognizant of/that	be aware of/that
be desirous of/that, wish	want, would like
be contingent upon	depend on
commence, initiate	begin, start
employ, utilize	use
eventuate, transpire	happen
execute, implement, perform	begin, complete, carry out, do
deem, envisage	think, regard, see
demonstrate, evidence, manifest	show
finalize, terminate	conclude, end, settle
furnish	give, provide
impact	affect, influence
prioritize	rank
quantify	measure
relinquish, render, surrender	give, give back, return
terminate	complete, conclude, finish
transmit	send

Two words, both of which are popular with technical writers, warrant comment: *impact* and *utilize*. The acceptability of *impact* when used as a verb depends on your audience and the type of writing you are doing. Many nontechnical writers insist that *impact* should be used only as a noun. But try to tell a Department of Natural Resources employee or an environmental engineer not to use *impact* in a sentence such as "Acid rain is impacting the water quality in the Great Lakes" and you'll get a puzzled, if not annoyed, look. (More than thirty years ago, writers were waging a similar debate over whether *contact* should be used as a verb.) The point is that what is common and perfectly acceptable in one style of writing may be considered poor usage in another.

Utilize presents a similar case. It is frowned on as a wordy variant of *use* by many nontechnical writers, but it is commonly used by technical writers—so commonly used, in fact, that many technical readers would be surprised to see *use* in its place. There is, however, a distinction worth noting between the two words. *Utilize* means not only to use, but to use well or to use in a novel way. So, for example, if a computer company were to donate ten computers to a teacher for classroom use, the teacher might say, "Thanks, but I am unable to *use* these computers because I don't have enough electrical outlets in my room." Or the teacher might say, "Thanks, but I am unable to *utilize* these computers because I don't know how to incorporate them into my teaching style."

Unless you have a good reason for using a fancy word, use a plain one. Avoid language that seems stilted or unnecessarily formal in favor of language that sounds natural and genuine to your ear. Trust the right word—whether fancy or plain—to do the job.

Avoid language that creates distance between you and your reader.

When you were in junior high, did you sit around the lunch table with your friends and say things like, "As per our phone conversation last night, I deem it imperative that we meet after school"?

I doubt it. So why do so many writers use such artificial-sounding language, particularly when they write on the job? Maybe they think that business writing requires a special kind of language, that if they don't toss in an occasional *as per* or *pursuant to*, they aren't doing their job.

Remember: Most readers prefer natural, everyday language. Most would rather read "Here is the brochure you requested" than "Enclosed please find the requested brochure." Do your friends and acquaintances go around saying "as per" and "enclosed please find"? Do they talk like that at lunch? If they did, I suspect you would look for new lunch partners.

Your reader feels the same way. If you write, "As you instructed, I have opened a new account for you," your reader is more likely to enjoy your company. But if you write, "In accordance with your instructions, establishment of a new account has been effectuated," your reader probably can't wait to get away from you.

It comes down to this: Certain words are likely to make you seem like a warm, caring human being, whereas others are likely to make you seem like a cold, heartless bureaucrat. Certain expressions are distance-reducing; others are distance-creating.

Compare, for example, "Thank you for your letter in which you express your dissatisfaction with our product" with "Receipt of your letter expressing dissatisfaction with our product is acknowledged." Imagine the kind of person who might have written each opening. Which writer seems more amiable and genuine? Whose company would you prefer on a cross-country hike?

There are certain distance-creating expressions that you should avoid. They include *as per, pursuant to,* and *in accordance with,* as well as any number of directional expressions, or words that point—expressions such as *above-referenced* and *below-listed.*

Even the expression *enclosed please find,* though a handy way to begin a letter, can be replaced with something more relevant and interesting to your reader. Compare "Enclosed please find our company brochure," for example, with "The enclosed brochure explains how our company can reduce your inventory maintenance costs by 25 percent."

Distance-creating language is commonly used not only in the openings but also in the closings of correspondence. Words and expressions to avoid include the following: *matter,* as in "Thank you for your assistance with this matter" (whether gray, cerebral matter or the stuff that collects in the corner of your eye, it's not a pretty word); *in advance,* as in "Thank you in advance for your assistance" (the phrase suggests the reader is not worth taking the time to thank later); and *contact* rather than *call,* as in "Please contact me at this number" (*contact* seems more appropriate to the relation-ship between an insect and your windshield than between you and your reader).

To conclude this chapter, I return to where I began: Word choice isn't everything—but it's pretty darn important, you know what I mean?

CHAPTER 3: ACTION

Use Action and Movement to Engage Your Reader
MAKE YOUR SENTENCES TELL STORIES.

USE VERBS TO ANIMATE YOUR DESCRIPTIONS.

USE SEMICOLONS AND ELLIPTICAL CONSTRUCTIONS TO
   SUGGEST MOVEMENT.

Prefer the Active Voice
USE THE ACTIVE VOICE FOR EMPHASIS AND ENERGY.

KNOW WHEN TO USE THE PASSIVE VOICE.

1. To emphasize the receiver of the action.

2. To de-emphasize the performer of the action.

3. To avoid responsibility.

4. To create smooth connections between sentences.

5. To maintain a consistent point of view or sequence of subjects.

Know How to Work With Verbs and Nouns
PREFER STRONG ACTION VERBS OVER NOMINALIZATIONS.

KNOW WHEN TO USE NOMINALIZATIONS.

1. When they are subjects that refer to previously expressed
   topics or actions.

2. When they replace the awkward phrase "the fact that."

3. When they save a few words by naming the object of a verb.

4. When they refer to a familiar concept.

DON'T VERB YOUR NOUNS.

AVOID NOUN STACKS.

CHAPTER THREE

{ Action }

Use Action and Movement to Engage Your Reader

If you were standing before a group of people giving a speech about dog sledding to the North Pole and a fly buzzed past your head, your audience would look away from you and watch the fly. It isn't that what you are saying is less interesting than the fly (one would hope), but that your listeners' attention naturally is attracted by movement. Any movement.

The same is true of your readers' attention. Depict a character moving from point A to point B, and your readers will want to know how your character made the journey, particularly if you create some obstacles along the way. Movement is one of the most compelling forces in writing. It arouses their natural curiosity: How are the two points connected? Why is this happening? How does the story end?

As an illustration of the power of movement, consider an example of the simplest kind: Imagine a ball rolling across the floor. If you were observing this event, you would naturally wonder: How far will the ball roll before stopping? Will it bump into anything along the way? If so, how will the collision alter its course? Will the ball take a little hop at the moment of contact? Will it completely reverse its direction, or will it glance off at an angle? It's not that these questions are necessarily significant, but in some elemental way they arouse our curiosity. Movement of any sort raises questions, and we want to know the answers.

Make your sentences tell stories.

The intrigue of movement accounts for the appeal of narrative and plot. Without movement of some kind, there is no story. Similarly, the principle that movement arouses curiosity applies to sentence structure. As Joseph Williams advises in *Style*, if you want your writing to be vigorous, make your sentences tell stories. You can do this by using your subjects to name characters and your verbs to name their actions.

Compare, for example, "An investigation was conducted concerning our accounting procedures" with "The IRS investigated our accounting procedures." The first sentence merely states a fact *(an investigation was conducted)*, but the second tells a story by naming a character *(the IRS)* and an action *(investigated)*. (Note also the change from passive to active voice, a choice I discuss below.)

To make your sentences tell stories, make sure they contain characters and actions. Rather than "It was my hope that a move to Paris would result in giving me time for writing," write "I moved to Paris, where I hoped to spend my days writing." Rather than "Our house at that time was in a village with a view of the river, the plain, and the mountains," write, as Ernest Hemingway does in *A Farewell to Arms*, "In the late summer of that year we lived in a house in a village that looked across the river and the plain to the mountains."

Now here's a sentence for you to invigorate by adding action: "A sudden decline in the stock market occurred."

How did you change it? My guess is that you introduced action by using the past tense of the verb *crash.*

If your sentence has no characters that can be used to create a story, you might have to introduce one. For example, you might rewrite "As per your request, an investigation of the feasibility of the mining of this area for iron ore is under way" by introducing pronouns: "As *you* requested, *we* have begun to investigate the feasibility of mining this area for iron ore."

Likewise, you might rewrite "The result of the examination of soil samples was the discovery of an incredibly rich vein of iron" like this: "When *the mining engineers* examined the soil samples, *they* discovered an incredibly rich vein of iron."

Or you might rewrite "Sometimes in the dark there was noise from the marching of troops under our windows and the movement of guns pulled by motor-tractors" so that it reads the way Hemingway wrote it: "Sometimes in the dark we *heard* the troops marching under the window and guns *going* past pulled by motor-tractors." (Emphasis added.)

As many technical writers have discovered, you can create movement by personifying an inanimate object. Rather than "The result of the tests was the discovery of an incredibly rich vein of iron," write "The tests *led* to the discovery of an incredibly rich vein of iron" or "The tests *revealed* an incredibly rich vein of iron."

Use verbs to animate your descriptions.

Imagine you are F. Scott Fitzgerald, a writer known for the beauty and power of his descriptions. You are sitting at your writing desk, perhaps feeling a little sluggish after last night's party, but it's time to work, so you settle down to the task at hand. You are writing a novel about Jay Gatsby's undying love for Daisy Buchanan, who—to Gatsby's eternal sorrow—is married to Tom Buchanan. You are puzzling over how to introduce Tom to your readers. You decide to set the scene for his grand entrance with a description of the Buchanans' mansion.

You write: "Their house was a huge Colonial. The lawn was expansive, with sun-dials and brick walks and flower gardens. There were vines on the sides of the house and French windows in front—and here's Tom, just back from riding his horse."

Well, you think, looking over what you have written, *there's not much grandeur there. This description is bland.* Fortunately, you remind yourself, this is only your first draft. *So,* you ask, *how can I make it more vivid and interesting?*

First, you decide to remind your reader that the scene is being presented from a particular point of view—in this case, your narrator's. (I discuss point of view in Chapter 7.) Second, you provide specific, concrete, colorful detail (as I discussed in Chapter 2) so that your reader can *see* the setting and the character. Third—and here is the lesson of this chapter—you create movement. You know that movement and action add energy to your writing and that this principle is particularly useful in bringing your descriptions to life. The way you see it, descriptions are not still photographs but moving pictures. Nothing is fixed; everything is in motion. With this approach in mind, you choose action verbs like *running* and *jumping* and *glowing* to animate the objects you are describing. You rewrite the passage this way:

Their house was even more elaborate than I expected, a cheerful red-and-white Georgian Colonial mansion, overlooking the bay. The lawn started at the beach and ran toward the front door for a quarter of a mile, jumping over sun-dials and brick walks and burning gardens—finally when it reached the house drifting up the side in bright vines as though from the momentum of its run. The front was broken by a line of French windows, glowing now with reflected gold and wide open to the warm windy evening, and Tom Buchanan in riding clothes was standing with his legs apart on the front porch.

Well, that's better, you tell yourself. *Now to describe Tom.*

For your first draft, you write: "His face had become harder since he was a student at Yale. He had big muscles. His body was strong and powerful—even cruel."

As before, you know your passage needs work. In your revised version, you again remind your reader that the scene is being viewed from the eyes of a narrator. You add specific detail, and you use active verbs to animate the objects you are describing:

He had changed since his New Haven years. Now he was a sturdy straw-haired man of thirty with a rather hard mouth and a supercilious manner. Two shining arrogant eyes had established dominance over his face and gave him the appearance of always leaning aggressively forward. Not even the effeminate swank of his riding clothes could hide the enormous power of that body—he seemed to fill those glistening boots until he strained the top lacing, and you could see a great pack of muscle shifting when his shoulder moved under his thin coat. It was a body capable of enormous leverage—a cruel body.

There. You're satisfied. In your description of Tom's imposing physical presence you have created a sense of unleashed energy, of movement about to burst forth, and you have set the stage for the scene in the next chapter, when Tom's mistress insists she has the right to say his wife's name, and

Tom—in response to her taunting—makes "a short deft movement . . . with his open hand" and breaks her nose. His movement is like the snap of a coiled spring.

Now, how can you, the real you, apply this lesson to *your* writing? How, for example, might you rewrite this sentence: "News of our boss's departure affected all of us"?

One possibility is "News of our boss's departure saddened all of us." Another is "When our boss announced he was leaving, we stomped our feet, pounded the table with our fists, and raised our voices in a chorus of unbridled joy and celebration." You may prefer one version over the other—depending on how you feel about your boss (or who your reader is).

Here's another example. Rather than "An emphasis on departmental problem solving would result in an increase in efficiency," write "If our department would emphasize problem solving, it would increase its efficiency." But you're not finished. Add a few details, and you get: "If our department would attend more carefully to solving little problems before they became big ones, it would meet its monthly production quota on a more regular basis."

One advantage of writing with action verbs is that they relieve you of an overreliance on adjectives and adverbs. Compare, for example, "The sales representative talked incoherently" with "The sales representative babbled," or—going back to that favorite person of yours—compare "My boss spoke continuously for forty-five minutes" with "My boss droned on for forty-five minutes." Modifiers such as *incoherently* and *continuously* have their place, but they usually convey meaning with less emphasis and power than verbs.

Use semicolons and elliptical constructions to suggest movement.

Few things are more pleasing to accomplished writers than the semicolon. It allows them to present their thoughts with particular subtlety. Humble, unpretentious, the semicolon announces its presence with simple dignity; its very abruptness gives pause and creates emphasis. Often confused with its purebred cousin the colon (a dot over a dot), the semicolon is neither here nor there; it indicates a pause greater than that of a comma and slighter than that of a period. Not quite a comma and not quite a period, this curious hybrid both connects and separates.

Because many writers are unsure of how to use the semicolon correctly, however, they simply avoid it. Such neglect, such utter disregard for so useful a punctuation mark, is sad commentary on the state of American writing. Unless serious semicolon-supporters stand solidly together, semicolons are at risk of disappearing from common usage altogether.

On a more serious note, I defend the semicolon in the context of movement and action because it enables the writer to create a particular type of movement, a type I call—for lack of a better expression—"mind travel." Mind travel is the mental leap the reader makes when creating connections between thoughts, or when filling in the gaps between words and sentences. The more you spell things out, the shorter the distance the reader must leap; the less you spell things out, the longer the distance the reader must leap.

A semicolon can provide just the right jumping distance. As Anne Stilman points out in *Grammatically Correct: The Writer's Essential Guide to Punctuation, Spelling, Style, Usage, and Grammar*, a semicolon used in place of a conjunction can create just the right effect. For example, rather than "Doreen was starting to worry *because* Leo was now two hours late," consider writing "Doreen was starting to worry; Leo was now two hours late." As Stilman explains:

> Aside from shaving off a word, an advantage to omitting conjunctions is that an overexactitude in spelling everything out can render your style a bit ponderous. Writing often comes through as subtler, more sophisticated, if you leave a few blanks for your readers to fill in for themselves.

Mind travel, in other words, is a mental activity your reader finds pleasing.

The same principle of using intentional gaps to create mental movement applies to elliptical constructions, or constructions in which certain words are omitted for stylistic effect. Compare "Susan caught the first fish, John caught the second fish, and Dan caught the third fish" with "Susan caught the first fish, John caught the second, and Dan caught the third." Now compare that sentence with an even more elliptical version: "Susan caught the first fish, John the second, and Dan the third." Though no longer visible, the omitted words still function. The missing verbs and fish have dropped to the subtext, where they still exist in the reader's mind. The reader traveling over the gaps created by their absence enjoys filling in the blanks and making the connections.

Prefer the Active Voice

The active voice is when the subject *performs* the action ("I wrote the essay"). The passive voice is when the subject *receives* the action ("The essay was written by me"). As you no doubt have been told by English teachers and programmed grammar checkers alike, the active voice is more direct, concise, and emphatic than the passive voice. As a rule, you should prefer the active voice over the passive voice.

Use the active voice for emphasis and energy.

Consider this sentence: "An attempt was made to make a determination concerning why there was a failure on the part of the contractor to bring the project to completion on time." Pretty awful, wouldn't you say?

To improve it, shift from the passive voice, where the subject of the sentence is acted upon, to the active voice, where the subject does the acting, and you get, "We made an attempt to make a determination concerning why the contractor failed to bring the project to completion on time."

That's better, but more revision is needed. (Or should I have written, "That's better, but you need to do more revising"?) Keeping in mind my earlier discussion of nominalizations, look for nouns *(attempt, determination, completion)* that could be expressed as verbs *(attempt, determine, complete)*. Here's the final revision: "We attempted to determine why the contractor failed to complete the project on time."

Try your hand at revising this sentence: "An improvement in writing that has too heavy a dependency on nouns can be achieved by making a circle around each noun and posing a question to yourself regarding whether a replacement of it with a verb could be made."

How did you do? One possible revision is, "To improve writing that depends too heavily on nouns, circle each noun and ask yourself if you could replace it with a verb." Much better, don't you think?

Here's another one for you to revise: "Our customers' complaints about poor service should lead us to make a determination about whether their complaints are warranted." One possible revision is, "When our customers complain about poor service, we should determine whether their complaints are warranted."

Despite the advantages of preferring the active voice over the passive and preferring verbs over nouns, it would be misleading to suggest that the passive voice and nominalizations should be avoided in all cases. To be sure, both can be used to good effect. But to illustrate the problem with overusing the passive voice: Consideration as to whether to show a preference for the active voice and active verbs over the passive voice and nominalizations generally should be given if improvement in your writing and vigor in your style are desirable.

Know when to use the passive voice.

Use the active voice to write with emphasis and vigor. Rather than "The account was handled by me," for example, write "I handled the account." That's good advice as far as it goes, but it doesn't go far enough. More complete advice would be to use the active voice—*unless* you have a good reason to use the passive voice.

There are five situations in which the passive voice is more effective than the active voice. Use the passive voice:

1. To emphasize the receiver of the action.

Use the passive voice when the receiver of the action is more important than the performer. Compare the active "Millions of people have read *The Hunt for Red October*" with the passive "*The Hunt for Red October* has been read by millions." Compare "Our employees routinely disregard the new quality control procedures" with "The new quality control procedures are routinely disregarded by our employees." The active voice would be preferable in a paragraph focusing on the employees, whereas the passive voice would be preferable in a paragraph focusing on the new quality control procedures. The question to ask yourself is, where do you want your emphasis? When the receiver of the action is more important than the performer, use the passive voice.

2. To de-emphasize the performer of the action.

When there is no advantage in the reader's knowing the performer of the action, use the "truncated passive voice," in which the performer is dropped from the sentence. Consider this sentence: "Our engineers have installed a more powerful CPU to give you faster processing." If the reader doesn't care who did the installing, use the passive voice: "A more powerful CPU has been installed to give you faster processing."

Similarly, when the performer of the action is either unknown or relatively unimportant, use the truncated passive. Compare "Everyone 'round the world heard the shot" with "The shot was heard 'round the world."

3. To avoid responsibility.

When the active voice seems indiscreet or when it calls unwanted attention to the performer of a negative action, use the "diplomatic passive voice." The passive voice allows you to avoid assigning responsibility for the action. Compare "You mishandled the account" with "The account was mishandled."

4. To create smooth connections between sentences.

Compare the following two passages:

> Management must decide whether it will insist on more flexibility in hiring part-time workers. The likelihood that the unionized workers will strike should influence its decision.

> Management must decide whether it will insist on more flexibility in hiring part-time workers. Its decision should be influenced by the likelihood that the unionized workers will strike.

When the active voice breaks the flow of thought from the previous sentence, use the passive voice.

5. To maintain a consistent point of view or sequence of subjects.

Compare these two passages:

> Our auditors have reviewed our accounting practices and found them to be adequate. We should convey this to our investors. The capital they provide allows us to operate.

Our accounting practices have been reviewed and found to be adequate. These findings should be conveyed to our investors, who provide us with operating capital.

When the active voice creates a disjointed sequence of subjects, use the passive voice.

So the next time you are criticized for using the passive voice—by either a human reader or computer-programmed grammar checker—don't submit passively to the indictment. Ask your critic to comment on whether your use of the passive isn't justified under one of the five situations described above. If your critic gives you a puzzled look or responds with a blank screen, you may want to stand behind your choice. After all, why would the passive voice exist if it served no useful purpose?

Know How to Work With Verbs and Nouns

Without nouns to name persons, places, things, or ideas, we would have great difficulty in communicating even the most basic information. An overreliance on nouns, however, can undermine a vigorous writing style. As a rule, when presented with the choice between using a verb or noun to express your thought, choose the verb.

Prefer strong action verbs over nominalizations.

Movement gives life to your writing, and the best way to create movement is to use verbs, those marvelous animators of language. To paraphrase Donald Hall, author of *Writing Well:* Verbs act. Verbs swing. Verbs cascade. Verbs explode. Verbs energize your style.

It's hard to imagine writing without verbs, and of course all writers use them. In *The American Way of Death*, for example, Jessica Mitford offers a catalogue of verbs to dramatize the gruesome details of embalming:

Alas, poor Yorick! How surprised he would be to see how his counterpart of today is whisked off to a funeral parlor and is in short order sprayed, sliced, pierced, pickled, trussed, trimmed, creamed, waxed, painted, rouged, and neatly dressed—transformed from a common corpse into a Beautiful Memory Picture.

Some writers, however, don't use verbs frequently enough, or they use the wrong kind. Rather than strong action verbs, they reach instinctively for nouns linked to weak verbs. Rather than *connect*, they *make a connection*. Rather than *investigate*, they *conduct an investigation*. Rather than *suggest*, they *make a suggestion*.

As I noted in Chapters 1 and 2, preferring nominalizations—or the noun form of verbs—over action verbs can result in wordiness and imprecision. Writers who routinely make this choice might think that the noun forms add authority to their writing, but rather than the weight of authority, nominalizations usually add the weight of dullness. The result: a noun-heavy style that is slow, ponderous, and (yawn) plodding.

Consider, for example, this sentence: "After the scientists undertook a study of the fossils, they made a change in their theory." The sentence exhibits a lumbering wordiness. Like a dinosaur stuck in a tar pit, it achieves little movement, and what movement it does achieve is ineffectual. Consider this version: "After the scientists studied the fossils, they changed their theory." Can you hear the difference?

Here are some more examples:

Noun-heavy style	Verb-energized style
Make a revision in this sentence.	Revise this sentence.
Please take under consideration my proposal.	Please consider my proposal.
The mallard offered protection to her ducklings when the raccoon made an approach.	The mallard protected her ducklings when the raccoon approached.

Note that nominalizations and verbs sometimes have identical spellings, as in *study/study* and *change/change*. Because the noun forms require extra words, however, they still damage (or do damage to) your style. Compare "We need to conduct a study of the problem and make changes in our strategy" with "We need to study the problem and change our strategy."

A related problem has to do with adjectives, or words that modify nouns and pronouns. As with nominalizations, choosing adjectives rather than verbs can obscure action and repress energy. For example, "These figures are *indicative* that our trade deficit is *dependent* on the strength of the dollar" vs. "These figures *indicate* that our balance of trade *depends* on the strength of the dollar."

For practice, revise these sentences:

1. The students voiced a complaint about the dorm food.
2. The intention of the pilot was to effect a landing on the grass field.
3. The scientists did some speculation about the reason for the explosion of the star.
4. The auditors conducted an investigation into the discrepancies and made a recommendation that we make a change in our procedure.
5. Knowledge and practice of certain principles of effective writing will give you the ability to make significant improvement in your style. (*Hint:* Create a subject for the verbs by beginning the sentence with *If you.*)

Here are some suggested revisions:

1. The students complained about the dorm food.
2. The pilot intended to land on the grass field.
3. The scientists speculated about why the star exploded.
4. The auditors investigated the discrepancies and recommended we change our procedure.
5. If you know and practice certain principles of effective writing, you can improve your style significantly.
   Or: Knowing and practicing certain principles of effective writing will enable you to improve your style significantly.

With these examples, I have offered a demonstration of the power of verb-energized writing. (You're not going to let that sentence go by without revising it, are you?)

Know when to use nominalizations.

Although you should usually choose the verb when given a choice between a verb and its noun form, there are certain circumstances when nominalizations are useful. In fact, as Joseph Williams points out, "We cannot get along without them."

Williams identifies four instances when nominalizations work to your advantage:

1. When they are subjects that refer to previously expressed topics or actions
For example, in the sentence, "This *decision* can lead to costly consequences," the nominalized word *decision* links the sentence to the one that precedes it, thus creating a more cohesive flow. Likewise, note the usefulness of the nominalization *discussion* in this sentence: "Although we debated the issue for hours, our *discussion* was inconclusive."

2. When they replace the awkward phrase "the fact that"
Compare "The fact that she denied what he accused her of impressed the committee" with "Her *denial* of his accusations impressed the committee." Compare "The fact that you were absent suggests that you are ambivalent" with "Your *absence* suggests ambivalence."

3. When they save a few words by naming the object of a verb
Compare "I failed to do what my boss expected me to do" with "I failed to meet my boss's *expectations*." Compare "She presented what we learned as a result of investigating the topic" with "She presented *the results* of the investigation."

4. When they refer to a familiar concept
Compare the following sentences:

Verb form	Nominalized form
I suggest you register when you arrive.	I suggest you register on arrival.
The Ph.D. candidate reviewed the material before she was examined orally.	The Ph.D. candidate reviewed the material before her oral examinations.
The right to speak freely is protected by the first amendment.	Freedom of speech is protected by the first amendment.

Verb form	**Nominalized form**
Being taxed when you're not represented is unjust.	Taxation without representation is unjust.

Despite their usefulness in these four instances, however, nominalizations should be used cautiously. As a rule, to energize your writing, don't nominalize; verbalize.

Don't verb your nouns.

As the comics character Calvin once said to Hobbes, "Verbing weirds language." I agree. Just as nouning makes dead your style, verbing weirds language. And it has been going on for a long time.

As I noted above, more than thirty years ago the noun *contact* was made into a verb, over the vehement objections of certain purists. Today we see the same thing happening to the nouns *impact* and *access.* They are being verbed. Thirty years from now, however, I suspect that few people will remember that anyone objected.

So could we dialogue for a moment about verbing language? Of course, as someone who instructions writing I would prefer written communication, but let's settle for conferencing.

Why do some writers like to verb their words?

For the same reason people wore powdered wigs in the eighteenth century and bell-bottoms in the 1960s. They think it makes them debonair or hip. I don't mean to argue that language should never change. Who would object, for example, to *fax* finding its rightful place in the English language, both as a noun and a verb? As our world—and our perception of our world—changes, so must our language.

Verbing your nouns is not always wrong. There are times when it's necessary to bend your words to suit your needs. Both in writing and in speech, this function shift is called inflection. But some writers go too far. What I object to is verbing words when doing so obscures rather than elucidates meaning. So don't verb your nouns just for the sake of verbing your nouns.

Avoid noun stacks.

A noun stack is a series of nouns, some of which have been created from verbs. Just as nominalizations can steal energy from a sentence, noun stacks—to use wording that illustrates my point—can cause energy elimination problems in your style.

The problem with noun stacks is that they alter the natural flow of thought in a way that momentarily suspends movement. For example, consider this noun stack: *an acquisition candidate identification process.* Note how the first three nouns (which have been impressed into service as adjectives) do not reveal their meaning until we come to the last word, *process.* Only then do the preceding words *an acquisition candidate identification* make sense. This suspension of natural movement creates an awkward pause in the sentence, a dead zone in which nothing is happening.

You can unstack those long, ungainly phrases by starting from the last word in the stack, or the right side of the phrase, and reversing the order. As you make your way through the stack, substitute verbs for nouns when appropriate, and add prepositions and pronouns as needed. (It's easier to do than it might sound.) *An acquisition candidate identification process,* for example, unstacks like this: *a process for identifying candidates for acquisition.* Here's another example: *software integrity validation specifications* unstacks as *specifications to validate the integrity of our software.*

Some noun stacks, of course, are not only acceptable, but also convenient and useful. The term *noun stacks* itself, for example, expresses the idea more definitely and more compactly than a *stack of nouns.* Many common expressions, such as *school year* and *workbench,* are actually noun stacks. Likewise, many technical and scientific terms, such as *vacancy rate, software validation, system availability,* and *heart palpitation,* are noun stacks put to practical use.

It isn't until you add a third or fourth noun to the stack that you begin to impede the natural progression and flow of a sentence in a way that damages your style. Although *software validation specifications* seems useful and only somewhat cumbersome, *software integrity validation specifications* definitely crosses the line. (Note that *integrity* and *validation* are redundant anyway.) Another consideration to keep in mind when weighing the value of compactness against the advantage of movement is frequency. Too many noun stacks have a cumulative effect that can weigh down your style and make it sound stiff, mechanical, and bureaucratic. So as a rule, practice noun stack construction avoidance—in other words, avoid noun stacks—for a lively style.

In a word, action is the key. Use action verbs, mind travel, and the active voice to create movement. Make your sentences tell stories, and don't let those nominalizations and noun stacks get in the way. Remember: To keep it interesting, keep it moving.

CHAPTER 4: MUSIC

Listen to Your Voice
Punctuate Your Beat

USE PERIODS TO PUNCTUATE YOUR THOUGHTS.

USE COLONS TO CREATE ANTICIPATION.

USE SEMICOLONS TO SUGGEST A CONNECTION.

USE COMMAS TO SEPARATE THE PARTS OF A SENTENCE.

USE DASHES TO PRODUCE A DASHING EFFECT.

USE EXCLAMATION POINTS TO SAY IT WITH GUSTO.

USE ELLIPSES TO TRAIL OFF.

Use Variety to Create Emphasis

VARY YOUR SENTENCE LENGTH AND STRUCTURE.

AVOID CREATING STRINGS OF SIMPLE DECLARATIVE SENTENCES.

REPEAT SHORT EMPHATIC SENTENCES FOR SPECIAL EFFECT.

ELABORATE BEFORE, WITHIN, OR AFTER THE MAIN CLAUSE.

AVOID THREE COMMON PATTERNS OF MONOTONOUS
  SENTENCE STRUCTURE.
  • Sentences beginning with a subordinate element.
  • Sentences ending with a subordinate element.
  • Sentences paired around the conjunctions *and, or,* or *but.*

FOLLOW A LONG SENTENCE WITH A SHORT, SNAPPY ONE.

USE SENTENCE FRAGMENTS FOR EMPHASIS.

INVERT THE USUAL ORDER.

Use Rhythm to Create Emphasis

PLACE IMPORTANT WORDS AT THE ENDS OF SENTENCES
  FOR CLOSING EMPHASIS.

USE ELLIPSES TO END SENTENCES ECONOMICALLY.

USE PREPOSITIONAL PHRASES FOR CONCLUDING FLOURISH.

Know When to Pause

CUT SPRAWLING SENTENCES DOWN TO SIZE.

1. Eliminate wordiness.
2. Break long, sprawling sentences into shorter units.
3. Condense clauses into phrases.

MANAGE LONG SENTENCES BY CONNECTING AND PAUSING.

1. Keep subjects and verbs close together.
2. Pause before elaborating.
3. Use parallel structure to make connections.

SUBORDINATE LESS IMPORTANT ELEMENTS.

Know Your Sentence Types

TO CREATE EXPECTANCY, USE PERIODIC SENTENCES.

- Use periodic sentences as engaging openings.
- Use periodic sentences for intensity.
- Use periodic sentences for concluding flourish.

USE LOOSE SENTENCES TO STATE YOUR POINT
DIRECTLY, THEN ELABORATE.

- Connect by modifying.
- Connect by repeating.
- Connect by restating.

USE BALANCED SENTENCES TO EMPHASIZE SIMILARITIES.

- Break the pattern for special effect.
- Omit words to accentuate the rhythm of parallel structure.

USE ANTITHETICAL SENTENCES TO JUXTAPOSE
CONTRASTING IDEAS.

- Balance antithetical elements to emphasize dissimilarity.
- Use paradox to get the reader's attention.

LEARN FROM OTHERS.

CHAPTER FOUR

{Music}

Listen to Your Voice

Of the five keys to great writing—economy, precision, action, music, and personality—perhaps the most easily overlooked is music. This oversight is not surprising given that the act of writing necessarily draws our attention to the characters or letters as they appear on the page or screen. As a result, we tend to forget that the symbolic system we are using, though marvelous in its way, is nevertheless limited and artificial. The written word is only a representation of our spoken, natural language, which is based not on the letters of the alphabet but on sound and expression, and the "sounding" of words that we do in our heads as we write and read is a poor substitute for actually speaking and hearing them.

When we speak, we sound happy. We sound angry. We sound upset. We sound worried. We communicate a great deal—and our audience infers a great deal—not only from what we say but also from the way we say it. Compared with the act of writing, speaking is a more direct, instinctive, intuitive, spontaneous form of communication. In writing, the more effectively we convey the nuances of our spoken language—our rate of delivery, volume, rhythm, inflection, mood, and passion—the more pronounced and engaging our style.

One of the most important things you can do to sharpen your style is to reawaken yourself to the sound of your words, to tune your ears to the rhythm and cadence and flow of your language. It is in this context that you should ask, How can I make this music more pleasing to my readers? What techniques can I learn from accomplished writers? What techniques can I discover on my own?

In this chapter, I invite you to listen carefully to the music of your language, to the alternation of strong and weak elements in the rhythm of your words, and to the cadence of sound and silence in the flow of your sentences.

As an infant, you learned to distinguish the sounds of language and to associate those sounds with particular meanings. Over time you learned to imitate what you were hearing and to produce your own words and sentences. In the process you also developed a distinctive way of raising or lowering the pitch of your voice as you spoke, a musical pattern called intonation that has stayed with you throughout life. At age seventy, you are likely to use the same basic patterns of intonation you used at age seven. Similarly, when you learned to write, you learned to arrange words in a certain order and to create various structures to convey increasingly complex meanings. Your repertoire of sentence structures was influenced not only by what you heard but also by what you read. As with patterns of intonation, you continue to rely on the basic sentence structures you learned early in life.

The question relating to style is this: How far have you developed your sentence repertoire beyond those basic structures? If you are constructing sentences made up entirely of main clauses (or clauses that are complete sentences) with no subordinate elements (or phrases and clauses that do not express a complete thought), your writing is likely to be perceived as elementary and uninteresting. Writing without subordinate elements is like speaking in a loud voice, without subtlety or variation, just as allowing your sentences to sprawl out of control, without shape or rhythm, can be compared to going without shaving or washing your hair. Your look might be viewed as a kind of natural style if you're able to pull it off, but most of us would simply look slovenly.

On the other hand, if you are incorporating a rich mixture of sentence types to create more complex and engaging rhythms, your writing is more likely to be perceived as refined and interesting. Your readers cannot hear your actual voice and intonation, but they *can* hear your written voice, a voice that is produced by word choice and sentence structure. That written voice is given a pleasing sound by the range and variety of your sentence types.

To determine if you are providing your readers with sufficient variety in sentence length, do this assessment: Randomly select a passage or paragraph from your writing. Count the words in each sentence. For a visual illustration, make a bar graph, numbering the sentences on the vertical axis and indicating the number of words in each sentence on the horizontal axis. If you are working on a word processor, you can simply rearrange the paragraph so that each sentence begins at the left margin. Now, look at your graph or your rearranged paragraph. If all of your sentences are approximately the same length as measured either by word count or by physical length, you probably are writing in a monotonous style, one that lacks sufficient variety to make your writing interesting.

Like sentence length, your sentence structure should be varied. An easy way to check for structural variety is to underline subordinate elements (phrases or clauses that are not complete sentences and that will not stand alone). In the paragraph you are reading, for example, I have underlined the seven subordinate elements. Again, if your paragraph consists solely of main clauses, the rhythm of your language is likely to be flat and boring. The key to an engaging style is variety, not only in sentence length but also in sentence structure.

To appreciate the importance of variety, try reading (preferably out loud) a paragraph that lacks variety. The preceding paragraph, rewritten to remove subordinate elements, sounds like this:

> Sentence structure is like sentence length. Both should be varied. An easy way to check for variety in sentence structure is the following: Underline subordinate elements. (Subordinate elements are a certain type of phrase or clause. They are not complete sentences and they will not stand alone.) Take the paragraph you are reading as an example. I have not underlined the subordinate elements. There are no subordinate elements in this paragraph. I want to make this point again. This paragraph consists solely of main clauses. The rhythm of the language in this paragraph is flat and boring. The key to an engaging style is variety. Variety is important both in sentence length and in sentence structure.

As an exercise, rewrite the following paragraph, which sounds flat because it lacks subordinate elements, into one that is rhythmically pleasing. If you're feeling energetic, take the time to copy or type it over. Then, as you revise it, look for main clauses to condense into subordinate elements.

> In my introduction I made an important point. Understanding a concept is one thing. Applying it is another. I am keeping this in mind now. I am illustrating its application here. I am providing you with another illustration. You are reading that illustration now. This paragraph consists entirely of main clauses. Do the following as an exercise: Add variety to the rhythm and flow of these sentences. Subordinate some of the main clauses. Do something else as well: Vary your sentence length. Mix in a few short sentences for emphasis. Go ahead. Try it. You will again see the importance of variety. Variety makes a dramatic difference in the sound of your language.

Here is one version of how the paragraph might be rewritten:

> <u>As I pointed out in my introduction</u>, understanding a concept is one thing; applying it is another. <u>With this in mind</u>, I am providing you with another illustration—<u>the paragraph you are reading, which [no longer] consists entirely of main clauses</u>. <u>As an exercise</u>, add variety to the rhythm and flow of these sentences <u>by subordinating some of the main clauses</u>. <u>While you're at it</u>, vary your sentence length. Mix in a few short sentences for emphasis. Go ahead. Try it. <u>Once again</u>, you will see <u>that variety makes a dramatic difference in the sound of your language</u>.

If you are writing with few or no subordinate elements, you are depriving your reader of variation in the flow of your sentences, the equivalent to speaking in a monotone. Many technical writers seem to fall into this pattern, perhaps because they are concentrating on presenting their material with clarity and precision rather than attending to the sound of their language. All writers, however, should keep in mind this simple principle: Variety in sentence structure adds energy to your writing.

Punctuate Your Beat

How do you feel about punctuation? Do you view it as an opportunity to express yourself with subtlety and precision, or as a necessary evil, a test that you either pass or fail? Do you think of those little marks and squiggles as a means of conveying the music of your voice, or as a minefield in which one false step will reveal your ignorance of the rules?

If, like many writers, you view punctuation more as an ordeal than an opportunity, I challenge you to take a fresh look: Think of punctuation not as your enemy, but as your ally. Those little marks and squiggles enable you to indicate in writing what your voice would be doing if you were speaking. Remember that not all punctuation is mandatory; in many situations punctuation is a matter of style, a means of exercising control over the rhythm and flow of your sentences. As you read my advice on how to use punctuation for stylistic effect, keep in mind that *to punctuate* means not only *to use punctuation* but also *to accentuate* or *to emphasize*.

When you speak, your inflection is a kind of song, and punctuation helps you capture in writing the musical features of your voice. When you say these words—"Would you like to go out for lunch?"—the listener can hear your voice rise in pitch, and this change indicates you are asking a question. But when you ask that question in writing, the reader can't hear your voice, so you use a question mark to indicate the higher pitch you would be using if you were speaking.

To appreciate the importance of nonverbal signals, listen to your voice as you say these sentences out loud: "That was smart." "That was smart?" "That was smart!" In each sentence the words are the same, but the messages are quite different. The first is a simple statement, the second a question that suggests a reproach, the third a sarcastic rebuke. The various meanings are conveyed by changes in your voice. Punctuation enables you to indicate these inflectional changes in writing.

When you communicate with someone in person, you use a whole range of nonverbal signals to convey your meaning. In addition to intonation (the rise and fall in the pitch of your voice) and inflection (the change in pitch or loudness of your voice), you use gestures, facial expressions, volume, and rate of delivery. Punctuation allows you to communicate in writing some of those nonverbal signals, signals that can have as much significance as the words themselves.

How does all this apply to you and writing with style?

If you appreciate the importance of voice in writing, you are more likely to use punctuation to your advantage. You are more likely to take the time to learn how to use those sometimes troublesome little marks to convey the music of your language. And you are more likely to listen to your own voice and recognize the features that make it distinctive.

Of less stylistic value are the marks of clarification—hyphens, quotation marks, and parentheses. (Note, however, that parentheses are often used to mark humorous asides or comments that undercut the statements that precede them.) Marks of clarification are useful, but they have more to do with mechanics than with style.

Of greater stylistic value are the marks of inflection—question marks and exclamation marks. They enable you to indicate the intonation you would use if you were speaking. Of particular value are the marks of separation—periods, commas, colons, semicolons, and dashes. They serve not only to separate words, phrases, clauses, and sentences, but also to create that most useful device of rhythm and variety: the pause.

Note, for example, the effect of the colon in the preceding sentence. Whenever you pause—whether in speaking or in writing—you create emphasis. The semicolon, which also marks a pause, creates an effect slightly different from that of the colon: "Understanding a concept is one thing; applying it is another." Even as the semicolon separates, it implies a link. The resulting pause is slight, perhaps providing just the right timing. (As I discussed in Chapter 3, the semicolon is a useful device for creating a little mental space over which the reader enjoys leaping.) Note that using a conjunction in place of the semicolon makes the sentence sound flat: "Understanding a concept is one thing, but applying it is another." Other punctuation marks produce their own special effects. The period produces a complete halt: "Understanding a concept is one thing. Applying it is another." The dash creates a more abrupt, emphatic pause: "Understanding a concept is one thing—applying it is another."

As you can see, punctuation, like musical notation, allows you to indicate timing and expression and to control the rhythm and flow of your sentences.

If you were a composer reading a book about how to write music, and if you were told that you would be permitted to use marks of clarification (such as time signatures and measures), but forbidden to use marks of inflection (such as crescendos, decrescendos, and accents) and forbidden to use marks of separation (such as full-note, half-note, and quarter-note rests), you would be miffed. You would feel deprived of your full expressive range because certain musical effects had been placed off-limits to you. If you are writing without using the full range of punctuation marks available to you, you are like a musician who never gets the timing right.

Use periods to punctuate your thoughts.

Periods do more than separate sentences. Periods punctuate. They create pauses, and pauses create emphasis. If you write nothing but long sentences, you offer your reader fewer points of natural stress and fewer breaks in the flow of your thought. On the other hand, if you mix in some short sentences, you offer more frequent pauses. Short sentences are emphatic. Don't underestimate their power.

Think of the period as a whole note rest or—as the British call it—a full stop. Use it at the end of a sentence to indicate that you have completed your thought. Take advantage of the pause it creates by placing an important word or phrase immediately before it. As I point out in my discussion of closing emphasis below, when you conclude your sentence with the words you want to emphasize, you give your reader a moment for their meaning to sink in.

Use colons to create anticipation.

The colon is a mark of anticipation. Like the period, it indicates a full stop. But rather than prompting the reader to look backward and reflect on what has been said, it leaves the reader leaning forward with a promise of more to come. When used as a stylistic device to create emphasis, the colon is most effective when it produces an abrupt or dramatic halt, as in "We met at the appointed time: midnight." A sentence fragment preceding the colon creates an emphatic, punchy style, as in "The result: a business boom that has lasted nearly a decade."

Think of the colon as a three-quarter note rest, shorter than the full stop of the period and longer than the pause of the semicolon.

Use semicolons to suggest a connection.

Part period and part comma, the semicolon is a hybrid mark that both separates and connects. If the colon is an open door, the semicolon is a door that stands ajar. It requires the reader to pause briefly before passing through.

Although commonly avoided by writers who don't know how to use it or who fear they might use it incorrectly, the semicolon is an indispensable mark for certain situations and sentence structures. As Strunk and White point out, the semicolon is particularly useful in showing a "close relationship" between two statements, especially when the relationship is one of "cause and consequence." They offer these examples:

Connecting with conjunctions	Connecting with semicolons
Stevenson's romances are entertaining, for they are full of exciting adventures.	Stevenson's romances are entertaining; they are full of exciting adventures.
It is nearly half past five, and we cannot reach town before dark.	It is nearly half past five; we cannot reach town before dark.

A student in one of my writing classes put the semicolon to good use when she used it in a short, snappy sentence intended to cap off a paragraph:

> Explaining how he got out the vote, Jesse [Ventura] said, "I convinced them that if they voted, they could get out of work. It's a federal law. And if you timed it right, say go at 3:30, you wouldn't have to go back to work." He connected; they voted.

Knowing when to use the semicolon is a matter of timing, and this student got it right.

Think of the semicolon as a half-note rest, a brief pause that separates even as it connects. It creates a pause shorter than the period, slightly shorter than the colon, and longer than the comma. To omit it entirely from your repertoire is to limit your range as a writer.

Use commas to separate the parts of a sentence.

The most frequently used (and misused) punctuation mark, the comma is perhaps the most expressive. Certain commas are required by grammar. Other commas are optional. As optional marks, they enable you to convey a range of expression and to indicate subtle variations in the rhythm and flow of your sentences. They help you capture the slight pauses and varying emphasis you use when speaking—and in both spoken and written language, timing is everything.

As a rule, the more commas you use in your writing, the more deliberate and reflective your style; the fewer commas you use in your writing, the faster-paced and more direct your style. Academic writers, for example, tend to use more commas than business writers. Whether you use commas in the following sentence, for example, is a matter of emphasis and style: "In 1990, we bought a fourteen-foot Hobie Cat from a man who, like many sailors, wanted a bigger boat."

Think of the comma as a quarter-note rest. It's a brief pause, a slight hesitation, rather than a full stop. Like the semicolon, it both separates and connects, but unlike the semicolon, it does so unobtrusively.

Use dashes to produce a dashing effect.

Use a dash—or a pair of dashes—to emphasize an abrupt interruption. Though sometimes used by writers as an easy substitute for careful sentence structure and more fully integrated thinking, the dash is a bold—if somewhat showy—way to indicate an abrupt change in the flow or continuity of a sentence. When more emphasis is desired than that produced by commas or parentheses, no punctuation mark is more striking—or more dashing—than the dash.

The dash is useful not only as a mark of style but also as a mark of clarification. You can use it to mark an aside or a parenthetical statement, particularly when the aside contains commas. Compare, for example, "Knowing the five keys to great writing, economy, precision, action, music, and personality, will help you convey your message with clarity and emphasis" with "Knowing the five keys to great writing—economy, precision, action, music, and personality—will help you convey your message with clarity and emphasis."

Use exclamation points to say it with gusto.

In terms of subtlety, the exclamation point is on the opposite end of the spectrum from the semicolon. Skillful writers usually find other ways, such as timing and sentence structure, to give their words emphasis. In certain types of writing, such as on-the-job writing, exclamation points are rarely used.

But when unabashed enthusiasm is what you want, go for it!

Use ellipses to trail off.

An ellipsis, consisting of three or four spaced periods, indicates an omission in quoted matter. (An ellipsis consisting of three periods indicates part of a sentence has been omitted; an ellipsis consisting of four periods is used at the end of a sentence to indicate that an entire sentence or more has been omitted.) An ellipsis (the plural is spelled *ellipses*) also can be used as a stylistic device at the end of a sentence to suggest a trailing off. For example, "If I only could remember my next point . . ."

Use Variety to Create Emphasis

Beginning writers treat the structure of each sentence as a freestanding unit, unaffected by what goes on before or after it. They pay little attention to how the sound of one sentence relates to that of another. For them, writing is a matter of finding words and creating sentences to express their thoughts, and arranging those sentences into some kind of coherent order, without regard to sound.

More advanced writers, on the other hand, do more than find the words and construct the sentences that convey their meaning. They attend to how various sentence structures sound in relation to each other. For them, writing involves creating sentence structures that not only connect their thoughts but produce a distinct rhythm and flow.

Vary your sentence length and structure.

A fundamental rule of style is that variety is interesting, monotony boring. To add energy and life to your writing, vary your sentence length and structure.

Avoid creating strings of simple declarative sentences.

This paragraph is made up entirely of simple declarative sentences. It is like an earlier paragraph. Perhaps you remember that paragraph. I asked you to revise it. It also was made up entirely of simple declarative sentences. A simple declarative sentence makes a statement. It has no subordinate elements. A string of simple declarative sentences creates monotony. Monotony steals life from your writing.

Repeat short emphatic sentences for special effect.

On the other hand, a series of short sentences can produce an insistent, emphatic tone. To produce this effect, repeat not only the sentence structure but also a word or phrase, as in this series of sentences: "Sometimes they fail. Sometimes they make mistakes. But seldom do their efforts go unnoticed." Note that progressing from shorter to longer sentences produces a pleasing rhythm, like the rising emphasis of a crescendo. (In Chapter 10 I discuss various schemes for ordering your material in the context of creating coherence.)

When I was writing my Ph.D. dissertation on the history of the Iowa Writers' Workshop, I wrote to writers who had taught in the program asking them to describe their experiences. In a letter responding to my request, Kurt Vonnegut used repetition to good effect: "I left my large family (six children) behind with my wife on Cape Cod, and lived alone out there for the first six months or so. I needed the time. I needed the stimulation. I needed the change in scene." As you can see, in the hands of a skillful writer, even a simple technique makes good music.

Elaborate before, within, or after the main clause.

Unless you are using repetition for special effect, however, vary your sentence structure. Change the flow. As in this sentence (the one you are reading), offer a preliminary element before the main clause. Or elaborate after the main clause, as I do here. Or offer an aside, a pause for reflection, within the main clause itself. As I discussed above, mark preliminary elements, asides, and afterthoughts with commas, parentheses, or dashes.

Accomplished writers are intentional. As they manage the rhythm and flow of their sentences—particularly as they create longer, more complex sentences—they always keep in step with their main clause. Whether moving toward, within, or away from the center, they are like dancers who never lose their balance.

Avoid three common patterns of monotonous sentence structure.

Although repetition can be used to create emphasis, careless repetition can have the opposite effect: It can create monotony and steal the energy from your writing. Be careful not to fall into three common patterns of monotonous sentence structure: sentences beginning with a subordinate element, sentences ending with a subordinate element, and sentences paired around the conjunctions *and, or,* and *but.* Listen for the monotonous effect produced by these patterns in the examples below.

Sentences beginning with a subordinate element:
As soon as I arrived at my office, I sat down at my desk. Before checking my E-mail, I booted up my computer. After answering the most pressing messages, I returned phone calls.

Sentences ending with a subordinate element:
I arrived at my office, ready to get to work. I checked my E-mail after booting up my computer. I answered the most pressing messages, hoping I would find time later to return phone calls.

Sentences paired around the conjunctions **and, or, and but:**
I walked into my office and sat down at my desk. I booted up my computer and checked my E-mail. Then I answered the most pressing messages and returned phone calls.

Follow a long sentence with a short, snappy one.

Wind it out slowly, then snap it back. This long-short combination makes you sound decisive: "We have waited years for the right time to expand our business. That time is now." A simple technique, it works every time, as it does for Casey Miller and Kate Swift when they write in *The Handbook of Nonsexist Writing:*

> For whatever reasons—goodwill, a sense of justice, an editor's instructions, the pursuit of clarity—a growing number of writers and speakers are trying to free their language from unconscious semantic bias. This book is intended for them.

It works the same way for Maya Angelou when she writes in *I Know Why the Caged Bird Sings:*

> If growing up is painful for the Southern Black girl, being aware of her displacement is the rust on the razor that threatens the throat.
>
> It is an unnecessary insult.

You also can create emphasis by writing a one-sentence paragraph, as Angelou does here.

But don't overdo it.

Use sentence fragments for emphasis.

Another way to create emphasis by varying your rhythm is to use sentence fragments. Because they bring an abrupt halt to the flow of complete senten- ces, they act as a sharp accent to punctuate the thought being presented. And because they seem to come as afterthoughts, they lend a conversational quality to your writing.

Consider, for example, the effect produced by the sentence fragment in the following passage from Sherry Sweetnam's *The Executive Memo: A Guide to Persuasive Business Communications:*

The number one priority when you're writing a letter of apology is: *Don't bury your apology.* Think about your own expectations for how you want to be treated. If a friend of yours promised to meet you at a restaurant at 6:30 and shows up at 7:00, the first thing you expect is an apology. Up front. Until you get one, you will not be completely open to listening to your friend. Once you get your apology, you can begin to have a good time.

Remember, too, that a sentence fragment preceding the colon creates an emphatic, punchy style, as in "My concern: Will people in our generation outlive their resources?"

Invert the usual order.

This simple technique lifts a sentence and breathes life into it. Rather than "Word choice is equally important," write "Equally important is word choice."

Subject-predicate inversion also can improve the coherence or flow of thought between sentences. When you move a thought that has been presented to the reader previously (*equally important*) from the right side to the left side of a sentence, you place it in a position where it serves as a transition. In the same way, when you move a thought that is new to the reader (*word choice*) from the left side to the right side of a sentence, you place it in a natural position for it to be developed in the following sentences. (I discuss coherence and Williams' principle of "something old, something new" in Chapter 10.)

For practice, change the word order in this sentence: "The marks of inflection—question marks and exclamation marks—are of greater stylistic value." (You'll find the inverted form of this sentence in the section titled "Punctuate Your Beat" on page 72.)

Use Rhythm to Create Emphasis

Like variety, rhythm is key to creating emphasis in your writing. You can use periods to punctuate your beat, as I discussed above. You also can heighten the effect of closing emphasis by using ellipses and prepositional phrases.

Place important words at the ends of sentences for closing emphasis.

As I pointed out when discussing techniques of economy in Chapter 1, there is a natural stress point, a position of prominence, at the beginning and ending of every sentence. To take advantage of this naturally occurring opportunity for emphasis, place important words at the beginnings and endings of your sentences, where they will receive the most attention. Compare "His co-workers appreciate the diplomacy he uses" with "His co-workers appreciate his diplomacy." Compare "These problems are temporary in nature" with "These problems are temporary."

It's a simple concept: To use sentence structure to your advantage, place the words or phrases you want to emphasize immediately before the period. A date, a deadline, a dollar amount, a particular word or phrase—anything you place at the end of your sentence will receive particular emphasis. The reason: As I pointed out above, the period—like the colon and the dash—creates a pause. And a pause creates emphasis.

Think of the last part of a sentence as a punch line to a joke: It counts more than the beginning and the middle. Your success—both as a writer and a comedian—depends on it.

Sometimes you take advantage of closing emphasis by rearranging your words. Compare "You need to write frequently to improve your writing" with "To improve your writing, you need to write frequently."

At other times, you can heighten closing emphasis by omitting needless words. Compare "Maybe it just sags in a downward motion" with "Maybe it just sags." Compare "Does it stink like rotten meat would smell to you?" with the way the poet Langston Hughes actually wrote the line: "Does it stink like rotten meat?"

As you can see, wordiness interferes with emphasis. Anything that gets in the way works against emphasis, so make every word count.

For example, compare the cluttered and uncluttered versions of this sentence (read it twice, first with the phrases in brackets and then without): "Because of the euphoria created by the booming economy [that currently exists], people who are well-off tend to forget the problems of people who are less fortunate [than they are]."

Here's a sentence for you to revise: "Loving you is easy 'cause you're a beautiful person." How does the uncluttered version go in the lyrics of the popular song? Where should the closing emphasis be?

So, for closing emphasis, rearrange and condense. Above all, be economical. And once you've made your point, stop.

Use ellipses to end sentences economically.

In managing your sentence endings for emphasis, you can use an ellipsis to good effect. As defined above, an ellipsis is the omission of a word or phrase that is suggested by the context and understood by the reader. An ellipsis tightens the rhythm of a sentence and heightens its closing emphasis.

Consider this passage: "If a man does not keep pace with his companions, perhaps it is because he hears a different drummer [than the rest of us hear]. Let him step to the music which he hears, however measured or far away [it may be from him]." Which way do you think Henry David Thoreau actually wrote the passage in *Walden?*

An ellipsis brings a sentence to a neat, emphatic conclusion. Note its effect in this sentence: "Although top correspondents generally have a good understanding of international affairs, many local reporters do not [have this understanding]."

Likewise, compare "A wonderful fact to reflect upon, that every human creature is constituted to be that profound secret and mystery to every other human creature" with the way Charles Dickens actually wrote the sentence in *A Tale of Two Cities:* "A wonderful fact to reflect upon, that every human creature is constituted to be that profound secret and mystery to every other."

Your turn. Use an ellipsis to compress the ending of this sentence: "I revised the first draft, but a friend revised the second draft." (*Hint:* The second draft is expendable—at least in this exercise.)

As Edward Corbett and Robert Connors point out in *Style and Statement,* an ellipsis "can be an artful and arresting means of securing economy of expression." Perhaps nowhere does economy of expression have more impact than in sentence endings.

Use prepositional phrases for concluding flourish.

If you want to end your sentences in a way that Joseph Williams calls "self-consciously dramatic," conclude your sentences (and your phrases) with prepositional phrases, particularly those introduced by the preposition *of*. Compare, for example, "We observe today not a party victory but a freedom celebration," with the way John F. Kennedy actually delivered the first part of the opening sentence in his 1961 inaugural address: "We observe today not a victory of party but a celebration of freedom."

Prepositional phrases (phrases introduced by prepositions, as in *of party* and *of freedom*) are effective in creating concluding emphasis because their structure leads naturally to a point of emphasis: The unstressed preposition (in this case, *of*) is invariably followed by words containing stressed syllables. It is the rhythm of this unstressed-stressed combination that adds concluding flourish and elegance. Rather than "An essay involves imagination," write, as Cynthia Ozick does in her article "She: Portrait of the Essay as a Warm Body," "An essay is a thing of the imagination."

Rather than "their successors' mistakes," write, as Henry Adams does in the concluding sentence of *The Education of Henry Adams*, "the mistakes of their successors." (Also, note the wording of Adams' title itself.) To appreciate the skill with which Adams uses prepositional phrases to manage his rhythm, read the entire sentence out loud:

> Perhaps some day—say 1938, their centenary—[the three friends] might be allowed to return together *for a holiday*, to see the mistakes *of their own lives* made clear *in the light of the mistakes of their successors;* and perhaps then, *for the first time* since man began his education *among the carnivores*, they would find a world that sensitive and timid natures could regard *without a shudder*. (Emphasis added.)

For practice, revise the following sentence so that it concludes with a prepositional phrase: "We arrived, experiencing no mishaps." (*Hint:* Reduce the sentence to four words, using the preposition *without* as the third word.)

Know When to Pause

There are many good reasons to avoid writing long sentences. They often lack clarity, take too long to get to the point, and sprawl out of control. Short sentences, on the other hand, are more likely to be clear and easy to follow. They set a fast pace and require less concentration on the part of the reader. And when the words are well-chosen and the rhythm pleasing, they produce a kind of unadorned eloquence, as in Thomas Paine's stirring pronouncement, "These are the times that try men's souls," or Hamlet's anguished declaration, "To be, or not to be: That is the question," or the stark beauty of the Bible's opening words, "In the beginning God created the heavens and the earth."

Despite the risks, there are good reasons to venture writing long sentences. Long sentences offer you an opportunity to write with flourish, to achieve a more intentional effect than the straightforward eloquence of a simple declarative sentence. As Williams points out, if our sentences "never went beyond twenty words, we'd be like a pianist who could use only the middle octave: We could pick out a few clear and simple tunes, but not much more." Long sentences, well managed, are a declaration of the writer's composure, a deliberate pause in a frenzied world of hurry and haste. They invite the reader to slow down, to reflect, to savor.

Don't be afraid to write long sentences. But make sure you don't let them sprawl. The key to keeping them under control is knowing when and how to pause.

Cut sprawling sentences down to size.

There are two basic ways to get long, sprawling sentences under control: Cut them down to size, or give them shape by changing their structures. You can make sentences shorter by using these three techniques:

1. Eliminate wordiness.

Wordiness obscures the rhythms and cadences of your sentences. If you make every word count (as I discussed in Chapter 1), you are left with the essential components, and the reader can see your sentence—and hear it— for what it is.

For example, if you eliminate the wordiness from this sentence—"The key thing to remember when looking at these and other recommendations is that timing is a very important issue that must be taken into consideration"—you are left with just four essential words, "The key is timing," or three: "Timing is key." (Note, by the way, the ellipses before and after the word *three*.) Either way, what was loose and sprawling is now short and emphatic.

2. Break long, sprawling sentences into shorter units.

Sentences often sprawl out of control because too much information is being presented without pausing. A good way to ensure that you are pausing frequently enough is simply to limit each sentence to a single main idea. For example, change "After his November 17th phone conversation with Mr. Green, Mr. Brownfield prepared a second letter, which also was signed by Mr. Carter and sent to Ms. Benjamin" to "After his November 17th phone conversation with Mr. Green, Mr. Brownfield prepared a second letter. That letter also was signed by Mr. Carter and sent to Ms. Benjamin."

The value of the period is that it allows your reader a mental pause, a moment to take in your meaning before proceeding to your next point. Despite its obvious usefulness, however, many writers are too sparing in their use of this boundary-setting marker. As William Zinsser observes, "There isn't much to be said about the period, except that most writers don't reach it soon enough."

3. Condense clauses into phrases.

Consider the following sentence: "Four telephone surveys *that have included questions about solid waste abatement programs* have been conducted this year." To make it less cumbersome, change the clause *that have included* to a participial phrase (*including questions*) or to a prepositional phrase (*with questions*) so that it reads, "Four telephone surveys *including questions about solid waste abatement programs* have been conducted this year," or "Four telephone surveys *with questions about solid waste abatement programs . . .*" Likewise, change "The hat *that is on the table* belongs to the little girl *who is wearing a brown coat*" to "The hat *on the table* belongs to the little girl *wearing a brown coat*."

Rather than "We were sitting in a nice little clearing *that was beside the trail after we had pitched our tents while we were eating our noodles and were savoring the exquisite pleasure of just sitting*, when a plumpish, bespectacled young woman *who was wearing a red jacket and who was carrying the outsized pack that is customary for hikers* came along," write as Bill Bryson does in *A Walk in the Woods: Rediscovering America on the Appalachian Trail:* "We were sitting in a nice little clearing beside the trail, our tents pitched, eating our noodles, savoring the exquisite pleasure of just sitting, when a plumpish, bespectacled young woman in a red jacket and the customary outsized pack came along."

Manage long sentences by connecting and pausing.

Another approach to controlling long sentences is altering the structural features that make them sprawl. Here are three techniques for managing structure:

1. Keep subjects and verbs close together.

Readers cannot make sense of a sentence until they see how the subject and verb connect. For this reason, sentences with subjects and verbs that are close together are easy to understand. Sentences with subject and verbs (and verbs and objects) that are far apart are taxing because they delay the moment of comprehension when the subject-verb or verb-object connection becomes clear.

Rather than "Approximately 430 sites that may contain mixed municipal, industrial, and hazardous materials are being inventoried," write "Approximately 430 sites are being inventoried because they may contain mixed municipal, industrial, and hazardous materials." Rather than "The writer who cares about style, in addition to choosing words carefully, preferring verbs over nouns, and using punctuation to control the rhythm and flow of sentences, tries to convey an authentic voice," write "In addition to choosing words carefully, preferring verbs over nouns, and using punctuation to control the rhythm and flow of sentences, the writer who cares about style tries to convey an authentic voice."

2. Pause before elaborating.

Meaning is conveyed in units (words, phrases, clauses, sentences, paragraphs, etc.), and sensing when your reader needs a break to let the meaning sink in requires a keen sense of timing.

Compare "Classical rhetoric is an oppositional style of persuasion that involves two parties presenting opposing arguments to a third party in a way that highlights differences" with "Classical rhetoric is an oppositional style of persuasion, one that involves two parties presenting opposing arguments to a third party. The point is to highlight differences."

3. Use parallel structure to make connections.

As I discuss in more detail below, writing with parallel structure involves presenting related thoughts in similar fashion or the same parts of speech. Creating these patterns helps the reader see how you are connecting your thoughts, and making the connections obvious to your reader is particularly important when you are writing long sentences. Beginning with one structure or part of speech then switching unexpectedly to another obscures those connections and makes it more difficult for your reader to grasp your meaning.

Compare "He is predictable, dependable, and a conscientious person" with "He is predictable, dependable, and conscientious." Likewise, compare "When debating how to manage our natural resources and the protection of our national heritage, we should not view theoretical models as tools that make perfect predictions, but they can help us make helpful predictions" with "When debating how to manage our natural resources and protect our national heritage, we should view theoretical models not as tools that make perfect predictions, but as tools that make helpful predictions."

Subordinate less important elements.

As I discussed above, some writers tend to express their thoughts in one main clause after another. They give equal emphasis to every statement, regardless of its relative importance. More accomplished writers, on the other hand, manage their emphasis by giving prominence to more important points and by subordinating less important points.

When you subordinate one part of a sentence, you throw your emphasis to the other part. Rather than present two thoughts in two main clauses of equal emphasis ("Kathy is the director of fund-raising, and she is in a good position to coordinate our efforts"), indicate which clause you consider more important ("As director of fund-raising, Kathy is in a good position to coordinate our efforts").

When writers fail to make these choices, they often misplace their emphasis. Compare, for example, the questionable stress in this sentence, "Our budget projections, which reflect this trend, are attached," with the more appropriate emphasis in this sentence, "Our budget projections (attached) reflect this trend."

Subordination affects not only emphasis but meaning. The following two sentences present the same information but make very different statements: "Although Jim is a good writer, he makes frequent errors in punctuation." "Although Jim makes frequent errors in punctuation, he is a good writer." Both sentences convey negative information, but the former is essentially negative, the latter positive.

Subordination is a mark of intelligent writing. According to Edward Corbett and Robert Connors in *Style and Statement*, it is "the most sophisticated of sentence patterns." Subordination is your declaration to the reader that you are making thoughtful choices, weighing the relative significance of your points, and indicating their relationships.

Know Your Sentence Types

As you build your sentences into more complex structures, keep in mind the following definitions. A *phrase* is a group of words that contains no subject or independent verb (though it may contain a verb form). For example, *inside the book, to read the book*, and *reading the book* are all phrases (prepositional, infinitive, and participial). A *clause*, on the other hand, contains both a subject and a verb. For example, *I want to read the book* and *After I read the book* are clauses. (Note that *After reading the book* is a phrase, whereas *After I read the book* is a clause—the difference is the lack of a subject and an independent verb in the phrase, and the presence of a subject and an independent verb in the clause.) Clauses come in two varieties: main clauses and subordinate clauses.

A *main clause* (also called an independent clause or a complete sentence) is one that has a subject and a verb, expresses a complete thought, and can stand alone. *I lost my shirt,* for example, is a main clause. A *subordinate clause* (also called a dependent clause or an incomplete sentence) is one that has a subject and a verb but does not express a complete thought and cannot stand alone. *After I lost my shirt,* for example, is a subordinate clause. (Note that adding a subordinating conjunction like *after* or *although* to a main clause subordinates it or, as the name implies, makes it less important.)

With those definitions in mind, consider three categories of sentences: functional, grammatical, and rhetorical. Within each category are four types of sentences.

Before I discuss the stylistic opportunities offered by the various categories and types, I think it would be useful if I provided you with a brief overview. (Pour yourself another cup of coffee or tea—or do whatever helps you stay alert. These definitions get a little complicated.)

The four basic types of *functional sentences* are declarative sentences (those that make a statement), interrogative sentences (those that ask a question), imperative sentences (those that issue a command), and exclamatory sentences (those that make an exclamation).

The four basic types of *grammatical sentences* are simple sentences (those with a single main clause, as in *I rode home on my bicycle*), compound sentences (those with two main clauses joined by a coordinating conjunction like *and* or *but,* as in *I rode home on my bicycle, and I slept in the hayloft*), complex sentences (those with one subordinate clause and one main clause, as in *After I rode home on my bicycle, I slept in the hayloft*), and compound-complex sentences (those with two main clauses, one of which contains a subordinate element, as in *I rode home on my bicycle, and I slept in the hayloft because I wanted to be alone*).

The four basic types of *rhetorical sentences* are periodic sentences (those with elaboration before the main clause, as in *Confused, overwhelmed, exasperated, the diligent reader plows on*), loose sentences (those with elaboration after the main clause, as in *The diligent reader plows on, though confused, overwhelmed, and exasperated*), balanced sentences (those with parallel elements, as in *What is read without effort is remembered without pleasure*), and antithetical sentences (those with contrasting elements, often in parallel structure, as in *I didn't promise you a rose garden; I promised you an adventure*). Of the three categories of sentences, rhetorical sentences are the most dependent on rhythm for their effect—and therefore are of the most stylistic value.

{ Sentence Types }

Functional Sentences:

1. declarative (statement)
2. interrogatory (question)
3. imperative (command)
4. exclamatory (exclamation)

Grammatical Sentences:

1. simple
2. compound
3. complex
4. compound-complex

Rhetorical Sentences:

1. periodic
2. loose
3. balanced (or parallel)
4. antithetical

So much for definitions. The point is that when you create sentences consisting of more than a single main clause, you have many options regarding the placement of your subordinate elements: You can elaborate before the main clause, within the main clause, or after the main clause, or, in more complex structures, in any two locations, or even in all three locations.

Your choice of whether to elaborate with phrases or with clauses alters the grammatical structure of your sentence. For example, if you added the phrase *After riding home on my bicycle* to the simple sentence *I slept in the hayloft,* the resulting sentence would still be simple because the verbal phrase is not a clause, whereas if you added the clause *After I rode home on my bicycle* to the simple sentence *I slept in the hayloft,* the resulting sentence would be complex. (Do you see the difference in the grammatical structures of the sentences?) Although adding the elaboration changes the grammatical structures, the difference in meaning, emphasis, and style is slight.

Where you choose to elaborate (before, within, or after the main clause), as opposed to *how* you choose to elaborate (with a phrase or clause), however, does have a significant impact on the rhythm, flow, and emphasis of your sentences. In fact, your method of elaboration, like your choice of words (discussed in Chapter 2) and your use of action verbs (discussed in Chapter 3), is a fundamental element of your style.

For example, if you elaborate—either with phrases or clauses—*before* the main clause, you create a periodic sentence. If you elaborate—either with phrases or clauses—*after* the main clause, you create a loose sentence. Although periodic sentences and loose sentences are mirror images of each other, each produces a distinct rhythm and effect.

In periodic sentences, the subordinate elements come before *the main clause*, which is usually short and emphatic. Delaying the main point until the end creates suspense and expectancy, like the effect produced by a Roman candle: After one flash of light, then another flash of light, then another flash of light, *there's a boom.*

In loose sentences, *the main clause* comes before the subordinate elements. Leading off with the main clause creates a structure that is less intentional, more relaxed, and more straightforward than that of periodic sentences. The effect produced is like an echo: *First you shout,* then you hear it again, hear it again, hear it again.

To create expectancy, use periodic sentences.

More self-conscious in structure than loose sentences, periodic sentences are better suited for some types of writing than others. Because they create intentional delay, and because this delay demands concentration and patience on the part of the reader, periodic sentences are more appropriate in carefully crafted writing (such as academic, legal, and creative writing) than in more routine or pragmatic writing (such as business and technical writing).

Use periodic sentences as engaging openings.

Periodic sentences make good leads for advertising copy, articles, essays, and narratives when the desired effect is to begin in the middle of things. (This narrative technique is sometimes referred to as *in medias res*). The periodic structure engages readers with a series of relevant details before revealing the main thought. The effect is to make readers feel involved even before they reach the main clause and comprehend the information being presented.

Consider, for example, the effect of beginning a story *in medias res* with this sentence: "Wandering out of the bookstore, distracted from my next shopping bargain, I sat down on the nearest bench to consider my next move." The effect of partial disclosure and gradual revelation—a common narrative technique—draws the reader into the scene by arousing the reader's curiosity about what is happening.

Although the delay in the next example tries the patience of the modern reader, note the periodic structure of an opening sentence in "The Custom-House," Nathaniel Hawthorne's "sketch of official life," which he uses to introduce *The Scarlet Letter:*

> In my native town of Salem, at the head of what, half a century ago, in the days of old King Derby, was a bustling wharf,—but which is now burdened with decayed wooden warehouses, and exhibits few or no symptoms of commercial life; except, perhaps, a bark or brig, half-way down its melancholy length, discharging hides; or, nearer at hand, a Nova Scotia schooner, pitching out her cargo of firewood,—at the head, I say, of this dilapidated wharf, which the tide often overflows and along which, at the base and in the rear of the row of buildings, the track of many languid years is seen in a border of unthrifty grass,—here, with a view from its front windows adown this not very enlivening prospect, and thence across the harbour, stands a spacious edifice of brick.

Hawthorne, who—even by the standards of his time—fancied periodic sentences and subject-predicate inversions perhaps to a fault, might simply have written:

> A spacious edifice of brick stands in my native town of Salem. It stands at the head of town where half a century ago there was a

bustling wharf, but now that area is burdened with decayed wooden warehouses, and it exhibits few or no symptoms of commercial life, except perhaps for a bark or brig discharging hides half-way down its melancholy length, or a Nova Scotia schooner pitching out her cargo of firewood nearer at hand. But as I was saying, this brick building stands at the head of this dilapidated wharf, which the tide often overflows and along which the track of many languid years is seen in a border of unthrifty grass at the base and in the rear of the row of buildings. This building has a view from its front window adown this not very enlivening prospect and thence across the harbour.

What is gained in clarity, however, is lost in elegance. The straightforward sentence structures are easier to understand (and therefore less annoying to a modern reader), but they lack the grace of Hawthorne's intentional delay and the richness of his gradual, unhurried, layer-by-layer disclosure of information.

If you want to explore the complexity of Hawthorne's sentence in greater depth—and if you have greater stamina and patience than Mother Teresa—copy his sentence over, study it, and write another just like it on another subject, matching the original sentence subordinate clause for subordinate clause.

Use periodic sentences for intensity.

The intentional delay that typifies periodic sentences creates two types of emphases: the emphasis of anticipation and the emphasis of compounding detail. The emphasis of anticipation results from the reader's eagerness to get to the delayed conclusion, to see how the sentence turns out or comes together. The emphasis of compounding detail is a product of rhythm: As each new thought is delivered, the cadence of succeeding phrases or clauses heightens intensity.

As an example of a skillfully rendered periodic sentence, consider this sentence from George Orwell's well-known essay "Shooting an Elephant": "The wretched prisoners huddling in the stinking cages of the lock-ups, the grey, cowed faces of the long-term convicts, the scarred buttocks of the men who had been flogged with bamboos—all these oppressed me with an intolerable sense of guilt."

To appreciate the emphasis created by placing the compounding elements before the main clause, simply recast Orwell's periodic sentence as a loose sentence—that is, as a sentence with the compounding elements coming after, rather than before, the main clause: "I was oppressed with an intolerable sense of guilt when I saw the wretched prisoners huddling in the stinking cages of the lock-ups, the grey, cowed faces of the long-term convicts, the scarred buttocks of the men who had been flogged with bamboos." The vivid details still evoke an emotional response, but the taut energy of the periodic structure is lost.

To gain a greater appreciation for the periodic sentence structure, you might want to create your own version of Orwell's sentence and experiment with moving its parts around.

Use periodic sentences for concluding flourish.

A third use for which periodic sentences are particularly well suited is summary and conclusion. The compounding elements of periodic sentences provide an effective means of pulling various thoughts together, and the main clause, because of its heightened emphasis, lends itself to creating a conclusive tone.

At a critical point in *The Elements of Style*—the first sentence of the book's final paragraph—E. B. White uses a periodic sentence for concluding flourish: "Full of his beliefs, sustained and elevated by the power of his purpose, armed with the rules of grammar, the writer is ready for exposure." The moment had come for a windup sentence, a grand finale, and White—with a stroke of elegance even his persnickety former professor would call a home run—uses the periodic structure to provide the requisite flourish.

For practice, see if you can recast the following periodic sentence as a loose sentence by reversing the order of the main clause (which I have underlined) and the elaborating elements: "For the eighteen-year-old high school senior, for a young person who is both naive and experienced, both child and adult, writing the college application essay is a time of reckoning."

If you reverse the order of the main clause and the elaborating elements, you change a periodic sentence (elaboration first, main clause last) to a loose sentence (main clause first, elaboration last): "Writing the college application essay is a time of reckoning for the eighteen-year-old high school senior, a young person who is both naive and experienced, both child and adult."

Use loose sentences to state your point directly, then elaborate.

As you can see in the example above, in contrast to periodic sentences, loose sentences are relaxed and straightforward. With their elaborating elements coming after—rather than before—the main clause, they lack the tautness produced by the intentional delay of periodic sentences. As their name implies, loose sentences usually seem more laid-back, or less self-consciously crafted, than periodic sentences.

Like periodic sentences, however, they rely on rhythm for their effect. The pause after the main clause, and—if there is more than one elaborating element—the pauses between the elaborating elements, divides a long sentence into more manageable units. These divisions give long sentences shape and prevent them from sprawling. For example, listen to the flat, unvaried sound of a sentence made up of successive relative clauses introduced by the word *that:* "We would like to explain our concerns about the proposed changes in the Sunshine Act that would allow agency commissioners to meet behind closed doors in a manner that would exclude tax-paying citizens." Compare the sentence when it is restructured as a loose sentence: "We would like to explain our concerns about the proposed changes in the Sunshine Act, changes that would allow agency commissioners to meet behind closed doors and exclude tax-paying citizens."

Although loose sentences are less dramatic than periodic sentences, they too can be crafted into rhythmically pleasing structures. John F. Kennedy, for example, began his 1961 inaugural address with a loose sentence: "We observe today not a victory of party but a celebration of freedom, symbolizing an end as well as a beginning, signifying renewal as well as change."

When you write loose sentences, however, make sure that what follows the main clause is indeed a subordinate phrase or clause rather than a second main clause. If you write two main clauses and you join them with a comma, you have created not a loose sentence, but a comma splice. For example, here is a loose sentence: "A comma splice is two main clauses joined with a comma, an error committed frequently by beginning writers." And here is a comma splice: "A comma splice is two main clauses joined with a comma, this error is committed frequently by beginning writers." Do you see the difference in the grammatical structures?

As Williams points out in *Style*, you can use one of three methods to connect the elaborating element (or elements) to the main clause of a loose sentence. All three methods involve using a comma after the main clause to attach the subordinate or trailing elements. Whichever method you use, note the usefulness of the pause: It allows the reader to take in the meaning of the main clause before proceeding to the elaboration. Here are the three methods:

Connect by modifying.

The first method of connecting the trailing element to the main clause is to use a modifier. When you extend your sentence in this way, you can use one of three types of modifiers: a present participle (the *-ing* form of verb), a past participle (usually—but not always—the same form as the past tense of the verb), or an adjective (a word that describes a noun or pronoun).

- **Modifying with a present participle:** "As a boy, Bix Biederbecke cared little about schoolwork, *preferring* the piano to a book."
- **Modifying with a past participle:** "Bix once sneaked aboard a riverboat, *drawn* by the seductive notes of the steam calliope."
- **Modifying with an adjective:** "Bix was happiest when he was playing the cornet, *oblivious* to everything but his music."

Connect by repeating.

A second method of connecting the trailing element to the main clause of a loose sentence is to repeat a word. This technique, which works best when the repeated word is worthy of emphasis, was used in the example above: "We would like to explain our concerns about the proposed *changes* in the Sunshine Act, *changes* that would allow agency commissioners to meet behind closed doors and exclude tax-paying citizens." Here, not only is the sentence given shape by the pause, but its main point (the suspect *changes*) is presented in a way that invites scrutiny.

Connect by restating.

A third method of connecting the trailing element to the main clause is with a word that restates or sums up what has been said, *a technique* I am using in the sentence you are reading now. (The word *technique* alludes to a previously expressed thought: the idea of using a word to restate or sum up.) This method involves repeating not only a word (as you do with the second method), but also a thought.

As Williams points out, this type of modifier (a connecting word he calls a "summative modifier") is useful in avoiding a common structural weakness that arises from the misuse of the relative pronoun *which*. As Williams explains, the summative modifier "lets you avoid the sprawl that sometimes occurs when you tack on a *which*-clause referring to everything that preceded." He is referring to a common misuse of *which*, a relatively weak connector that is easily overtaxed.

To avoid this faulty construction (common in conversation but to be avoided in writing), use *which* to refer only to the word or phrase immediately preceding it rather than to the general thought of the preceding clause. Compare, for example, the proper use of *which* in this sentence, "I found my glove, which I had dropped in the snow" (here, *which* refers unambiguously to *glove*), with the improper use of *which* in this sentence, "I found my glove, which was fortunate" (here, *which* refers awkwardly to the act of finding the glove).

Likewise, compare "A third method of connecting the trailing element to the main clause is with a word that restates or sums up what has been said, *which* I am using in the sentence you are reading now" with the sentence as it appears above: "A third method of connecting the trailing element to the main clause is with a word that restates or sums up what has been said, *a technique* I am using in the sentence you are reading now." Not only does the summative modifier *technique* avoid the ambiguity of the misused relative pronoun *which,* but it also creates a more pronounced and emphatic pause.

If you are feeling somewhat confused by all this, allow me to offer a word of encouragement: It's not as complicated as it may seem. In fact, applying this technique is easier than explaining it. Just look for a word that summarizes the point of your main clause and use it to introduce your trailing element.

Use balanced sentences to emphasize similarities.

Like subordination, a "balanced" (or parallel) sentence is a sign of accomplished writing, a declaration to the reader that the writer is attending to the musical qualities of language. It involves the balancing of grammatically similar or related elements. Parallelism is also called "coordination," and sentences with parallel elements are called "balanced" or "coordinated sentences."

The principle of parallelism, or parallel structure, is based on a simple premise: The reader expects and appreciates consistency. When related or coordinate ideas are expressed in parallel structure, they have more emphasis, and the reader finds them more memorable.

Here's how parallelism works: If you begin making a list with adjectives, for example, you enter a contract with the reader to complete your list in like fashion. If you switch to a different part of speech somewhere in your list, you break the contract, and the breach jars the reader.

For example, if Benjamin Franklin had written, "Early to bed, early to rise, makes a man healthy, wealthy, and a CEO," we wouldn't be quoting him today. Instead, he began his list with two adjectives, *healthy* and *wealthy*, and completed it not with a noun, *CEO*, but with a third adjective, *wise*, thereby maintaining parallel structure and rendering his maxim memorable.

The point is to be consistent. Create an expectation in the reader's mind, and then meet that expectation. It's a nice trick. It tells the reader you know what you're doing.

Here's another sentence that breaks the pattern: "She is capable, experienced, and often works late at night." Here, the writer breaks the contract with the reader by shifting from a series of adjectives, *capable* and *experienced*, to a verb phrase, *often works late at night*. The result is a break in rhythm, a loss of momentum.

To honor the contract, the writer should have written, "She is capable, experienced, and dedicated"—or "talented" or "brilliant" or whatever adjective came to mind, as long as it was another adjective. If, on the other hand, the writer was partial to the verb phrase, if the writer liked the sound of it and didn't want to give it up, the sentence could have been rewritten this way: "A capable and dedicated employee, she often works until late at night." Either way, the writer avoids a common writing error, the sentence is vastly improved, and the reader doesn't feel cheated.

Here's another example: "The volume of business depends on an institution's delivery method, production time, and whether or not it is open or closed." Can you hear where the parallel structure breaks down? To eliminate the breach in contract, the series should be concluded as it was begun—with a third noun phrase, like this: "delivery method, production time, and hours of operation."

Sometimes the break in parallel structure is glaring: "I like opera, poetry, and playing golf on Sundays." Sometimes the break is subtle: "Many young people dream of getting married, the birth of a child, and buying a home." Either way, the pattern is broken. The point is to be consistent.

Correctly used, parallelism can make your writing memorable, as illustrated by Samuel Johnson (who wrote one of the first dictionaries of the English language) when he declared, "What is written without effort is in general read without pleasure," and when he quipped to an aspiring author: "Your manuscript is both good and original; but the part that is good is not original, and the part that is original is not good." Though uncharitable in its sentiment, Johnson's pronouncement is impressive in its execution.

Henry David Thoreau created a balanced sentence when he wrote, "Any fool can make a rule and every fool will mind it." Likewise, President Kennedy used parallel elements in his 1961 inaugural address when he proclaimed, "We shall pay any price, bear any burden, meet any hardship, support any friend, oppose any foe to assure the survival and the success of liberty." In these examples, the rhythm and cadence of language work to the writer's (and the orator's) advantage.

The conclusion of Abraham Lincoln's "Gettysburg Address" offers another case in point: "It is for us the living . . . to be here dedicated to the great task remaining before us—that from these honored dead we take increased devotion to that cause for which they gave the last full measure of devotion—that we here highly resolve that these dead shall not have died in vain—that this nation, under God, shall have a new birth of freedom—and that government of the people, by the people, and for every single one of us, shall not perish from the earth."

Obviously, that's not the way it went.

Like any great orator—and any great writer—Lincoln knew how to use parallel structure to good effect. He not only constructed a balanced sentence consisting of four coordinate *that* clauses, but he imbedded a second parallel element in the final clause: "government of the people, by the people, and for the people."

Parallelism is uncommonly versatile in its applications. It can be used for many purposes, whether to declare independence from Great Britain ("We hold these truths to be self-evident, that all men are created equal, that they are endowed by their Creator with certain unalienable Rights, that among these are Life, Liberty, and the pursuit of Happiness"); to honor the 23,000 Union soldiers—not to mention the 25,000 Confederate soldiers—who were killed or wounded during three days of fighting on July 1—3, 1863, near Gettysburg, Pennsylvania ("But, in a larger sense, we cannot dedicate—we cannot consecrate—we cannot hallow this ground"); or to announce the purpose of next week's staff meeting ("Please come prepared not only to react to my proposal but also to offer your own ideas and suggestions").

Similarly, note the power generated by the Reverend Martin Luther King, Jr., when he punctuated his famous speech with, "I have a dream that one day . . . I have a dream that one day . . ." The effect of parallelism is to add a rising crescendo of emphasis. As the Roman statesman and orator Marcus Tullius Cicero knew, parallel structure allows you to take an ordinary thought ("You should do something for your country instead of always thinking about what your country can do for you") and express it so memorably ("Ask not what your country can do for you; ask what you can do for your country") that a certain American president decided to use the same line two and a half millenia later. It's a beautiful thought, beautifully rendered.

Break the pattern for special effect.

Sophisticated writers sometimes break parallel structure deliberately, as the English novelist Somerset Maugham did when he wrote: "There are three rules for writing a novel. Unfortunately, nobody knows what they are." In fact, skillful writers—and skillful humorists—know how to play with their audiences. They use parallel structure to create a certain expectation and then offer a conceptual twist, as Dorothy Parker did when she said, "The best way to keep children home is to make the home a pleasant atmosphere—and let the air out of the tires."

Ingrid Bergman employed the same technique: "Happiness is good health and a bad memory." Mark Twain did likewise: "Familiarity breeds contempt—and children."

Omit words to accentuate the rhythm of parallel structure.

As I pointed out in Chapter 3, elliptical constructions heighten the effect of parallel structure. Omitting words that are suggested by the context slows and intensifies the rhythm of the balanced elements, as when the poet and memoirist Patricia Hampl writes in "Look at a Teacup," "Her eyes were closed, her arms [were] heavy and soapy."

One type of ellipsis (called "asyndeton") is achieved by omitting the *and* at the end of a series, as in "She felt hopelessly lost, unloved, [and] abandoned." Kennedy uses asyndeton in the sentence quoted above: "We shall pay any price, bear any burden, meet any hardship, support any friend, [and] oppose any foe to assure the survival and the success of liberty." In both examples, the omissions slow the pace, tighten the rhythm, and render the point more deliberately.

Use antithetical sentences to juxtapose contrasting ideas.

Like the three other types of rhetorical sentences (periodic, loose, and balanced), the antithetical sentence relies on its structure to produce its distinctive effect. An antithetical sentence is one that places contrasting ideas side by side, often in parallel structure. The resulting juxtaposition creates emphasis. Consider, for example, these sentences, from a memo by Thomas Watson, Jr.: "IBM wasn't built with fuzzy ideas and pretentious language. IBM was built with clear thinking and plain talk." Note that when the contrasting ideas of an antithetical sentence are presented in parallel structure (in other words, when dissimilar thoughts are expressed in similar rhythms), content and structure seem to move in opposing directions, and the resulting tension heightens the emphasis.

Balance antithetical elements to emphasize dissimilarity.

Again taking J.F.K. as an example, his 1961 inaugural address is characterized—and made memorable—by his skillful use of antithesis. (For a detailed stylistic analysis of his speech, see Corbett and Connors' *Style and Statement.*) His opening sentence is not only loose but antithetical. It is not only antithetical but balanced. And it is balanced around not one but three pairs of contrasting ideas: "We observe today not a victory of party but a celebration of freedom, symbolizing an end as well as a beginning, signifying renewal as well as change."

Later in the same speech he uses a rhetorical scheme called "antimetabole" when, in juxtaposing and balancing contrasting ideas, he repeats certain words in reverse grammatical order: "Let us never negotiate out of fear, but let us never fear to negotiate." He uses the same device in the most memorable line of the speech (quoted above), "And so, my fellow Americans, ask not what your country can do for you; ask what you can do for your country." In the next sentence he uses a similar scheme called "chiasmus." Like antimetabole, chiasmus heightens the effect of antithesis by reversing grammatical structures, but unlike antimetabole, it does so with no repetition of key words: "My fellow citizens of the world, ask not what America will do for you, but what together we can do for the freedom of man." In all three examples, J.F.K., using the rhythm of balanced sentences to intensify the effect of antithesis, does more than capture the spirit of the times: He does so with carefully crafted eloquence.

For practice, revise this sentence so that the antithetical elements are more neatly balanced: "I didn't mean to hurt your feelings; my intention was merely to help." (*Hint:* Begin the second clause with "I only wanted . . .")

Use paradox to get the reader's attention.

Like antithesis, paradox takes its effect from the presentation of unlike ideas. But paradox presents ideas that are more than contrasting. Paradox presents ideas that are contradictory (or that appear to be contradictory).

Ellen Goodman uses paradox to good effect in "Putting In a Good Word for Guilt." She leads off with an attention-getting paradox: "Feeling guilty is nothing to feel guilty about." Later she again uses paradox when she writes, "The last thing we need more of is less conscience," and when she writes, "This worst emotion, in a sense, helps bring out the best in us."

Although usually direct and emphatic, paradox also can be subtle. It can be a mere suggestion of contradiction or incongruity, as when a student in one of my classes wrote, "I remained unemployed and optimistic." As with antithesis, when the contradictory elements are presented in parallel structure, content and structure seem to move in opposing directions, and the effect is heightened.

Paradox engages our attention by appealing to our intellect. It invites us to solve a puzzle, to take a closer look, to examine the contradiction, to see if it is apparent or real. We are intrigued by the invitation, perhaps because we tend to assume that beneath the contradiction lies a deeper truth.

Learn from others.

Although some of the techniques presented in this chapter may seem complicated, the overall lesson is simple: You can improve your style by listening carefully to the sound of your language, by tuning your ear to the musical quality of your words and the rhythm of your sentences. The principles and techniques I have identified will help you make that sound more pleasing. If you are committed to developing your style, to expanding your repertoire of stylistic devices and effects, I suggest that you do three things: Study those principles and techniques, watch for their appearance in the writing of others, and try them out in your own writing.

I also urge you to do what developing writers have done for centuries: Imitate accomplished writers. Select a sentence or passage you think is beautifully written and study it, read it out loud, copy it over, and write another passage that incorporates its stylistic features. Select a subject of your own and use words of your own choosing, but copy everything else. Imitate the defining characteristics of your model—the sentence structures, the punctuation, the rhythm, the figures of speech, the types of words—phrase by phrase, comma by comma, and metaphor by metaphor.

Don't be concerned that imitating the styles of other writers will make you sound too much like them or that your style will become indistinguishable from theirs. The point of imitating the style of an accomplished writer is to expand your knowledge of various stylistic possibilities, to try them out and see how they work—and perhaps in the process to discover some of your own. Over time, as you learn to incorporate these techniques into your own writing, your own distinct voice will emerge.

With this approach in mind, consider the following passage by Karal Ann Marling, professor of American Studies at the University of Minnesota and author of *Blue Ribbon: A Social and Pictorial History of the Minnesota State*

Fair. Note how she captures the wistful mood associated with a passing season in her description of the Minnesota State Fair:

> Fairs come at the twilight of the year, when the harvest is in and the year's work is almost done, when the land prepares for its long winter sleep. The final event of the departing summer, the Minnesota State Fair marks a time of celebration, a time of optimism and satisfaction with a job well done. Like a warm, soft Minnesota night, it is a time of rest and play and renewal, a time for learning and contemplation and wonder, a time for dreaming.

What techniques does Marling use to convey the mood so effectively?

The answer—at least in part—is her evocative use of metaphor (*the twilight of the year* and *its long winter sleep*). But it is also the *sound* of her language. It is the rhythm and cadence of her sentences, the refrain of repeated phrases beginning with the words *when* and *a time*. If you look closely at the passage (better yet, if you read it out loud), you will hear the effect of this repetition: *When, when. A time, a time. A time, a time, a time.* The beat goes like this: One, two. One, two. One, two, three. And in the last sentence you will hear a kind of counterpoint, a rhythm within the overall rhythm, with three adjectives in the introductory phrase *(Like a warm, soft Minnesota night)* and a series of three nouns, another three nouns, then one noun after the repeated words *a time: Rest and play and renewal. Learning and contemplation and wonder. Dreaming.* Once established, the beat ends abruptly, suggestively: One, two, three. One, two, three. One, two, three. One.

A student in one of my classes did the following study based on Marling's passage:

> Quiet comes at mid-evening, when Alexis becomes serene and asks to read a book, when her eyes finally close in peaceful sleep. Her day comes to a close, a day full of activity, hours filled with promise and possibilities. Her face is a sleeping memory, of toys that offered new enjoyments, of places revisited and explored, of grandparents who clung to her every word, of love.

Nicely done, wouldn't you say?

CHAPTER 5: PERSONALITY

Be Lively, Unpredictable, Playful, and Genuine

Add Color and Unpredictability With Figurative Language

EXPRESS YOUR ORIGINALITY BY MAKING UNLIKELY
  COMPARISONS.

USE ANALOGIES TO CLARIFY OR REINFORCE YOUR MEANING.

CHOOSE BETWEEN SIMILE AND METAPHOR DEPENDING ON THE
  DESIRED EFFECT.

DON'T FORCE YOUR COMPARISONS.

EVALUATE YOUR SIMILES AND METAPHORS ON THE BASIS OF
  THEIR APTNESS, NOVELTY, AND SIMPLICITY.

COME BACK TO YOUR METAPHORS.

PREFER THE UNEXPECTED TO THE FAMILIAR AND THE CLICHÉD.

USE PERSONIFICATION TO ADD LIFE TO YOUR WRITING.

Be Playful

AS A RULE, AVOID INVOLVED NARRATIVE JOKES
  ENDING WITH A PUNCH LINE.

USE PUNS OR PLAYS ON WORDS ONLY WHEN APPROPRIATE.

USE WIT (FROM THE OLD ENGLISH *WITAN*, "TO KNOW").

USE IRONY TO POINT OUT THE DISPARITY BETWEEN
  WHAT IS REAL AND WHAT IS PERCEIVED.

USE UNDERSTATEMENT (OR MEIOSIS) FOR A MORE
  REFINED STYLE OF HUMOR.

USE OVERSTATEMENT (EXAGGERATION OR HYPERBOLE) FOR A
  MORE OUTLANDISH STYLE OF HUMOR.

USE SELF-DEPRECATING HUMOR.

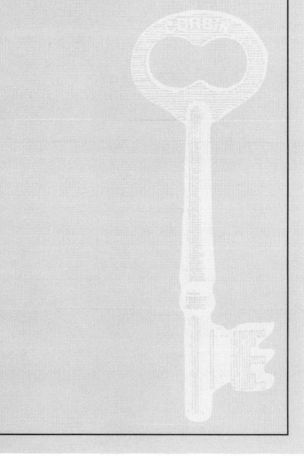

Be Genuine

VALUE SUBSTANCE OVER STYLE.

TAKE A DEFINITE STAND.

APPROACH WRITING AS SELF-REVELATION, AND STYLE
AS SELF-REALIZATION.

AVOID A BUREAUCRATIC STYLE.

DON'T HIDE BEHIND YOUR WORDS.

BE A COMPLETE PERSON.

CHAPTER FIVE

{Personality}

Be Lively, Unpredictable, Playful, and Genuine

When you think of Whoopi Goldberg presiding over the Academy Awards, what traits come to mind? Liveliness? Unpredictability? Humor?

If you're talkin' personality, Honey, that woman's got it.

Now, when you think of someone *writing with personality*, what traits come to mind? I would argue the same. Whether conveyed in person or in writing, personality is associated with—among other traits—liveliness, unpredictability, and humor.

The writer, however, faces certain challenges that the oral communicator does not. Unlike Whoopi Goldberg before a live audience and a camera, the writer cannot rely on inflection, expression, gestures, body language, and flamboyant costumes to make a vivid impression. The writer must convey the traits of personality as features of written language.

Writing with personality and style can be achieved by learning the techniques I have presented in the first four chapters of this book. To review some of those techniques, consider the following:

- **Make every word count.** Rather than "The fact that you are reading this book is an indication that you have an interest in writing," write "Your reading this book indicates an interest in writing."
- **Use natural language.** Rather than "A strong union affords strength and protection; a weak alliance engenders vulnerability," write "United we stand; divided we fall."
- **Use words and images that appeal to the five senses.** Rather than "They spat into the water behind the riverboat, feeling their oats," write, as

Rita Dove does in her poem "The Event," "They spat where the wheel / churned mud and moonlight, / they called to the tarantulas down among the bananas to come out and dance."

- **Use action verbs to invigorate your writing.** Rather than "Make a revision in this sentence," write "Revise this sentence."
- **Use variety, pauses, and rhythm to make your sentences memorable.** Of the various techniques relating to sentence structure discussed in Chapter 4, five are particularly useful for making a vivid impression on your reader.

    1. Follow a long sentence with a short, snappy one. This long-short combination creates emphasis and makes you sound decisive.

    2. Pause for emphasis. To bring a sentence to a dramatic halt, use punctuation. Particularly useful are the dash and the colon.

    3. Use occasional sentence fragments. The reason: They change the pace. Note the effect of a sentence fragment before a colon. You also can use a sentence fragment after a complete sentence. Like an afterthought. Be careful, though. Not to overuse this device. It can become. Distracting.

    4. Invert usual word order. Particularly useful is inversion, a technique called "anastrophe" by classical rhetoricians. Without its inverted structure, for example, the sentence you just read would sound like this: "Inversion, a technique called 'anastrophe' by classical rhetoricians, is particularly useful."

    5. Use parallel structure. Rather than "You better work hard on your writing if you want to please your reader," write "The harder you work on your writing, the more likely you will please your reader," or write, as the lexicographer Samuel Johnson did (and as I quoted him in my foreword), "What is written without effort is in general read without pleasure."

But style, in its deeper meaning, goes beyond technique. There is something incalculable about style, an intangible quality that has to do with the way language conveys the writer's personality, self, values, and character. In this chapter I build on the keys and techniques discussed so far in an attempt to explore style in this deeper sense.

Add Color and Unpredictability With Figurative Language

Sometimes the best way to make your point is to say what you don't mean—or rather, to say what you mean but to say it nonliterally and unconventionally, in a way that surprises and delights your reader.

Imagine, for example, that you are a writer and humorist named Garrison Keillor and you are describing the newly elected governor of the state of Minnesota back in his days as a professional wrestler. You want to capture the essence of this peculiar type of entertainer in all his garish glory. How do you go about it?

You do two things. First, you come up with some colorful and vivid details. Then, to cap off your description, you conclude with an unanticipated comparison: "You see him cavorting around the ring, 6 feet 4 inches, 225 pounds, with a fringe of peroxided hair, wearing sort of tie-dyed tights, a man in a grotesque cartoon body. . . . He's got a mustache and long, dangling earrings. He looks like a CPA at Mardi Gras." It's that last twist—an image that is at once outlandish and apt—that renders your description memorable.

Of all the things you do as a writer, perhaps none is more challenging than offering the right comparison. To do so requires nonrational thinking, a particular type of inventiveness based on playfulness and imagination, a willingness to wander beyond conventional boundaries. It was for this reason that Aristotle declared, "By far the greatest thing is to be master of metaphor. It is the one thing that cannot be learned from others. It is a sign of genius, for a good metaphor implies an intuitive perception of similarity among dissimilars."

To take another example, let's say you are a newspaper columnist named James Lileks and you want to give your reader a feeling for the ludicrously oversized dimensions of the governor's vehicle of choice, the Lincoln Navigator. Rather than offer an objective, point-by-point inventory of features, you stretch things a bit to capture the spirit of both the vehicle and its owner:

> The Navigator . . . seats about forty. I've been in smaller movie theaters. . . . If SEALS spent a lot of time jumping out of planes, they'll appreciate the view from the driver's window. The last time I was that high up someone offered me peanuts and a compli-

mentary beverage. . . . Acceleration is instantaneous: Step hard
on the gas, and you feel as if you're riding the back of a terrified
ox. . . . There are enough air bags for the truck to qualify as a
Senate subcommittee.

Well, you get the idea. Outlandish comparisons are fun. But they can be
more than entertaining. Comparisons—whether they be analogies, metaphors, or similes—can lead to a deeper, more profound understanding than
can literal description and objective detail. When you want to add a light
touch, illuminate a complex situation with clarity, or cap off a description
with a memorable image, offer a comparison.

Express your originality by making unlikely comparisons.

Be the person who first thinks to question someone's intelligence by saying,
"He's a few sandwiches short of a picnic." Rather than "Duplication of effort
was the reason for the cost overrun," write "Duplication of effort was the
cost overrun culprit." Rather than "The practice may not be illegal, but it
isn't ethical," write "The practice may not be illegal, but it doesn't pass the
smell test." And rather than "I like E-mail because it's efficient and direct,"
write, as a student in one of my classes did, "I like E-mail because it's efficient
and direct. No receptionist, no voice mail, no elevator music." Do as F. Scott
Fitzgerald does when he makes that imaginative leap in describing Jay Gatsby's
mansion in *The Great Gatsby* as a place where music was heard "through the
summer nights" and where "men and girls came and went like moths among
the whisperings and the champagne and the stars."

When the time seems right—when you really want to drive home your
point—abandon the realm of rational thought. Give in to your creativity and
playfulness. Appeal to your reader's imagination. Venture a metaphor.

Use analogies to clarify or reinforce your meaning.

When you offer a comparison or analogy, you help your reader understand
your meaning on a different—sometimes simpler, sometimes more profound—level. Rather than "This manual is poorly written," write "Following

these instructions is like putting together a jigsaw puzzle with three pieces missing." Rather than "Our sales representatives have trouble setting up an unfamiliar display unit," write, as a student in one of my classes did:

> Have you ever tried repairing a flat tire when you didn't have the right jack? You might get the tire changed, but it's cumbersome. That's how it feels for our sales representatives when they're trying to set up a display unit different from the one they are accustomed to using.

Use analogy to help your reader grasp a complex idea, particularly when the concept is abstract or technical. Indeed, one measure of a technical writer's effectiveness is the extent to which he or she is able to make complex ideas comprehensible to the nonspecialist. In an article that appeared in the May 6, 1999, *Minneapolis Star Tribune*, for example, John Mather, senior astrophysicist at NASA's Goddard Space Flight Center in Greenbelt, Maryland, described how the Hubble telescope is changing the way scientists think about cosmology and the evolution of the galaxies. With Hubble orbiting above the obscuring effects of the Earth's atmosphere, he explained, astronomers can look back in time to when galaxies were forming. Said Mather:

> We thought galaxies formed just like they are. But now we think they grew, they assembled themselves from smaller pieces. It might have been like rain on the side of a hill. First you get little rivulets that flow together into a larger stream.

In a follow-up article that appeared a few weeks later, Robert Kirshner of Harvard University was quoted as saying that scientists "used to disagree by a factor of two concerning the age of the universe." That was a huge gap, he explained, like "arguing about having one foot or two." But now the range of difference has been narrowed to a mere 10 percent, which is more "like a difference of one toe. This is good to plus or minus one piggy."

Creativity and playfulness of this sort come as a relief to your readers, especially when the information being conveyed is complex or difficult to understand.

As another example, compare—as Lynn Quitman Troyka does in the *Simon and Schuster Handbook for Writers*—two descriptions of the common wart. The first is from a medical encyclopedia, the second from Lewis Thomas, a physician and author known for his ability to render technical information in a colorful, accessible style:

> The common wart usually occurs on the hands, especially on the backs of the fingers, but they may occur on any part of the skin. These dry, elevated lesions have numerous projections on the surface.

> Warts are wonderful structures. They can appear overnight on any part of the skin, like mushrooms on a damp lawn, full grown and splendid in the complexity of their architecture.

Although the first description provides specific and objective information, the second creates a better feeling for the unusual features of these curious afflictions.

If you are a technical writer, your foremost concerns are clarity, precision, and accuracy. But don't be so bound by the demands of objectively perceived, precisely rendered detail that you neglect a powerful tool of communication: your imagination. Rather than "Combining atoms from different molecules is difficult because of nearly intractable differences in their physical properties," consider writing "Combining atoms from different molecules is like mixing vinegar and oil." Use imaginative analogies to help your reader get the point.

The creative writer likewise can put analogy to good use. In *Memoirs of a Geisha*, for example, Arthur Golden uses unadorned comparisons, often to the natural world, to convey the nuances of complex human emotions, as when his narrator observes:

> Grief is a most peculiar thing; we're so helpless in the face of it. It's like a window that will simply open of its own accord. The room grows cold, and we can do nothing but shiver. But it opens a little less each time, and a little less; and one day we wonder what has become of it.

Later, in describing a turning point in her troubled relationship with her rival and nemesis Hatsumomo, the narrator says:

> I don't think I realized it at the time, but after Hatsumomo and I quarreled over my journal, her mind—as the Admiral would have put it—began to be troubled by doubt. She knew that under no circumstances would Mother take her side against me any longer; and because of that, she was like a fabric taken from its warm closet and hung out of doors where the harsh weather will gradually consume it. . . .
>
> And another thing: she was no longer as beautiful as she'd once been. Her skin was waxy-looking, and her features puffy. Or perhaps I was only seeing her that way. A tree may look as beautiful as ever; but when you notice the insects infesting it, and the tips of the branches that are brown from disease, even the trunk seems to lose some of its magnificence.

Choose between simile and metaphor depending on the desired effect.

Use similes (or comparisons using *like* or *as*) for a more conscious, calculated effect ("He works like a horse"); use metaphors (or comparisons not using *like* or *as*) for a more insistent, surprising effect ("He is a horse"). Compare, for example, "When I came home to my family after my freshman year, I felt like a stranger in a small town," with "When I came home to my family after my freshman year, I was a stranger in a small town."

Don't force your comparisons.

Perhaps more than any other aspect of writing, expressing your thought in figurative language draws on your creativity and imagination. There is no easy formula to help you create a good metaphor. Making an apt comparison is more the work of the unconscious than the conscious mind. It has more to do with an image or idea coming to you than you searching it out. Perhaps the best advice is to be open to that part of yourself that you associate with reverie and dreams. As Donald Hall advises in *Writing Well,* "Try to activate the daydreaming mind." Let your thoughts wander.

Evaluate your similes and metaphors on the basis of their aptness, novelty, and simplicity.

Although your journey cannot be charted easily, your arrival can be readily determined. Your reader knows at a glance if your metaphor works or fails, if it succeeds in clarifying and reinforcing your message or if it detracts from it.

A good metaphor has three qualities: aptness, novelty, and simplicity. Some of the most enduring metaphors in the English language are the most natural and unaffected. Consider, for example, Shakespeare's metaphor "All the world's a stage," or these similes (metaphors that use *like* or *as*): "O my love's like a red, red rose" (Robert Burns), "My heart is like a singing bird" (Christina Rossetti), and "I wandered lonely as a cloud" (William Wordsworth).

Consider this metaphor: "The state is at a crossroads." It was written by a budget analyst in the Minnesota State Department of Finance. Although the comparison with a crossroads is familiar—so familiar, in fact, it could be considered a cliché—the writer puts it to good use: to emphasize the need to choose between a policy based on lower spending and one based on higher taxes.

Consider a bad metaphor: "We want to hire only the best applicants, so we are cherry picking the cream of the crop." That was written by a personnel manager of a trucking firm. Consider this series of terrible metaphors: "Given our employees' tendency to fly off the handle, we must nip their outbursts in the bud before they run rampant." That was written by me. I present it here to illustrate how a rotten metaphor can be made even worse by mixing images. And as William Safire advises, "Take the bull by the hand, and don't mix metaphors."

Just for the fun of it, here are a few similes that are so bad they're good. They were posted on the Internet under the title "Winners of the worst analogies ever written in a high school essay." Among the best of the worst were these:

The hailstones leaped from the pavement, just like maggots when you fry them in hot grease.

His thoughts tumbled in his head, making and breaking alliances like underpants in a dryer without Cling Free.

McNeil fell twelve stories, hitting the pavement like a Hefty Bag filled with vegetable soup.

The politician was gone but unnoticed, like the period after the Dr. on a Dr Pepper can.

Her vocabulary was as bad as, like, whatever.

My favorite was this one: "Her hair glistened in the rain like nose hair after a sneeze." Now that's what you might call an explosive simile.

Not to ride a gift horse until you make it puke, but usually the metaphors that flop are the ones that are overdone, contrived, outlandish, or simply inappropriate to the subject or context. There is a critical difference between a metaphor that makes a gentle turn in the road and one that reaches out a giant hand and slaps you in the face. (Ouch!)

Be creative, but not contrived. Rather than "At last week's meeting I felt as if everyone turned against me the way the populace stormed the Bastille during the French Revolution," write "At last week's meeting I felt like a dart board." The point is, be imaginative, be creative, be daring—but don't overdo it. Use metaphors that reinforce or clarify your meaning but that don't distract from your message or intrude on the flow of your development. Show restraint, even as you exercise your imagination. Too many metaphors, even good metaphors, will work against you. As Hall observes, "The liveliest prose moves from analogy to analogy without strain. It takes practice to learn how to invent, and practice to learn when to stop inventing." Know when enough is enough. A little metaphor goes a long way.

Come back to your metaphors.

As every good essayist and storyteller knows, returning to an earlier metaphor enhances coherence. Whether it is a green light at the end of Daisy Buchanan's dock, which appears early on and again at the end of *The Great Gatsby*, or the fat pitch in E. B. White's introduction to *The Elements of Style*, a reappearing metaphor conveys structure and craft. It provides a frame that leaves your reader (or listener) with a satisfying sense of order and completion.

Prefer the unexpected to the familiar and the clichéd.

If it sounds familiar and commonplace to you, it probably sounds familiar and commonplace to your reader. Search for the new, the unusual, the un-anticipated, the unpredictable. Find words that have retained their freshness, words like *conifer, conjure, succulent,* and *sapsucker,* rather than words like *tree, predict, juicy,* and *bird.*

The person who first looked out the window and exclaimed, "Look! It's raining cats and dogs!" introduced a wonderful figure of speech into the English language. (Some sources claim that the phrase describes an actual event that occurred when the family pets, kept atop a thatched roof, had difficulty maintaining their footing in a heavy rain.) Whatever its origins, to use the image of animals tumbling pell-mell from the sky to capture the feeling of a downpour was unexpected. It was a brilliant metaphor (a figure of speech containing an implied comparison)—when it was used for the first time. But now, after millions of repetitions, this imaginative comparison has become a cliché.

Not that familiar, common expressions are necessarily a poor choice. Cli-chés offer the advantage of being easily comprehended. They link your thoughts to readily accessible images, sometimes quite colorfully ("A bird in the hand is worth two in the bush" and "Nothing ventured, nothing gained"). But after repeated use, these expressions fail to awaken and surprise. They're like tarnished gems that over time have lost their luster.

Of more consequence to the writer seeking authentic expression, clichés can trivialize complex thought and suppress genuine emotion. They offer a facile connection between meaning and words, a connection that cheapens the writer's relationship to language.

For these reasons, use clichés sparingly. Resist the temptation to settle for the familiar and the commonplace. Rather than attach your thoughts and feelings to ready-made images, travel the opposite direction: Reach deep within yourself. Explore the nuances and subtlety of what you find there, or as Donald Hall says, "Push yourself to discover the true specifics of your feeling."

If you approach writing as an occasion to discover truth, and you think of word choice as a search for true expression, you'll find that clichés usually stand in your way. It's not that they're false, but that they're generic. Try to grasp the particular before the universal. Seek to understand the enormity of a single fact. As the poet Walt Whitman advised, look for truth in a blade of grass.

Use personification to add life to your writing.

Personification is figurative language that ascribes human attributes to inanimate objects, ideas, abstractions, and animals, as you do when you get fed up with your programmed grammar checker and yell, "I'm sick of my computer scolding me for using the passive voice!" Just as personification brings inanimate objects to life, it can add life to your writing.

Rather than "After the trees drop their leaves in the fall, the intricate design of their branches gives them a new look," write "After the trees drop their leaves in the fall, their branches speak a new language." Rather than "As I listened to the sounds of the wilderness, I realized I myself was making noise," write "As I listened to the sounds of the wilderness, I realized the wilderness was listening to me."

In Chapter 3 I advised you to make your sentences tell stories. As you look for characters that you might depict as performing actions, don't limit yourself to people. Use your imagination and you'll find that any object or any thing will serve quite well. So let the blizzard attack, the house shudder, the walls groan, the pines claw at the windowpanes, and the old oak rocker cry for a place in the living room, right over there by the warm caress of the fire.

Now you give it a try. I'll begin a sentence listing personified objects and you continue the series. Don't work too hard at it. Just use your imagination and see where it takes you: "So leave your desk and let the computer hum its joyless tune, the chair beg for a companion, the unopened mail . . ."

Do five or ten of these exercises a day and you'll get the hang of it in no time.

Be Playful

Use humor to have fun with your reader. Like figurative language and analogy, humor is a powerful tool for connecting with your reader. Humor allows you to reveal the creative, playful, imaginative side of your personality in a way that your reader is likely to find appealing. Humor works on many levels. It:

- **Appeals to your audience's intelligence.** Humor, by its nature, operates on multiple levels. As a result, it calls for your reader to be alert. This heightened state of attention is what every writer hopes to elicit from every reader. Think of the best teachers you have known. Did any of them *not* use humor?
- **Alleviates boredom.** Humor makes monotonous tasks less arduous. Whether reconciling budget figures or stacking sandbags, people usually find that a little levity lightens the load.
- **Reveals your human side.** Humor exposes your vulnerability. When you make an attempt at being humorous, you let down your defenses. You take a risk, especially if the humor is self-deprecating. When you attempt humor, you are asking for your audience's acknowledgment and approval.
- **Signifies your membership in, or allegiance to, a group.** Laughter emphasizes commonality. It reinforces bonds. Frequent laughter is a sign of a closely knit group.

Certain types of humor seem to work better than others. Of the following common types of humor, the first two are the riskiest.

As a rule, avoid involved narrative jokes ending with a punch line.

Few people can tell such jokes well, and the time and space they require may try your reader's patience. A poorly told joke, whether delivered orally or in writing, is awkward for both teller and audience.

Use puns or plays on words only when appropriate.

Some people love them; others hate them. The British, for example, consider a good pun a sign of intelligence; Americans tend to groan. Like Samuel Johnson, I find them punishing.

Use wit (from the Old English *witan*, "to know").

John Locke defined this all-inclusive type of humor as "The assemblage of ideas, and putting those together with quickness and variety." The effect is a comic twist or surprise, as when Dorothy Parker said, "I can't write five words but that I change seven," or when Peter De Vries said, "I love being a writer. What I can't stand is the paperwork."

Use irony to point out the disparity between what is real and what is perceived.

Sometimes called "Socratic irony" because Socrates liked to play dumb when asking his students hard questions, irony is the use of words to express something other than their literal meaning. Rather than open an article about life in a northern climate by writing "Contending with snow can make your commute to and from work unpleasant," write "There's nothing like a blizzard to add a little excitement to your morning commute."

Irony often involves saying the opposite of what you actually mean, as when you say, "Nice job," in response to someone messing up. Of the two common types of irony, understatement (as in "This assignment required more than a minute") generally is perceived as being more subtle than overstatement (as in "This assignment took forever").

Use understatement (or meiosis) for a more refined style of humor.

Rather than "This is costing us millions," write "This is costing us more than a Happy Meal at McDonald's." Rather than "I can't believe they canned me on my birthday!" write "Getting fired on your birthday is not the present one normally hopes for."

Use overstatement (exaggeration or hyperbole) for a more outlandish style of humor.

If the governor of your state accuses you of ripping him off for writing an unauthorized story about his days as a pro wrestler, rather than respond by saying, "You might have a point," respond the way Garrison Keillor did to Jesse Ventura. Call him a "GREAT BIG HONKING BULLET-HEADED SHOVEL-FACED MUTHA WHO TALKS IN A STEROID GROWL AND DOESN'T STOP." That will get his attention.

Use self-deprecating humor.

In the spirit of fair play, rather than describe yourself as "a tall, handsome intellectual type with glasses and a way with words," describe yourself as Keillor did, as "a tired old hack with a gecko face and thinning hair and a body like a six-foot stack of marshmallows." (Just don't get into any wrestling matches with large people who don't care for your sense of humor. You might get your marshmallows toasted.)

Making a joke at your own expense is one of the safest types of humor. The only possible problem is overdoing it to the point that you portray yourself as a buffoon.

Despite the risk of being misunderstood or having your attempts at humor fail, consider using humor when the time seems right. Look for details and situations that reveal the ludicrous or absurdly incongruous elements of daily life and our earthly existence. Humor reminds us of what we have in common as human beings. It makes us feel close when we otherwise might feel distant.

Be Genuine

In addition to the three traits I have been discussing—liveliness, unpredictability, and humor—there is a fourth trait of personality: sincerity. To care about your subject, to be committed to your craft, to be genuine in your expression—these are the deeper, less immediately visible attributes of writing with personality. The other traits may please your reader on the short term, but without sincerity your writing will seem superficial.

Value substance over style.

Style without substance accomplishes little. Kurt Vonnegut had this point in mind when he declared in an essay on style, which appeared in *Palm Sunday,*

"Did you ever admire an empty-headed writer for his or her mastery of the language? No." If you want to do more than make a good first impression, have something to say. To the writer committed to developing a "winning literary style," Vonnegut offers this advice: "Find a subject you care about and which you in your heart feel others should care about. It is this genuine caring, and not your games with language, which will be the most compelling and seductive element in your style."

Taking as his premise the point that "your eloquence should be the servant of the ideas in your head," Vonnegut urges writers to follow this simple rule of style: "If a sentence, no matter how excellent, does not illuminate my subject in some new and useful way, scratch it out."

Take a definite stand.

To make a definite impression, take a definite stand. Be decisive. Assume a position and defend it. Write with a discernible voice, tone, or point of view. (I discuss the implications of point of view in Chapter 7.) When you speak at full volume, people are more inclined to perceive you as confident and self-assured, two traits commonly associated with personality. Whatever you think about Whoopi Goldberg, for example, you wouldn't accuse her of lacking personality.

Approach writing as self-revelation, and style as self-realization.

When you write, you reveal who you are to your readers. You let them in on your secrets, your perceptions, your values, your ways of thinking, and your habits of speech. As E. B. White reminds us, writing is not just communication, but "communication through revelation—it is the Self escaping into the open." If you are honest and courageous, you write about the things that matter most to you. At its best your writing gives your reader a sense of who you are, a feeling for the person behind the words.

Writing is also a journey, an opportunity for self-exploration, for you, the writer. As you experiment with language, as you study and practice techniques of style, trying out various expressions and constructions, learning to adapt them to your own purposes, and figuring out which ones work for you and which ones don't, you discover who you are. More than that, you are led to ask, Who would I like to be? What persona or symbolic representation of myself would I like to create and present to the world—and perhaps someday, in real life, come to be? Just as writing is self-revelation, developing style is a creative process of self-realization.

Avoid a bureaucratic style.

To write in a bureaucratic style is to write without sincerity and commitment. The word *bureaucracy* comes to us from the Old French *burel,* the name of a woolen cloth used to cover desks, which became known as *bureaux.* In time, the word *bureaux* was associated with the office, then with the occupants of the office. Add *-cracy* (from the Greek *kratos* meaning *power*), and you've got *bureaucracy.*

Bureaucratese is writing characterized by general inscrutability, lifelessness, and lack of humanity. More specifically, its traits include:

- **Overuse of the passive voice.** Sentences in which the subject is acted upon, as in "The report was written by me," or "A new method for effecting the dephosphorization of taconite pellets was developed by the University of Minnesota."
- **Excessive use of nominalizations.** Nouns created from verbs, such as *contribution, recommendation,* and *consideration,* as in *make a contribution, offer a recommendation,* or *take into consideration,* rather than *contribute, recommend,* and *consider.*
- **Long compound noun phrases.** Series of nouns used as adjectives, such as *an acquisition candidate identification process* rather than *a process for identifying candidates for acquisition.*
- **Long and unnecessarily complex sentences.** As in "Although preliminary proposals must be processed through the Office of Research Administration (ORA) prior to submission to the sponsoring agency to ensure that University and agency requirements have been considered, and that proper University endorsement is affixed, the requirement to complete the BA Form 23 ('Application for External Research or Training Support') is not necessary in these instances."

Not only does bureaucratic writing fail to convey commitment, but it also fails to take into account the advice about listening to language I presented in Chapter 4. Bureaucratese is language without music.

This superficial approach to language may explain why on-the-job writing often seems so lifeless and dry, as though it were written by a machine rather than a human being. When people write on the job perhaps they assume that they must use someone else's language, that being a professional requires them to resort to a kind of high-blown, unnatural language that is supposed to establish their prowess and their intelligence by its very obscurity and detachment. Maybe business writers believe they are responsible to some higher authority that requires them to write *It is my recommendation that we take action at the earliest possible time* rather than *I think we should act immediately.*

People who write this way fail to realize a simple truth about most on-the-job writing: The reader wants to hear a human voice, not some abstract construct of how business writing is supposed to sound.

If you want to connect with your reader, you should avoid language that seems stilted or unnecessarily formal in favor of language that sounds natural and genuine to your ear. As I said in Chapter 2, unless you have a good reason for choosing a fancy word, use a plain one. Think of writing as a personal transaction between you and your reader. The words are the medium, nothing more than the means of creating a relationship between you and your audience. The real subject is you—your thoughts, ideas, and values.

Consider this sentence: "I deem it advisable that you and I should continue to interface in positive ways on this matter until such time as a solution can be found." Admittedly, that's an extreme example of puffed-up, overdone, fancy language, but I would wager that you've probably come across something like it. (You even may have *written* something like it—not to point any fingers.)

Does the language in that sentence give you a sense of the person behind the words? Perhaps more to the point, are you comfortable with that person? Would you enjoy spending time with that person?

Compare this version of the sentence: "I am eager to continue working with you to solve this problem." Do you hear how this more natural language makes a better impression? A person who uses this kind of language seems more real, easier to be with, a more pleasant companion than someone who puffs up his or her thoughts with phony, inflated language.

Perhaps the best way to avoid bureaucratic writing is simply to use natural language. Without sacrificing precision and clarity, try to capture the flow and rhythm of natural speech. Although some audiences and situations do require a more formal style, don't be more formal than the occasion requires, and, in any case, remember that formality does not require awkwardness. (I discuss the need to maintain a consistent level of formality in Chapter 7.) As Patricia Westheimer advises in *The Executive Style Book*, in all but the most formal writing, "Write the way you speak—conversationally and naturally."

So the next time you find yourself struggling over whether to use the word *commence* or *begin*, remember the golden rule as it applies to writing: "Write unto others as you would have them write unto you."

Don't hide behind your words.

Your goal as a writer is to connect with your reader, not to create distance through artificial-sounding language. At its best, your writing should convey a sense of your individuality, your humanity, your warmth. Communication goes deeper than language. It goes to the heart of human interaction. To write with a sense of humanity is to recognize writing as a personal transaction between writer and reader. Your reader should never be allowed to forget that behind your words, behind this artifice of language, is a real person, an authentic human being. As William Zinsser points out in *Writing With a Word Processor*, "Readers identify first with the person who is writing, not with what the person is writing about. . . . We may think we are responding to the writer's 'style'; actually we are responding to his personality as he expresses it in words."

The secret to connecting with your reader is to be yourself. It may take confidence, even courage, to reveal who you are, but your reader wants to know. Don't hide behind your words.

Be a complete person.

There are times, of course, when you must show restraint. In many types of professional, technical, scientific, and academic writing, you, the author, are not the focus of attention. But when the time is right, when you are permitted a broader range of expression, seize the opportunity. Invite your reader to share your company—to think with you, to laugh with you, to enter your imaginative world. Reveal not only your thoughts but your feelings. Share your inner self, your insights, your humor. Be playful. Have fun with your reader. Write with heart. Bare your soul.

{PART TWO}

Elements of Composition

CHAPTER 6: PURPOSE

Know What You Want to Say

CHOOSE A SUBJECT YOU CARE ABOUT.

DETERMINE YOUR PURPOSE.

FOR MOST TYPES OF WRITING, FORMULATE A THESIS STATEMENT.

PROVIDE CONTEXT AND BACKGROUND.

Determine a Persuasive Strategy

SELECT A MODE OF DISCOURSE.

- Use description to provide information about a person setting, scene, or object.
- Use narration to tell a story.
- Use exposition to inform your reader.
- Use persuasion to induce your reader to think, act, or feel a certain way.

ANALYZE YOUR AUDIENCE.

ASSESS YOUR CREDIBILITY IN THE EYES OF YOUR READER.

DECIDE WHEN AND HOW TO STATE YOUR PURPOSE.

WRITE TO EXPLORE AND DISCOVER.

CHAPTER SIX

{Purpose}

Know What You Want to Say

The first part of this book, a discussion of five keys to great writing, was about how to make your writing more vivid, emphatic, colorful, musical, and memorable. The second part of this book, a discussion of five elements of composition, has more to do with *what* than with *how*. What is your purpose in writing? What is your topic? What material—what information, thoughts, insight, or experience—do you want to relate to your reader, and why? It also has to do with *how*, though not in the sense of *how to say it* but *how to arrange it*—how to present your material; how to work with it; how to approach, organize, illustrate, support, and connect it; how to make it appealing to your reader; and how to make it flow. Just as Part 1 concentrated primarily on language, Part 2 concentrates primarily on content.

Having begun with techniques relating to word choice or expression, we are, in a sense, traveling backward. As Aristotle and other classical rhetoricians taught writing, there are three phases in discourse: invention or the discovery of arguments, arrangement or the organization of arguments, and style or the verbalization of arguments. When you are working your way through a particular writing assignment, you proceed in that order.

My reason for beginning with the third phase was to emphasize the importance of an aspect of writing that is frequently neglected. Too often writers concentrate almost exclusively on organization and arrangement without attending to expression, or *how* you say something, which can be as important as *what* you say. To attend to the five keys to great writing—economy, precision, action, music, and personality—is to reorient yourself to language, to train your ear to its rhythms, and to awaken yourself to its possibilities.

I turn now, however, to those more fundamental questions of content and arrangement: purpose, point of view, organization, support, and coherence. What is your topic—why did you choose it (or why was it chosen for you), how is it significant to you, and how can you make it relevant to your reader? What is your relation to your material and to your reader? Given your purpose and point of view, what is the most effective way to arrange your material? What is the best way to illustrate and support your points? And how can you make your thoughts flow so that one point connects logically to the next?

Choose a subject you care about.

Assuming you are in the enviable but challenging position of choosing your own subject rather than having it chosen for you, how should you go about finding a worthy subject, one that has significance for you and relevance for your reader, and one that you are capable of managing? In evaluating the worthiness of your subject and your ability to handle it, ask three questions:

- Do you know enough about your subject to write about it meaningfully?
- Do you care enough about your subject to devote the time needed to find out what you need to know and to complete the assignment?
- Are you able to present your subject in a way that will be interesting, fresh, relevant, or useful to your intended audience?

Asking these questions will help you gauge your interest and commitment to a subject. Beyond a checklist approach, of course, you should simply listen to your heart. You might find that a certain idea or theme commands your attention so compellingly that you are unable to let go of it. (Some authors would say it's more a question of an idea or theme not letting go of them.) If this is the case, you probably have a subject that is worth exploring.

Determine your purpose.

As you settle on a subject, you need to clarify your purpose. What is your reason for writing about this subject? What is your goal? What do you hope to accomplish?

It could be argued that all discourse falls into one of three categories: to inform, to persuade, or to entertain. The purpose of every written or spoken sentence is to perform one of these functions. Although most written communication includes aspects of more than one category, you may find it helpful to identify your primary goal as one of these three.

There are, of course, other ways of defining purpose. Composition theorist James Britton, for example, takes a less reader-centered, more writer-centered approach to defining purpose when he describes written discourse in terms of three "function categories": expressive, transactional, and poetic. In *expressive* writing, your purpose is to articulate your inner feelings and make them intelligible. In *transactional* writing, you write interactively to solve a problem, to accomplish a specific task, to conduct business, or to make something happen. In *poetic* writing, your purpose is to explore, to analyze, and to understand.

A somewhat similar approach is taken by the theorist James Kinneavy, whose model of communication is based on the three points of a communication triangle—writer, audience, and subject—plus the medium or the triangle itself, language. According to Kinneavy, if your preoccupation is with yourself, the writer, your purpose is *expressive* (as in Britton's function category). If your focus is on the audience's ideas, concerns, and feelings, your purpose is *persuasive*. If your primary interest is a particular subject, your purpose is *reference*. And if your main concern is the creation of a work of literature, your purpose is *literary*.

Combining these theories and approaches (and allowing for some overlap) produces six basic purposes for writing:

1. to inform your reader
2. to entertain your reader
3. to persuade your reader
4. to transact business (or accomplish a task)
5. to express yourself
6. to create a literary work.

My combined grouping overlooks the nuances of each approach, but it also gives us a more complete view of the motives for writing. Note that three of the purposes—to inform, to entertain, and to persuade—focus on the reader, and the other three—to transact business, to express yourself, and to create a literary work—focus on the writer.

Also note that the third and fourth purposes—to persuade your reader and to transact business—differ from the others in an important regard: They involve getting the reader to take a desired action (and so, in a sense, they involve an element of manipulation). This emphasis characterizes what is commonly referred to as "business writing" but what might be described more accurately as "on-the-job writing" or, to use Britton's term, "transactional writing."

Note: The limited and misleading nature of the term "business writing" becomes apparent when it is applied to a budget request written by a librarian, for example, or to a letter of recommendation written by a chemistry professor. The problem with referring to on-the-job or work-related writing as "business writing" is that it suggests that only those students majoring in business need concern themselves with learning how to write a memo or a proposal.

Mary Munter emphasizes the importance of persuading the reader to take a desired action in the opening of *Guide to Managerial Communication* when she writes:

> Managerial communication is different from other kinds of communication. Why? Because in a business or management setting, a brilliant message alone is not sufficient: You are successful only if your message leads to the response you desire from your audience.

In short, the interactive, pragmatic nature of the third and fourth purposes—to persuade your reader and to transact business—distinguishes them from the others.

Given this emphasis on communication resulting in action, you will be more likely to succeed if you are clear in your own mind about the action you want your reader to take, whether that action is to refund your money, acknowledge receipt of your shipment, pack up and clear out of the office by three this afternoon, contribute five hundred dollars to your cause, or vote for you. Whether you state your purpose directly or indirectly depends on your persuasive strategy.

Whatever your purpose, you should have a clear sense of it as you begin to write. Here's a simple test to determine if you are writing with a clear sense of purpose: See if you can state your purpose in a simple declarative sentence. Whether you are writing a memo to reschedule next week's staff meeting or composing a thousand-page book on nineteenth-century English romantic poetry, you should be able to state your purpose in a single, simple declarative sentence. If you are unable to do so, you probably lack a clear sense of why you are writing or what you are attempting to accomplish.

Writing with a clear sense of purpose will help you not only write clearly, but also make all the other decisions required of you during your journey— choices regarding approach, mode of discourse, method of development, rhetorical strategy, point of view, organization, and type and amount of detail used to illustrate your points and support your argument.

For some types of writing, formulate a thesis statement.

Do you remember when you were in high school—your teacher at the front of the room, the fragrant spring air wafting through the open windows—and the only thing between you and a carefree summer, or between you and graduation, was your research paper? Before you could begin writing that paper, however, you had to come up with a good thesis or central argument, and that could be tricky.

A good thesis has to be a debatable proposition, a statement that is neither too narrow to be argued ("Monday is the first day of the week") nor too broad to be adequately developed in a reasonable number of pages ("Capitalism offers many advantages"); neither a nonstarter ("The U.S. is a democracy") nor a nonstopper ("There are many systems of government in the world").

It has to be something like "Of all modern economic systems, capitalism has proven itself most efficient at producing goods and services with minimal impact on the environment."

Once you have formulated your thesis, your next task is to delineate it. To delineate is to outline the boundaries of something, to limit your scope, to indicate your intended lines of development, to declare your point of view. The process goes like this: First you state your general topic, then you state your more particular concern. It's a logical, two-step progression.

Not all types of writing, however, require an explicit statement of purpose. In various genres of creative writing, for example, an explicit thesis statement ("The purpose of this novel is . . .") would seem clumsy and out of place. As Diana Hacker points out in *A Writer's Reference*, "A personal narrative, for example, may have a focus too subtle to be distilled in a single sentence, and such a sentence might ruin the story."

But for most types of persuasive writing, a thesis statement is an integral component of the argument. Although it can appear anywhere in the opening material, the thesis usually appears after the lead as the last sentence in the introduction.

Provide context and background.

To help your reader understand the significance or implications of your thesis, purpose, or subject, you need to establish a context. Your ideas will have more meaning for your reader if you present them in relation to a particular set of circumstances, especially when you are writing to inform, to transact, or to persuade. It stands to reason that if your reader has firsthand experience with the circumstances you are describing, your reader will be more likely to understand your message and accept your point of view. With this in mind, you should try to find common ground between yourself and your reader, and for all types of writing, you should provide sufficient background information to make your subject relevant and interesting to your reader.

Determine a Persuasive Strategy

Having selected your subject, determined your purpose, and—depending on the type of writing you're doing—formulated a thesis statement, your next step is to choose your approach. As with most journeys, there is usually more than one route that will take you to your destination.

Select a mode of discourse.

In determining your approach, you have four basic choices or modes of discourse to choose from: description, narration, exposition, and persuasion.

Each mode has certain distinguishing characteristics, and each offers certain advantages. For most writing you will employ a combination of their features. The point is to be intentional. As you consider your purpose, audience, and subject, choose the mode that is most likely to help you accomplish your goals.

Use description to provide information about a person, setting, scene, or object. Description is a good way to show the reader rather than tell the reader, and as I discussed in Chapter 2, descriptions that appeal to the five senses tend to have the greatest impact. Those that offer concrete detail tend to be more vivid and memorable than descriptions based on more abstract observations.

Although there is an element of subjectivity in all human perception, descriptions vary according to the degree of their objectivity. In scientific and technical writing, description is more objective. It is usually based on empirical observation and characterized by specificity and thoroughness. In fiction and poetry, description is more subjective. The information provided is usually selected for its value in creating a mood or capturing a state of mind.

To appreciate the differences between the two types of description, try this exercise. Describe the contents of your refrigerator, first objectively, then subjectively. In your objective description, compile a precise inventory, relying on specific detail. In your subjective description, select detail for its value in reinforcing a certain theme or creating a particular impression.

At the end of this paragraph, I provide examples from two students who did this exercise in one of my writing classes (but I suggest that you do the exercise yourself before you read the examples). Here they are:

- **Objective description.** My refrigerator contains the following items: one red pepper, one lemon, two Fireside apples, one apple pie, a container of sour cream, a container of plain yogurt, two cans of pop, two bottles of beer, a wedge of Parmesan cheese, various condiments, a half a head of lettuce, five carrots, containers of cream cheese, one container of Jello, half a loaf of sourdough bread, leftover pizza, seltzer water, and fresh herbs.

- **Subjective description.** If you took a look inside my refrigerator and started to poke around a bit, one word would come to mind: old. My refrigerator suffers the plight of a busy single user. In the spot in the door where eggs usually go I have a wrinkled red pepper that I keep meaning to use or freeze, but it just keeps getting more shriveled and soft. Next to the pepper is a mottled lemon, which I picked up on sale a month ago, thinking I could always use a lemon for something. On the shelves near the lemon are various Ziploc bags filled with parsley, mint, lemon mint, Italian parsley, oregano, thyme, and marjoram. These I cut from my father's garden when it was still warm outside, with intentions of making an herb-roasted chicken, mint and garlic red potatoes, and other delectables. . . . Below are Schweppes mixers, one bottle of club soda, one bottle of lemon sour. My best friend sent these home with me after a late-August cocktail party celebrating her upcoming move to Chicago. Next to the mixers is half of a taco pizza, delivered from Lake Harriet Pizza the other night when I didn't feel like making something of all the less-than-fresh food in my refrigerator. Surveying my refrigerator, I imagine the chagrin of my agricultural ancestors, lamenting all the wasted food in my life.

- **Objective description.** On the top shelf are the tall items including three half gallons of skim milk, a bottle of wine, Log Cabin Lite Syrup, ketchup, a half gallon of orange juice, a pitcher with baby formula in it, and a half full baby bottle. On the middle two shelves are the medium-small items including cottage cheese, two very out-of-date yogurts, two jars of pickles, a crock of butter, sour cream, three bottles of beer (each a different kind), and six cans of caffeine-free Diet Coke, five of which are closed and one of which is opened. In the meat drawer we have an unopened package of Healthy Choice medium cheddar cheese, an opened package of beef jerky, a brick of mild cheddar cheese, and some deli cheese. In the vegetable bin you will find six Red Delicious apples, two bruised nectarines, and more than ten tomatoes from the garden. In the refrigerator door you will find "door items" such as eggs, salad dressings, mustard, soy sauce, relish, and an occasional bottle of medication such as cough syrup or Nyquil.

- **Subjective description.** Although the sun has yet to come up, I find myself, once again, trying to sneak in a two-minute breakfast before my baby wakes up. As a working, new mommy, I'm still trying to figure out how to get the basic care needs such as feeding, washing, dressing, and changing done efficiently for two people all before 7:00 A.M. Upon scanning the contents of my refrigerator, I'm thrilled to discover the frozen waffles in the freezer door. Calorie laden? Who cares? They're fast. Once I position them in their designated places in my toaster, I move on to preparing the condiments. I have butter and I have syrup. However, on this particular morning, removing the syrup from the top shelf of the refrigerator was tricky because there is a little pool of sticky syrup battening down the bottle to the shelf. I suppose I hadn't completely closed the cover, or heaven forbid, wiped the bottle down thoroughly before I put it back in the refrigerator as my mother had so drilled into my head. My mother—the obsessive-compulsive housekeeper. She would have a home-maker's hernia if she saw our refrigerator right now. Besides the gluey, goopy maple syrup, she would have scorned the chocolate stopped in mid-stream on the bottle of chocolate syrup, or the open Diet Coke can. How about the perfectly round imprint on the shelf left shamelessly by a jar of jelly? She would have shaken her head in disgust looking at the two nectarines bearing their longevity scars in the vegetable drawer. And there's no doubt she would warn me of the terrible diseases my child would surely get if I were to feed him the half-full bottle from last night's feeding. My mother. She walked around her kitchen with a washcloth sewn onto her hand. She was prepared to sterilize anything that showed, or didn't show, the slightest signs of being sticky, goopy, gloppy, or smelly. Anything removed from our refrigerator was bathed, brushed, and buffed prior to reentrance.

Note how much more engaging the subjective descriptions are. And note too how both descriptions serve to introduce characters (the writers themselves as well as members of their families). As you can see, carefully rendered description tells its own story.

Whether objective or subjective, nearly all description depends on a keen eye—as well as ear, nose, mouth, and hand—for relevant detail. The amount of detail, or the length of description, is determined by your purpose and the audience for whom you are writing.

Use narration to tell a story.

Storytelling is an art. Its success depends on many factors, from a clear sense of purpose to a keen awareness of audience. But perhaps its most important requirements are that the narrative voice and structure arouse the reader's interest in the story. Narrative voice depends on a recognizable, consistent point of view that conveys to the reader the writer's caring, concern, or commitment to the subject and characters. Narrative structure depends on a sense of timing, which means relating the events of the story in a way that holds the reader's interest, heightens drama, or creates dramatic tension.

Of particular usefulness to the writer is the anecdote. This kind of mini-story is useful in nearly every type of writing, including exposition (where it is used as a means of explanation or clarification) and persuasion (where it is used to reinforce a point or to demonstrate the consequences of an action).

Note how Malcolm Cowley uses anecdote to good effect in *The View From 80:*

> They gave me a party on my 80th birthday in August 1978. First there were cards, letters, telegrams, even a cable of congratulation or condolence; then there were gifts, mostly bottles; there was catered food and finally a big cake with, for some reason, two candles (had I gone back to very early childhood?). I blew the candles out a little unsteadily. Amid the applause and clatter I thought about a former custom of the Northern Ojibwas when they lived on the shores of Lake Winnipeg. They were kind to their old people, who remembered and enforced the ancient customs of the tribe, but when an old person became decrepit, it was time for him to go. Sometimes he was simply abandoned, with a little food, on an island in the lake. If he deserved special honor, they held a tribal feast for him. The old man sang a death song and danced, if he could. While he was still singing, his son came from behind and brained him with a tomahawk.
>
> That was quick, it was dignified, and I wonder whether it was any more cruel, essentially, than some of our civilized customs or inadvertencies in disposing of the aged.

Anecdotes are effective because they appeal to your reader's natural curiosity about narrative (How does the story turn out? Why did it happen this way? Could this happen to me?). Anecdotes also enable you to use point of view to your advantage. When you tell a story, you invite your reader to see the story the way you see it, and this invitation tends to create sympathy and understanding for your perspective.

Use exposition to inform your reader.

Expository writing is writing that explains. Its primary aim is to convey information or to enlighten your reader. Because expository writing or exposition often incorporates elements of the other three modes of writing (description, narration, and persuasion), it is the broadest of the four categories. Exposition includes writing that is both objective and subjective, as well as writing that conveys both an impersonal and a personal tone. It ranges from minutes of meetings to procedures, news articles, travel writing, and personal essays. It also includes the nonpersuasive writing of every field and profession, from scientific and technical writing to academic and legal writing.

There are six types of exposition: example, process analysis, division and classification, comparison and analogy, cause and effect, and definition. (I comment on these six types when I discuss organizational issues in Chapter 8.)

Use persuasion to induce your reader to think, act, or feel a certain way.

Like exposition, persuasion often incorporates aspects of the other three categories of writing, but compared to exposition, its features are more closely bound by a unifying purpose. That purpose is to influence the thinking, actions, or feelings of your reader. Just as exposition is more focused on the subject, persuasion is more focused on your reader. Every decision—from word choice to tone, detail, and structure—is based on its intended impact on the reader. In this sense, in persuasive writing every choice you make is strategic. (Because persuasive strategy has implications for point of view and structure, I also discuss it in Chapters 7 and 8.)

Analyze your audience.

Your reader's attitude toward your subject and toward you, the writer, should be taken into account as you decide on an approach or persuasive strategy.

The main thing you need to determine about your audience when writing persuasively is whether they are sympathetic, skeptical, or hostile to your message, and whether they have relatively high or low esteem for you, the writer.

In *Guide to Managerial Communication,* Mary Munter suggests four basic questions to ask when analyzing your audience:

- **Who are they?**
- **What do they know?** (What do they need to know? What are their expectations and preferences?)
- **What do they feel?** (How interested are they in your message? What is their probable bias: positive or negative? Is your desired action easy or hard for them?)
- **How can you motivate them?** (Can you motivate through audience benefits, such as tangible benefits, career or task benefits, ego benefits, group benefits? Can you motivate through credibility . . . ?)

The more you know about your readers, the more likely you will succeed in connecting with them.

Assess your credibility in the eyes of your reader.

A second important consideration is your readers' opinion of you. Do you have high credibility or low credibility? Or are your readers neutral about your credentials or reputation? Although it isn't always possible to know how you are perceived by your readers, you usually know when your credibility is very high or very low, and your assessment will affect your tone and approach. If you are a best-selling novelist or the leading sales representative in your district, you are more likely to present your ideas and conclusions without a great deal of justification or explanation. If you are a graduate student or a newly hired employee, you are more likely to explain your reasons and thinking to justify your ideas and conclusions.

Mary Munter makes a helpful distinction between initial and acquired credibility. The former is based on credentials and reputation; the latter is earned by the effectiveness and professionalism of your communication. From her distinction one might draw the obvious conclusion: If you think your credibility is low, establish your credentials early on. If you think your credibility is high to begin with, don't blow it.

Decide when and how to state your purpose.

When you state your purpose, and how directly or indirectly you present your conclusion, depends on your analysis of your audience and your assessment of your credibility. These considerations will help you determine a rhetorical strategy and approach. Here's the rule of thumb: When writing to a sympathetic audience, state your purpose directly (first conclusion, then evidence). When writing to an unsympathetic or hostile audience, state your purpose indirectly (first evidence, then conclusion).

Unless you are conveying bad news or writing to a hostile or unsympathetic audience, the best way to introduce a routine business communication is to open with a clear, straightforward statement of your purpose.

Write to explore and discover.

When Alice asked the Cheshire Cat which way she ought to go, the cat said, "That depends a good deal on where you want to get to."

"I don't much care where—" said Alice.

"Then it doesn't matter which way you go," said the Cat.

"—so long as I get *somewhere*," Alice added as an explanation.

"Oh, you're sure to do that," said the Cat, "if you only walk long enough."

How can you get to where you want to be if you don't know where you're going? The Cheshire Cat's advice to Alice works fine in wonderland, but not in real life. For most types of writing, you need to begin with a clear sense of purpose. If you are clear about your purpose, you are more likely to communicate clearly to your reader. If you know what you want your readers to do as a result of reading your message, you are more likely to succeed in persuading them to take the desired action.

There are some types of writing, however, when it is better just to start writing, without a clear plan or set destination, and see where your thoughts take you. Even in the most intentional, most carefully planned writing, you should be willing to depart from your outline if, in the process of writing, something new and valuable occurs to you. After all, one of the reasons we write is to discover what we think. The English novelist Graham Greene said it well when he asked, "How can I know what I think until I see what I write?" In *On Writing Well*, William Zinsser makes the point this way:

> Don't fight [an unanticipated] current if it feels right. Trust your material if it is taking you into terrain that you didn't intend to enter but where the vibrations are good. Adjust your style and your mood accordingly and proceed to whatever destination you reach. Don't ever become the prisoner of a preconceived plan. Writing is no respecter of blueprints—it is too subjective a process, too full of surprises.

If you keep your mind open to the unanticipated, you might be surprised to discover what you really think.

Perhaps the best approach is to begin writing with your head, but once you are underway allow your heart to suggest an unexplored path. Because writing is as much a question of intuition and instinct as it is decision making and intellect, it makes sense to begin by thinking carefully—take time to reflect, do some planning, maybe make an outline—but don't try to plan everything in advance. Leave something for the writing. Follow your thoughts or feelings. Allow yourself to be surprised. Sometimes you'll do your best, most fluent writing if you allow yourself to go with the flow.

The creative process cannot—and should not—be confined to declared goals and predetermined lines of development. One of the great pleasures in creative writing is to hear a character say something you hadn't planned for the character to say. It is as though this created being, this figment of your imagination, has taken on a mind and personality independent of you, its creator. To lose control over your material in this way is a singular achievement, for it means that you have surrendered yourself to the mystery of the creative imagination.

CHAPTER 7: POINT OF VIEW

Establish Your Relationships.
USE AN APPROPRIATE VANTAGE POINT, TONE, AND LEVEL OF
   FORMALITY.
MAINTAIN A CONSISTENT LEVEL OF FORMALITY.
USE A PERSONAL TONE IN MOST CORRESPONDENCE.

Consider Your Options in Narrative Writing
USE A LIMITED POINT OF VIEW TO CREATE INTRIGUE AND KEEP
   YOUR READER GUESSING.
USE A SUBJECTIVE POINT OF VIEW TO HEIGHTEN DRAMA.
USE A LIMITED POINT OF VIEW TO CREATE HUMOR AND IRONY.
USE CONTRASTING POINTS OF VIEW TO ADD INTEREST.
USE A PERSONA FOR EFFECT.

Maintain a Consistent Point of View
EXERCISE YOUR FIRST-PERSON OPTION EARLY ON.
MAINTAIN UNITY IN NARRATION.

Use Point of View to Your Advantage in Persuasive Writing

ADOPT A REASONABLE TONE.

KNOW WHEN TO HEDGE AND WHEN TO INSIST.

- Hedges
- Intensifiers
- Overqualification
- Overintensification
- Hollow hedges
- Hollow intensifiers

USE THE *YOU VIEWPOINT* TO INVOLVE YOUR READER.

USE ANECDOTES TO CREATE SYMPATHY FOR YOUR PERSPECTIVE.

Use Point of View for Special Effect

USE DISPARITY TO CREATE HUMOR AND IRONY.

USE A PERSONAL POINT OF VIEW TO REVEAL YOUR FEELINGS.

CREATE A PERSONA TO ACCOMPLISH YOUR PURPOSE.

DEVELOP THE PERSONA YOU WOULD LIKE TO BE.

CHAPTER SEVEN

{Point of View}

Establish Your Relationships

Writing is a matter of establishing relationships. With your first few sentences of your opening, you declare your relationship with your subject and, either directly or indirectly, with your reader. Deciding on your point of view is a matter of deciding whose story you are telling, from what perspective you are telling that story, and what attitude or feelings you want to convey regarding that story.

Where and how you position yourself in relation to your subject and your reader has a great deal to do with your success or failure as a writer. You indicate those relationships through your use of point of view, which has three dimensions: person, vantage point, and attitude.

Person is the *who*. It is the narrator or observer from whose eyes the story is told or the subject is viewed. The *who* may be first person *(I* or *we)*, second person *(you)*, or third person *(he, she, it, one,* or *they)*.

First person and second person are frequently used in transactional or business writing, correspondence, newsletter articles, and instructional writing, including procedures, manuals, and how-to books like this one (as in "*I* hope *you* are finding this analysis useful"). Third person is commonly used in more formal types of on-the-job writing and in scientific, technical, academic, and legal writing (as in "Consequently, *the Court* shall award all personal property in each party's possession to themselves, and *the Court* shall consider the division as equitable"). Both first and third person are commonly used in narrative writing.

In fiction and other types of literary writing, a first-person narrator's point of view is limited by what the narrator perceives by observing and interacting with the characters. A third-person narrator may be either an uninvolved observer or a participant in the action (one of the characters). When a third-person narrator knows everything that needs to be known about the unfolding of the story and has access to the thoughts, feelings, and motives of all the characters, the narrator is said to be omniscient. When a third-person narrator knows only what is perceived or known by a character (or a few characters) within the story, the narrator is said to be limited.

If *person* is the *who*, *vantage point* is the *when* and the *where*. It is the location or frame of reference from which the narrator relates the story or the observer views the subject. Vantage point has two dimensions: *temporal* (both the observer and the subject are located in time—past, present, or future) and *spatial* (the observer and the subject are located in physical relationship to one another—close or distant).

Person and vantage point are particularly significant in narration, as illustrated by the following three scenarios involving a limited third-person point of view. If a mother is watching her children playing in the backyard while standing in her kitchen, she is viewing present action relatively close-up through her kitchen window. If a mother is watching a home video of her children playing in the backyard, she is viewing past action recorded relatively close-up through the eye of the camera. And if a mother is watching a home video taken from her front porch of her children getting off the school bus at the end of the block, she is viewing past action recorded from a slight distance through the eye of the camera. In each example, what the mother is feeling—her thoughts and emotions—may be reported in the past tense or in the present tense (or, hypothetically, in the future tense). In other words, both the observer (or the act of observation) and the subject are located in time and place.

Likewise, in each example, the mother's frame of reference—whether she is viewing past or present action, from close-up or far away—is limited. She perceives only what she can see through her kitchen window or the eye of the camera. If the children leave the backyard, or if the camera shifts to her children's grandparents, and if she has no other means of gathering information, she no longer knows what her children are doing. As is evident in these examples, person and vantage point play a significant role in determining what information is conveyed to the reader.

The third dimension of point of view, *attitude*, is the *how*. It is the tone conveyed by how the narrator or the observer feels toward the action, subject, or thing being observed. A mother in her seventies viewing a video taken fifty years ago of her children getting off a school bus is likely to experience strong feelings of love and perhaps wistfulness for times gone by, whereas a mother watching her children get off the bus after having received a call from the principal informing her that they had been caught smoking during recess is likely to feel something quite different. As we know from real life, the same event may be experienced and portrayed from various perspectives in markedly different ways. The nature of that portrayal is determined not only by person and vantage point but also by attitude.

All of these considerations contribute to your reader's having a sense of your authorial voice and authorial presence, which is at the heart of what we mean by an author's style. Behind the choices regarding person, vantage point, and tone, the reader senses, to use M. H. Abrams words in *A Glossary of Literary Terms,* "a pervasive authorial presence, a determinate intelligence and moral sensibility, who has invented, ordered, and rendered all these literary characters and materials in just this way." To a great extent, the effect of literary writing (as well as persuasive writing and, in some cases, transactional writing) depends directly on the reader's sense of authorial voice and authorial presence—or what I like to call the reader's sense of the person behind the words. As Abrams and others point out, this presence plays an especially important role in engaging the interest and guiding the imaginative and emotional responses of the readers to whom the work is addressed. In other words, authorial presence, which is created in large part by point of view or the author's relationship with subject and reader, is an integral feature of style.

Point of view is most often discussed in relation to narration and literary works, but it has implications for all types of writing, including description, exposition, and persuasion. All writing—even writing in which point of view is not readily apparent—imparts a sense of the writer's voice or authorial presence, and in all writing, point of view may be used to the writer's advantage.

Use an appropriate vantage point, tone, and level of formality.

Vantage point and tone, as revealed by your word choice, determine your level of formality. A distant vantage point and a less personal tone are associated with more formal writing. For example, you may place yourself at a distance from your subject ("It is recommended that . . .") or close to your subject ("I recommend that . . ."), just as you may place yourself at a distance from your reader ("I regret to inform you that . . .") or close to your reader ("I'm really sorry that . . .").

Closely linked to vantage point is tone, which conveys your attitude toward your subject and audience. You may adopt a formal, respectful tone ("I must take issue with your position"); a formal, disrespectful tone ("I find your position absurd"); an informal, respectful tone ("I'm afraid I disagree with you on this one"); or an informal, disrespectful tone ("You gotta be kidding").

Maintain a consistent level of formality.

A friend once told me she realized she was spending too much time with young children when she caught herself saying to an adult friend, "Oh, look at the moo-moo cows!" Sometimes writers—especially on-the-job writers—make the same mistake. They use vocabulary that is inappropriate to their audience.

Whenever you communicate, you adjust your word choice—either consciously or unconsciously—to suit your audience and situation. When you speak to a three-year-old child, for example, you don't use the same vocabulary that you use when you talk with your boss—unless, of course, you have a boss who doesn't handle complexity well. In written communication, your opening words do more than convey meaning: They also establish a certain level of formality. Once that level has been established, you should use words that are consistent with that style.

If you begin a letter of recommendation with the words, "It is with great pleasure that I recommend . . . ," for example, you establish a relatively formal tone, and it would be inappropriate later in your letter to write, "Can we talk turkey?" Similarly, if you open an E-mail message with "Hey, Joe. How's it going?" you establish an informal tone, and it would strike your reader as odd if later in your message you wrote, "Despite our adversary's implacable determination to offer no ostensible resistance, one can nevertheless discern a subtle shift in tactics."

Abrupt shifts in tone and style are awkward. In the following letter, for example, see if you can identify which words and phrases seem inconsistent with the letter's relatively formal style and replace them with more appropriate wording:

> Dear Mr. Smith:
>
> Thank you for inviting me to present a proposal for increasing thrust in your A91 series of propellers.
>
> Although the higher production costs are nothing to sneeze at, I believe they are justified by the increased efficiency of the blade. (Check out my redesign of the leading edge!)
>
> I'll touch base with you next week to see if you have any questions.
>
> Best,
> Sue

One way to revise the letter to give it a more consistent tone would be as follows: Replace *nothing to sneeze at* with *not insignificant;* replace *Check out* with *Note;* replace the exclamation mark with a period; replace *I'll touch base with you* with *I will call you;* and replace *Best* with *Sincerely.* The revised letter reads:

> Dear Mr. Smith:
>
> Thank you for inviting me to present a proposal for increasing thrust in your A91 series of propellers.
>
> Although the higher production costs are not insignificant, I believe they are justified by the increased efficiency of the blade. (Note the redesign of the leading edge.)
>
> I will call you next week to see if you have any questions.
>
> Sincerely,
> Sue

In the following E-mail message, see if you can identify which words and phrases seem out of keeping with an informal style:

> Hi, Susan.
>
> I am writing to acknowledge receipt of your proposal for increasing thrust in our A91 series of propellers. Your imaginative redesign of the leading edge of the blade is impressive, and the increased production costs proposed therein seem reasonable.
>
> Please be assured that your proposal will receive all due consideration.
>
> Sincerely,
> Bob

To maintain an informal style throughout, replace *I am writing to acknowledge receipt of your proposal* with *Thanks for your proposal;* replace *costs proposed therein* with *costs that you propose;* replace *Please be assured that your proposal will receive all due consideration* with *I assure you that your proposal will receive serious consideration,* or simply *We will seriously consider your proposal;* and replace *Sincerely* with *Thanks* or *Best.* The revised memo reads:

> Hi, Susan.
>
> Thanks for your proposal for increasing thrust in our A91 series of propellers. Your imaginative redesign of the leading edge of the blade is impressive, and the increased production costs that you propose seem reasonable.
>
> I assure you that your proposal will receive serious consideration.
>
> Thanks.
> Bob

In your on-the-job correspondence with readers outside your company or organization, you are likely to use a style that linguists call standard English, a style that falls somewhere between formal and informal English. Formal English (which is appropriate for academic and literary writing as well as some forms of public and political discourse) uses words like *to admonish, to feign,* and *impetuous;* whereas standard English (which is appropriate for most forms of business and technical writing) uses words like *to scold, to pretend,* and *rash*; and informal English (which is appropriate in casual situations when you know your reader well, as in most E-mail correspondence) uses words and expressions like *to lay into, to fake,* and *brainless.*

To some extent, your effectiveness as a writer depends on your ability to gauge the level of formality required by your audience, your purpose, and your subject, and to communicate comfortably and consistently at that level.

Use a personal tone in most correspondence.

Rather than "As per our conversation," write "As we discussed." Rather than "The above-referenced payment is overdue," write "Your payment is overdue." And rather than "It is regrettable that we were late in sending your shipment," write "I'm sorry that your shipment was delayed."

Consider Your Options in Narrative Writing

The options regarding point of view in literary works are more numerous and complicated than they are in other types of writing. In literary writing, which usually involves narrative, the question of point of view is not limited to person (first, second, or third). It also includes degree of power to enter the minds of the characters (omniscient or limited), role of the narrator (an uninvolved observer or a participant in the action), temporal vantage point of the narrator (describing present action or past action—the *when* mentioned above), spatial vantage point of the narrator (close to the action or far from the action—the *where* mentioned above), degree of presence of the narrator (intrusive or unintrusive), trustworthiness of the narrator (authoritative or unreliable), and attitude of the narrator (the *tone*—as mentioned above—toward subject, theme, setting, characters, story, and reader).

In determining attitude or tone, the writer has nearly limitless choices. As M. H. Abrams points out in *A Glossary of Literary Terms*, tone "can be described as critical or approving, formal or intimate, outspoken or reticent, solemn or playful, arrogant or prayerful, angry or loving, serious or ironic, condescending or obsequious, and so on through numberless possible nuances of relationship and attitude."

As an illustration of how point of view is established, consider the following examples. If you write, "Nothing had prepared me for what I saw when I opened that door," you declare yourself a first-person narrator participating as a character in the story. You are describing past action from a limited point of view, and you are writing a narrative lead intended to arouse the curiosity of your reader. If you write, "She seemed surprised by what she saw when she opened the door," you declare yourself a third-person uninvolved observer (as opposed to a first-person participating narrator), and you are describing past action from a limited point of view. If you change "seemed surprised" to "was surprised" and you enter the mind not only of this character, but of any character whose thinking is relevant to the unfolding of your story, you declare yourself a third-person omniscient rather than limited narrator. If you add the phrase "Unprepared as always" to the main clause, "she was surprised by what she saw when she opened the door," you not only declare *who* (third person ominiscient), *where* (close to the action), and *when* (depicting past action), but also *how* you feel about the character (critical, perhaps unsympathetic, even condescending).

The options relating to point of view, when taken at a glance like this, may seem overwhelming. But as you try to determine the most effective point of view for your purpose, audience, and subject, keep in mind two points. First, remember that writing represents spoken language and that written discourse is a type of utterance or a mode of speech. If you think of point of view as something you convey whenever you speak, the correct choices may seem more obvious. As Abrams reminds us, "To conceive a work as an utterance suggests that there is a speaker who has determinate personal qualities, and who expresses attitudes both toward the characters and materials within the work and toward the audience to whom the work is addressed." Second, in the early stages of conceptualization, trust your intuition. As Stephen Minot advises in *Three Genres: The Writing of Poetry, Fiction, and Drama*, "When a story idea first comes to you, it will probably be a mix of personal experience and invention. Let it run through your head like a daydream. Don't concern yourself at this early stage about the means of perception, person, and focus. If you analyze too much too soon, you may lose the feel of the story."

Use a limited point of view to create intrigue and keep your reader guessing.

A writer's power is determined not only by what is revealed but also by what is withheld. Partial disclosure and gradual revelation are time-tested principles at the heart of all storytelling. Consider, for example, George Orwell's use of a limited third-person point of view in *1984*. Orwell opens his book with these sentences:

> It was a bright cold day in April, and the clocks were striking thirteen. Winston Smith, his chin nuzzled into his breast in an effort to escape the vile wind, slipped quickly through the glass doors of Victory Mansions, though not quickly enough to prevent a swirl of gritty dust from entering along with him.

In these sentences Orwell establishes person, vantage point, and attitude toward his subject or—more particularly—toward his setting, which is made to appear bleak, surreal, and unwelcoming, but he doesn't tell everything. Although the landscape is subjectively drawn (the reader senses the narrator's attitude toward it), Orwell doesn't tell the reader what to think, at least not directly. It isn't until a few paragraphs later that Orwell moves inside the head of his third-person narrator: "Winston kept his back turned to the telescreen. It was safer; though, as he well knew, even a back can be revealing." By moving only gradually to his character's perspective, and then offering only a single thought rather than revealing everything his character is thinking, Orwell creates intrigue.

Flannery O'Connor uses the same technique of delayed and incomplete disclosure to create intrigue in the opening of *Wise Blood:*

> Hazel Motes sat at a forward angle on the green plush train seat, looking one minute at the window as if he might want to jump out of it, and the next down the aisle at the other end of the car.

O'Connor might have chosen to reveal more directly what her character was thinking, perhaps rewriting her opening to read:

> Hazel Motes sat at a forward angle on the green plush train seat. Uneasy about his reasons for traveling to Taulkinham, he looked one minute at the window, fighting an impulse to jump out of it, and the next down the aisle at the other end of the car, looking desperately for some avenue of escape.

Instead, she withholds information, leaving the reader to surmise from her character's actions, dialogue, gestures, and expressions what he is thinking and feeling.

Use a subjective point of view to heighten drama.

Both Orwell and O'Connor use third-person narrators (that is, they refer to their characters as *he* and *she* rather than *I* or *you*) who possess limited power to enter some, but not all, of the characters' minds. Both narrators report on the action without being part of it. In contrast, in *The Great Gatsby*, F. Scott Fitzgerald tells the story through the eyes of a first-person narrator, Nick Carraway, who mostly observes the action but occasionally participates as a character. Everything the reader knows about the thoughts, motives, and feelings of Jay Gatsby and Tom and Daisy Buchanan is reported by Nick Carraway. What Fitzgerald loses in access to the other characters' thoughts, he gains in tone, subtlety, and nuance from the richness and subjectivity of his limited first-person narrator's view:

> When I came back from the East last autumn I felt that I wanted the world to be in uniform and at a sort of moral attention forever; I wanted no more riotous excursions with privileged glimpses into the human heart. Only Gatsby, the man who gives his name to this book, was exempt from my reaction—Gatsby, who represented everything for which I have an unaffected scorn. If personality is an unbroken series of successful gestures, then there was something gorgeous about him, some heightened sensitivity to

the promises of life, as if he were related to one of those intricate machines that register earthquakes ten thousand miles away.

Through the filter of Nick's perspective, the story gains subjectivity and color.

Use a limited point of view to create humor and irony.

In *The Adventures of Huckleberry Finn*, Mark Twain uses a limited first-person narrator who playfully walks the line between what is real and what is fiction:

> You don't know about me without you have read a book by the name of *The Adventures of Tom Sawyer;* but that ain't no matter. That book was made by Mr. Mark Twain, and he told the truth, mainly. There was things which he stretches, but mainly he told the truth.

Compared to Fitzgerald's first-person narrator, Twain's narrator is more central to the story, but he is also less trustworthy. Huck's limited perspective—that of an "unsivilized," mischievous, naive, but essentially good-hearted teenage boy—results in his frequently misreporting the motives of the duplicitous and corrupt adults he encounters, a misapprehension that serves as the book's principal source of irony and humor. His gullibility, however, is punctuated by moments of keen insight and realization. Although both Huck and Jim are taken in by the stories told by the Duke and the King, and are "so glad and proud" to have them on board the raft with them, Huck soon recognizes the two men as imposters:

> It didn't take me long to make up my mind that these liars warn't no kings nor dukes at all, but just low-down humbugs and frauds. But I never said nothing, never let on; kept it to myself; it's the best way; then you don't have no quarrels, and don't get into no trouble. If they wanted us to call them kings and dukes, I hadn't no objections, 'long as it would keep peace in the family; and it warn't no use to tell Jim, so I didn't tell him. If I never learnt

nothing else out of pap, I learnt that the best way to get along with his kind of people is to let them have their own way.

Here, and throughout the book, the narrative tension is created by the interplay among three perspectives: what the narrator perceives to be real, what the reader suspects to be real, and what the author actually thinks. When these three perspectives converge, as they do at different points in the story, the author speaks through his narrator to the reader with heightened intensity and authority.

Use contrasting points of view to add interest.

Sometimes your reader will enjoy the contrast between two sharply differing points of view. The contrast is a pleasing reminder of how much we differ in our perceptions and experiences, a reminder of the quirkiness of human nature, of what it is to be human. "I was quite pleased with the stylishness of my new golf outfit," you might write. "My children, of course, thought I looked ridiculous." Or, to turn the tables: "The engine hummed with power and the car leaned into the curve as though it were holding the road in a tight embrace, to Scott's delight and his mother's alarm." In an essay comparing her own experience with pregnancy with that of the mother of Jesus, a student in one of my classes wrote: "Being told by an angel that she was pregnant had to be a perplexing moment, one that is difficult to fathom. It makes my moment of watching the stick turn blue seem meager."

Use a persona for effect.

All writing involves a degree of role-playing. When we write a letter of application, we assume the role of the experienced, eager, and successful worker. When we write the minutes of a meeting, we assume the role of the objective, detail-oriented, precise observer. In narrative writing, however, role-playing tends to be more subtle, and the disparity between what is reported and what the reader perceives to have actually taken place is sometimes more pronounced. Adopting a particular point of view to achieve one's purpose is integral to the genre, and the reader is more consciously aware of possible disparity between the author's true voice and the author's assumed voice. The fictitious voice is known as the *persona*, which as Abrams reminds us is "the Latin word for the mask worn by actors in the classical theater."

The degree of similarity or dissimilarity between the author and persona depends on the type of writing and the individual work. As Abrams points out, personas vary from "entirely fictional characters very different from their authors" to speakers in autobiographical works "where we are invited to attribute the voice we hear, and the sentiments it utters," to the author. Part of the complication (and the fun) of interpreting literature arises from the fact that the narrator's point of view may or may not coincide with the author's point of view. The writer's challenge is to create intrigue; the reader's is to determine the degree of similarity or divergence between the two points of view and, based on that determination, to interpret the author's true message.

Maintain a Consistent Point of View

Once you have established your point of view, stay with it. As I pointed out when discussing parallel structure in Chapter 4, the reader expects consistency. Unexpected shifts in person, subject, voice, and tense interfere with the coherent presentation of thought. It isn't that you can't use more than one person in a particular piece of writing, but that you should not switch back and forth without good reason.

Exercise your first-person option early on.

Your reader assumes you are writing in the third person unless you indicate otherwise. If you are thinking in the first person, use *I* or *we* in your opening, or at least relatively early on. If you wait until your closing to use *I* or *we,* the reader will be surprised by what appears to be a shift in person. In an article written in the third person on how acid rain is affecting the water quality of the Great Lakes, for example, don't surprise your reader by concluding, "As you consider the implications of the trends I have described, I'm sure you will find them as disturbing as I do."

Maintain unity in narration.

Despite the number and complexity of your options in narration, your point of view is—or at least should be—readily apparent to your reader. As with other types of writing, once you have declared your point of view, you should maintain it throughout your narrative. This consistency gives your story focus and coherence.

For deliberate effect, however, you can add complexity and richness to your story by telling it from more than one character's point of view, as William Faulkner does in *As I Lay Dying*, Louise Erdrich does in *The Beet Queen*, and Ernest Hemingway does in "The Short Happy Life of Francis Macomber," where the perspective shifts not only from character to character but even to an animal (a wounded lion). These sorts of shifts, however, are an intentional narrative device and should be thought of as an exception to the rule.

Use Point of View to Your Advantage in Persuasive Writing

What is the most appropriate and effective tone in persuasive writing? Is it unabashed assurance? Is it hesitant uncertainty?

You have been taught that good writing is vigorous writing, to present your points forcefully and emphatically. But you can lose an argument by overstating your case. Sometimes you need to qualify your assertions to make them credible.

"Each profession has its own idiom of caution and confidence," writes Joseph Williams in *Style*. Your persuasiveness "depends a good deal on . . . how successfully you tread the rhetorical line between timidity and arrogance." (And as Williams also points out, he chose to qualify that statement with the phrase *a good deal on*.)

Adopt a reasonable tone.

Avoid hyperbole and intemperate language. Rather than "If you had a brain, you would take it out and play with it," write "You should have attended more closely to the details of this project."

Know when to hedge and when to insist.

As I discussed in Chapter 1, modifiers intended to qualify or intensify a statement are sometimes "hollow" or devoid of meaning, and thus a source of wordiness. When used properly, however, these modifiers are an important means of creating a reasonable, measured tone and a more accurate statement.

Rather than "The problem *is* that you haven't worked hard enough to connect with your reader," write "The problem *may be* that you haven't worked hard enough to connect with your reader." Rather than "You *never* do the dishes," write "You *almost never* do the dishes."

Here are some examples of hedges and intensifiers, as well as two common problems associated with each:

Hedges

Hedges are used to qualify assertions. Common hedges include *usually, sometimes, perhaps, apparently, in some respects, seem,* and *appear.* As Williams points out, "The verbs *suggest* and *indicate* are particularly useful in making a claim about which you are less than 100 percent certain, but confident enough to propose." Compare "The evidence *proves* we need to adopt my proposal" with "The evidence *suggests* we need to adopt my proposal." Compare "This trend *demonstrates* that small businesses are more competitive" with "This trend *indicates* that small businesses are more competitive."

Intensifiers

Intensifiers are used to create emphasis. Common intensifiers include *indeed, clearly, absolutely, unquestionably, invariably, always, every, any,* and *all.* Compare "Rapid growth causes inflation" with "Rapid growth *invariably* causes inflation." Compare "A good writer needs a good editor" with "*Every* good writer needs a good editor."

Overqualification

Overqualification creates a tone of uncertainty and timidity. Compare "*In certain circumstances it seems fairly likely that* a confident tone *might* carry your argument" with "A confident tone can carry your argument." Compare "Excuses mean *almost* nothing to the customer" with "Excuses mean nothing to the customer."

Overintensification

Overintensification or overstatement may lead your reader to question your reasonableness or fair-mindedness. Compare "Tone is *absolutely* everything" with "Tone is everything." Compare "*Every* faculty member is against redefining tenure" with "*Nearly every* faculty member is against redefining tenure." Compare "We *never* make mistakes" with "We *rarely* make mistakes." As these examples suggest, absolutes are *always* problematic. (Don't you think?)

Hollow hedges

Hollow hedges are meaningless expressions such as *rather, somewhat, sometimes, virtually,* and *actually.* As with all modifiers, you need to distinguish between those that convey meaning and those that do not. Often context makes the difference. Read the following sentences out loud, first with and then without the italicized words. "We are *rather* concerned about your tardiness." "We are at a *virtual* crossroads." "Our count *actually* varies from yours."

Hollow intensifiers

Hollow intensifiers come in two varieties: redundant (*basic fundamentals, end result, final outcome, important essentials*) and meaningless (*effectively, certainly, altogether, literally*). For the latter group, good usage again is determined by context. Read the following sentences with and without the italicized words. "These are the *important* essentials of persuasive writing." "This *effectively* limits our ability to respond quickly." "Your description is *altogether* fitting." "We took *very* immediate action." "When asked to work overtime, he *literally* exploded"—a messy scene, as you can imagine. Note that "She *literally* fell off her chair" means she in fact fell off her chair.

In persuasive writing, moderately stated claims usually carry the most weight. Depending on your audience and material, the most effective tone lies somewhere between confidence without arrogance and diffidence without timidity.

Use the *you viewpoint* to involve your reader.

Refer to your reader's particular interests, concerns, motivations, or feelings, especially in your openings and closings. Recognizing your reader as an individual will make your message seem more relevant and interesting.

Sometimes referred to as *direct address* and the *you viewpoint*, the second person provides an effective means of emphasizing and involving the reader.

Use anecdotes to create sympathy for your perspective.

As I mentioned in Chapter 6, anecdotes can be used as a means of explanation, clarification, and persuasion. Because they invite the reader to see things from the storyteller's point of view, they tend to create sympathy—or at least understanding—for that perspective.

Use Point of View for Special Effect

Although you often write to express what you think and reveal how you feel, you don't necessarily say what you think and feel directly. In fact, the more comfortable you are with disparity, incongruity, and irony, the wider your range of expression and the more engaging you are likely to be as a writer.

Use disparity to create humor and irony.

Humor takes its effect in large part from incongruity in perspective. Often, the more sharply drawn the difference between what is anticipated and what actually occurs, the more humorous the effect. As I discussed in Chapter 4, one method for emphasizing incongruity in perspective is to create an expectation and then deliberately fail to meet it, as Somerset Maugham did when he wrote, "There are three rules for writing a novel. Unfortunately, nobody knows what they are."

Disparity in point of view accounts for the effect produced by a particular type of humor called *irony*. Irony can take many forms, but the two principal ones are *verbal* (or Socratic, which I discussed in Chapter 5) and *structural* (or situational). In verbal irony, the reader senses a difference between literal meaning and intended meaning. In structural irony, the reader senses a difference between what is perceived to be true—often by a naive narrator like Huckleberry Finn—and what is actually true. Both types of irony, as well as humor in general, involve working on more than one level of meaning, an approach that appeals to the reader's intelligence and playfulness.

Use a personal point of view to reveal your feelings.

When you are writing in the first person, think carefully about how much distance you want to create between yourself (or your persona) and your reader. The trend in modern writing is to give the reader a close, personal look. Generally, the more forthright you are in expressing your thoughts, feelings, and emotions, the stronger reaction you will elicit from your reader. This advice does not mean that you should write without subtlety (or irony, for that matter), but that you should take a definite position. Let the reader feel your presence. Don't hide behind your words. Have the courage to let the reader know who you are.

Create a persona to accomplish your purpose.

As I explained above, in narrative writing the narrator's voice and the writer's voice are never exactly the same. Through a variety of techniques and devices, the writer reveals the degree of difference between persona and true self. To some extent, this difference cannot be overcome entirely. Even in the most brutally honest confessional writing, there is still an element of contrivance and artifice.

Given that all writing is to a degree fictitious—writing, after all, can only *represent* reality, it can never *be* reality—it makes sense to use the element of artifice to your advantage. At times you will want to project an image of yourself that is as close to your true self as you can possibly make it. But at other times you will want to base your persona on your purpose and your assessment of how your reader is likely to respond to that created self. If portraying yourself as polite and respectful is more likely to accomplish your goals, present yourself as polite and respectful. If portraying yourself as frustrated and angry is more likely to accomplish your goals, present yourself as frustrated and angry.

Develop the persona you would like to be.

In addition to using persona to achieve a specific goal in a particular piece of writing, you can use this fictional representation of yourself in a way that has far-reaching implications for you, not only as a writer but also as a person. As John Steinbeck once said, "I can say now that one of the big reasons [for writing] was this: I instinctively recognized an opportunity to transcend some of my personal failings—things about myself I didn't particularly like and wanted to change but didn't know how." As you re-create yourself in writing, consider who you want to be. When you write, you have an opportunity to cultivate an image of yourself, to imagine the person you would like to become in real life.

To create a persona—to explore the similarities and differences between real and imagined people, and between your real self and your imagined self—is to explore some of the more interesting and subtle issues in writing. When you write, you create, and in creating you acquire a kind of unlimited power. You can be anyone you want to be. It's a marvelous freedom. Have fun with it.

CHAPTER 8: ORGANIZATION

Plan Your Writing

THINK IN PARAGRAPHS.

CHOOSE YOUR METHOD OF DEVELOPMENT.

1. Example
2. Process analysis
3. Division and classification
4. Comparison and analogy
5. Cause and effect
6. Definition

MAKE AN OUTLINE.

- When to outline
- Advantages of outlining
- Rules of outlining
- Steps in outlining

Persuasive Writing: Arrange Material to Your Advantage

WHEN WRITING TO A SYMPATHETIC AUDIENCE,
TAKE A DIRECT APPROACH.
WHEN WRITING TO AN UNSYMPATHETIC OR HOSTILE AUDIENCE,
TAKE AN INDIRECT APPROACH.
WHEN DELIVERING BAD NEWS, TAKE AN INDIRECT APPROACH.
ADAPT THE STANDARD FIVE-PART ARGUMENT TO YOUR PURPOSE
AND AUDIENCE.

1. Opening
2. Background and context
3. Presentation of argument
4. Refutation
5. Closing

STRENGTHEN YOUR ARGUMENT BY ACKNOWLEDGING THE
OPPOSITION.
IN PERSUASIVE CORRESPONDENCE, RECOGNIZE YOUR READER
AND OFFER TO TAKE THE NEXT STEP.

- Opening
- Body
- Closing
- Presentation

Concentrate on Beginnings and Endings

WRITE A GOOD INTRODUCTION.
USE YOUR LEAD TO ENGAGE YOUR READER.
USE THE FIRST SENTENCE OF A PARAGRAPH TO ANNOUNCE YOUR
TOPIC OR CREATE A TRANSITION.
USE THE LAST SENTENCE OF A PARAGRAPH FOR SPECIAL EFFECT.
CONCLUDE CONCLUSIVELY.

CHAPTER EIGHT

{Organization}

Plan Your Writing

As a child, you probably spent some time with blocks. You pushed them around. You stacked them up. After a while, you began to experiment with various arrangements and designs to see which were likely to stand and which were likely to fall.

As you grew older, maybe your parents or teachers gave you blocks in different sizes and colors—even blocks made of plastic that could be snapped together—and you attempted new, more intricate designs. But your basic activity remained the same: fitting individual pieces into some type of coherent whole.

Like block-building, writing is a matter of arrangement. It involves combining letters into words, words into sentences, sentences into paragraphs, and paragraphs into documents or finished pieces. It helps, of course, if you have some good words—or cool-looking blocks—to work with, but how you arrange your words is what sets you apart from other writers and other constructionists—or deconstructionists, as the case may be.

Think in paragraphs.

Imagine reading text that contained no sentence or paragraph divisions. What would it be like to make your way through a report, a story, or a book whose entire text was run together in an unbroken string of sentences? Imagine reading this chapter if it weren't divided into paragraphs.

Reading text written without breaks would be like living in a world without pauses. It would be like working an eight-hour day without getting up from your desk, or trying to swim across a one-hundred-meter pool without lifting your face out of the water. You probably wouldn't make it, and if you did, you would arrive desperate, your lungs bursting for air.

A world without paragraphs would be a daunting and confusing place. Your reader needs to know how things are organized, grouped, and connected. In the words of William Zinsser, "Writing is the logical arrangement of thought." Paragraphs are the building blocks that give your reader a sense of that arrangement.

Paragraphs range from tightly structured to loosely structured. Any scheme will do as long as the paragraph seems to hold together. Many paragraphs begin with a topic sentence or generalization, followed by a clarifying or limiting statement and one or more sentences of explanation or development. Some conclude with a resolution statement. Others delay the topic sentence until the end. Others have no topic sentence at all. Each paragraph should be designed to achieve its particular purpose.

The most tightly structured paragraphs, common in on-the-job writing (where paragraphs tend to be shorter—usually two to four sentences), follow a three-step approach: topic, development, resolution. These paragraphs state a topic, develop it with explanations and examples, and offer a conclusion. A paragraph beginning with "I recommend we change our policy for three reasons," for example, might then enumerate the reasons ("First . . . Second . . . Third . . ."), and then conclude with a statement of benefits.

A second standard structure, common in persuasive writing, is to follow the three steps of a syllogism, a basic pattern in deductive thinking: major premise, minor premise, conclusion. A paragraph using this deductive approach might offer as a major premise, "Every company needs to offer quality products at a competitive cost," then as a minor premise, "Our company, however, is offering substandard products at noncompetitive costs," and then as a conclusion, "Therefore, I recommend that we improve our quality control and cut our costs of production, distribution, and advertising."

Whatever form it takes, a good paragraph has three attributes: unity, coherence, and development. *Unity* involves linking the subordinate ideas to the main idea so that the paragraph has a single main purpose. *Coherence* results from connecting the sentences and arranging them in a logical pattern. And *development* has to do with supporting the main idea with sufficient examples and adequate detail.

Writing is rarely easy. Usually it's hard. But don't make it harder than it needs to be. Write in sentences, and think in paragraphs. Take it one step at a time.

Choose your method of development.

As I discussed in Chapter 6, there are four primary modes of discourse: description, narration, exposition, and persuasion. The third mode, exposition or expository writing, includes six basic methods of development: example, process analysis, division and classification, comparison and analogy, cause and effect, and definition.

1. Example

Using *example* to clarify, illustrate, and support your points is a basic principle of effective writing. As I will discuss in more detail in Chapter 9, your evidence will have its greatest impact on your reader when it is specific, detailed, colorful, relevant, and adequate. Anecdotes, analogy, metaphor, and direct quotes are all means of illustrating your points.

2. Process analysis

Process analysis is a step-by-step explanation of how something works or how to do something. Incorporating an element of narration into exposition, process analysis is the method of development you would use to explain a procedure from beginning to end, whether that procedure is auditing a branch office or assembling a hang glider. By its nature, process analysis is methodical and demanding. As Kim and Michael Flachmann point out in *The Prose Reader*, "No other thinking pattern will force you to slow down as much as process analysis, because the process you are explaining probably won't make any sense if you leave out even the slightest detail." To skip a step or to fail to explain one clearly could have serious repercussions for an auditor or hang glider alike.

The main disadvantage of process analysis is that it tends to become monotonous. (Imagine your state of mind when reading step 85 in a 100-step process.) Its main advantage is that it is easy to follow—provided the steps are presented in a consistent format and provided parallel structure is maintained throughout. A good way to check for parallel structure is to read the first few words of every item in the series. If some items begin with verbs and others with nouns, or if some items are complete sentences and others are fragments, the format is nonparallel. Consider the following two examples:

Assess compliance of our Tennessee operation on the following points:
1. Are collection efforts delayed?
2. Petty cash policy
3. Is on-site concurrent review performed?
4. Incomplete provider contract files

Assess compliance of our Tennessee operation on the following points:
1. Are collection efforts delayed?
2. Is there a policy for handling petty cash?
3. Is on-site concurrent review performed?
4. Are provider contract files complete?

Which list is nonparallel? Which is easier to read and understand?

3. Division and classification

Division and *classification* are methods of dividing and grouping. In a sense, they move in opposite directions. Division is the separation of something into its component parts; classification is the grouping of those parts into related categories. For example, you might divide workers in an automobile assembly plant according to their technical skills (division), or you might group them according to which part of the car they work on (classification). Your choice would depend on your purpose. Use division to identify differences, classification to emphasize similarities.

4. Comparison and analogy

Comparison and *analogy* are useful ways to clarify your meaning, particularly when the subject is complex and the reader's knowledge is relatively limited. The most effective comparisons and analogies often link what is unfamiliar and complex to what is familiar and simple, as when a scientist likens the formation of the galaxies to rivulets forming streams after a rain shower. As I discussed in Chapter 5, this type of exposition, which includes metaphor and simile, also provides you with an important means of conveying your personality and originality.

Comparisons and analogies that are more than brief references require an organizational structure. That structure can be whole by whole or part by part. The whole-by-whole approach addresses all relevant characteristics of one thing before addressing the other thing; the part-by-part approach compares all relevant features one by one. Whole-by-whole comparisons generally are easier for the reader to follow because they require less switching back and forth. Part-by-part comparisons, though more likely to become tedious, generally are more useful in determining a precise inventory of advantages and disadvantages, strengths and weaknesses, or similarities and differences. If your intent is to offer an overview of similarities and differences between gasoline-powered and natural gas–powered vehicles, for example, you might choose the whole-by-whole approach. And if your intent is to produce a point-by-point comparison of maintenance and costs, you might choose the part-by-part approach.

5. Cause and effect

Cause and effect involves analyzing connections. The most common problem in this type of writing is making false connections. Unlike process analysis, which addresses *how* something happens, causal analysis discusses *why* it happened and *what* the result was. You would use process analysis, for example, to explain how to tie the lacing on a pair of snowshoes, whereas you would use cause and effect to discuss the features that make longer snowshoes more suitable for use in the Arctic tundra and shorter snowshoes more suitable for use in the North Woods of Minnesota.

6. Definition

Definition involves limiting the frame of reference for the purpose of achieving precise and efficient communication. A definition can take the form of a phrase, sentence, or paragraph. An extended definition might include elements of all six types of exposition as well as description. For example, in defining swing dance, you might use process analysis to demonstrate how the various moves all depend on the same basic step, division and classification to identify its distinguishing features, and cause and effect to explain the reasons for its resurgence as a popular form of dancing.

Make an outline.

Outlining isn't exactly the most exciting, exhilarating, satisfying thing you might do in a day's work. For many writers, outlining is a sensible but bothersome form of preparation. It's like reviewing the minutes of the last meeting before attending the next one. You know you should do it, but you're tempted to wing it instead.

You may be less prone to skip this important stage in writing, however, if you think of outlining as formulating a plan of action for achieving your goals. It's an opportunity to gather your thoughts and organize your thinking before beginning that sometimes arduous task of producing text—of searching for the most precise language to convey your meaning. Outlining not only can make your document more effective, it also can save you the frustration of making false starts and doing hours of rewriting later on.

When to outline
1. When the subject is complex.
2. When the material is lengthy or involves multiple components.
3. Whenever you feel the need to gather and organize your thoughts.

Advantages of outlining
1. Helps clarify your thinking about purpose, audience, and material.
2. Provides a structure (at its most basic, a beginning, a middle, and an end).
3. Makes it easier to deal with large, complex subjects by breaking them into smaller, more manageable parts.
4. Helps you identify key points and decide how much emphasis to give them.
5. Promotes coherent development by helping you see how your various points relate to each other and to your central argument.
6. Helps you detect errors in logic and organization.
7. Makes it easier to rearrange and experiment with different structures.
8. Helps you decide what to include and what to exclude.
9. Helps you check for completeness.
10. Helps you write with more focus and precision.

Rules of outlining

1. Present all items in parallel structure.

Not this:	**But this:**
a. Advantages of Outlining	a. Advantages of Outlining
b. Know When You Should Outline	b. When to Outline
c. Rules of Outlining	c. Rules of Outlining
d. There Are Three Steps in the Outline Process	d. Steps in the Outlining Process

2. When dividing categories into subcategories, divide each unit into at least two subunits.

Not this:	**But this:**
a. First category	a. First category
1) First subcategory	1) First subcategory
	2) Second subcategory
b. Second category	b. Second category
1) First subcategory	1) First subcategory
2) Second subcategory	2) Second subcategory

3. In formal outlines, use this hierarchy of labeling:

I.

     A.

         1.

            a.

               i.

                   (a)

                   (b)

               ii.

            b.

         2.

     B.

II.

4. Use Roman numerals correctly; the first twenty are I, II, III, IV, V, VI, VII, VIII, IX, X, XI, XII, XIII, XIV, XV, XVI, XVII, XVIII, XIX, XX.

Steps in outlining

1. Identify your primary purpose (write your thesis or purpose statement in a simple declarative sentence).
2. Identify any secondary objectives (make a list).
3. Devise a working title (make it descriptive or functional rather than creative, such as "The advantages of ecosystem-based management in protecting northern hardwood-coniferous forests" rather than "Healthy forests: Taking the broader view").
4. Determine broad categories to use in classifying your information and material.
5. Arrange your categories according to hierarchy (vertical method) or sequence (horizontal method).
6. Evaluate your outline for logic, order, extraneous elements, and completeness.
7. Once you begin writing, modify and depart from your outline as you think appropriate.

Persuasive Writing: Arrange Material to Your Advantage

Effective writing is, to some extent, a matter of presenting your thoughts in the right order. Consider, for example, the following premise of persuasive writing.

If you think your reader is sympathetic to your ideas, be direct: Offer your conclusion first, then present your evidence. If you think your reader is unsympathetic or hostile to your ideas, be indirect: Present your evidence first (and perhaps rebut the opposing point of view), then offer your conclusion. The rationale behind this premise is that a sympathetic reader is more likely to accept your conclusion on face value. An unsympathetic reader, on the other hand, wants to hear your reasoning and evidence before considering your conclusion.

When writing to a sympathetic audience, take a direct approach.

A direct approach can be used to determine both the order of the paragraphs in an argument and the order of the sentences in a single paragraph. A paragraph taking a direct approach might look like this:

> One of the best ways to improve your writing is to study and imitate the writing of others. It is only by close attention to other writers' stylistic techniques that you will gain an appreciation for the full range of options available to you, options ranging from sentence structure to figurative language and point of view. Although some would argue that close study of this nature will result in a derivative style, you will find that the techniques you are examining and exploring quickly become your own.

Note the order: The paragraph opens with an assertion or a conclusion (*One of the best ways to improve your writing* . . .), supports that assertion with a second assertion (*It is only by close attention* . . .), offers some examples (*options ranging from* . . .), recognizes an opposing point of view (*Although some would argue* . . .), and closes with a rebuttal (*you will find* . . .).

When writing to an unsympathetic or hostile audience, take an indirect approach.

A paragraph presenting essentially the same arguments to an unsympathetic audience, on the other hand, might look like this:

> Some would argue that studying and imitating the writing of others will result in a derivative style. They claim that attending to other writers' stylistic techniques will prevent you from developing a distinct voice and style of your own. In practice, however, you will find that the techniques you are examining and exploring quickly become your own. Furthermore, it is only by close attention to the writing of others that you will gain an appreciation for the full range of options available to you, options ranging

from sentence structure to figurative language and point of view. For these reasons, learning through study and imitation is one of the best ways to improve your writing.

Taking an indirect approach, the paragraph opens with an opposing statement (*Some would argue . . .*), presents a rebuttal (*In practice, however . . .*), offers some examples (*Furthermore . . .*), then closes with a broader assertion or conclusion (*For these reasons . . .*).

When delivering bad news, take an indirect approach.

As a rule, you should be clear, concise, and to the point in your writing. When writing a memo, for example, you might follow this commonly used three-step formula: purpose, background, proposed action. But sometimes, for the sake of tact and diplomacy, you can't say straight out what's on your mind. Consider, for example, a memo that delivers its message in this way: "You're fired. Despite your thirty-five years of exemplary service to our company, we no longer need your services. Please pack up and clear out by three o'clock this afternoon." That memo is clear, concise, and brutally direct.

When you are delivering bad news or writing about a delicate topic, rather than use the conventional three-step approach—purpose, background, proposed action—to organize your message, consider opening and closing with a goodwill statement. The bad news in the heartlessly written memo above, for example, could be softened somewhat by opening with an expression of appreciation for the employee's good service or an explanation of the circumstances that led to the decision to terminate employment. This less direct approach, sometimes referred to as opening with a "buffer," helps prepare your reader for the bad news that follows. Concluding with a goodwill statement also is good practice because it enables you to end on a positive note.

Adapt the standard five-part argument to your purpose and audience.

The following five-part approach represents a standard way to organize an argument. You can use it to take a direct approach in presenting an argument to a sympathetic audience or, by reversing steps 3 and 4, to take an indirect approach in presenting an argument to an unsympathetic audience.

1. Opening
- Announces the topic or purpose and—depending on the author's strategy—the conclusion.
- Prepares the reader intellectually and emotionally for the argument that follows.
- Establishes the author's credentials as someone who is knowledgeable, reasonable, and fair-minded.

2. Background and context
- Presents the relevant background and history to make the topic understandable.
- Explains the significance and broader implications of the topic or recommendation.

3. Presentation of argument
- Presents the thesis (an assertion or proposition) as a debatable or argumentative statement.
- Offers specific points of proof or examples supporting the thesis.
- *Optional indirect approach:* Presents the *proof* first, then the *thesis* when the reader is likely to be skeptical or to disagree.

4. Refutation
- Acknowledges the opposing view.
- Points out the weaknesses of the opposing view.
- *Optional indirect approach:* Presents the *refutation* before the *presentation of argument.*

5. Closing
- Restates the main assertion in terms slightly different from the original statement.
- States the recommendation or recommendations.

The order in which you present your argument depends on your assessment of your reader's openness to your point of view. For example, you would likely present argument before refutation if you were recommending Wheaties over Frosted Flakes to parents of hyperactive children, but you would likely present refutation before argument if you were talking to a five-year-old child ("I know Frosted Flakes tastes good, but cereals coated with sugar . . ."). As is usually the case, your rhetorical strategy depends as much on your reader as your material.

Strengthen your argument by acknowledging the opposition.

Whatever your assessment of your audience's receptivity to your argument, a good persuasive strategy is to acknowledge the reader's point of view before presenting your own. In a letter to a store manager, for example, your complaint about poor service will carry more weight if you first acknowledge the other side of the argument:

> I understand that it isn't always possible to predict how busy you will be on any given day. I also realize that the two clerks on duty Saturday morning were doing their best to help dozens of customers as quickly as possible. Nevertheless, I think it unreasonable that I had to wait nearly an hour just to pay for my purchases.

When you recognize another person's perspective, you indicate you have considered the issue from both sides, and this approach makes you seem reasonable and fair-minded.

In persuasive correspondence, recognize your reader and offer to take the next step.

The secret to accomplishing your goal in persuasive correspondence is to leave nothing to chance. Unfortunately, when you're trying to get—and keep—the attention of a hurried reader, the odds are against you.

Chances are (a) your reader won't read your memo or letter carefully; (b) your reader won't read your memo or letter at all; or (c) your reader, even if persuaded by your argument, won't get around to taking the action you desire. How can you beat these less-than-favorable odds?

Here's what M.B.A. students in the University of Minnesota's Carlson School of Management and graduate students in the Management of Technology program are taught: Use every component of a memo to your advantage. If you're not thinking strategically, you're not thinking clearly.

When I assign and grade persuasive memos, for example, I emphasize the following points:

Opening

- **Make your subject line informative.** Your subject line is the title of your story. Use it to capture your reader's attention. Make it descriptive, specific, and succinct. A busy manager is less likely to read a memo titled "Morale problem" than one titled "High employee turnover is damaging our quality control."
- **State your purpose clearly.** Tell your reader why you are writing. Briefly summarize sufficient background detail to explain the situation. Convey a sense of urgency, if warranted.
- **Recognize your reader's interests and concerns.** Use the "you approach." Talk directly to your reader. Refer explicitly to something your reader has said or done ("As you requested, I am . . ."; "Knowing your commitment to quality control, I want to . . ."). If you haven't addressed the reader as an individual, you haven't used the "you approach."
- **Explain your organization.** Provide a road map. Even in a one-page memo, it's good practice to tell the reader where you're going: "After examining the causes of this dramatic increase in employee turnover, I will demonstrate how turnover is damaging our quality control and explain what we can do about it." Offer your organizational statement as the last sentence of your opening.

Body

- **Present your main points in informative, descriptive headings.** Word your headings so that a busy reader can see your key points at a glance. Rather than generic headings such as *Background, Consequences, Solution,* provide headings that emphasize your principal points: *Low wages are hurt-*

ing employee morale. High turnover is damaging quality control. New employee incentives are needed.

- **Present a well-organized, logically developed, carefully supported argument.** Organize your material into tightly structured paragraphs. Support your main points with specific detail (sufficient data, examples, and illustrations). Rebut opposing arguments.

Closing

- **State your recommendation(s) and action request explicitly.** Be clear and direct. If you are presenting multiple recommendations, number them in a vertical list.
- **Explain how the reader will benefit.** As in your opening, recognize your reader's interests and concerns.
- **Give and justify a deadline.** Like a department store advertising a thirteen-hour sale, give the reader a reason for acting now. Explain *why* prompt action is necessary. Otherwise, you might convince your reader of the validity of your argument but fail to persuade your reader to take action.
- **Offer to take the next step.** Take the initiative to follow up: "I'll call you Monday to see what you think"; "With your permission, I'd like to present my proposal at Friday's staff meeting." If you don't conclude with the ball in your court, you might have won the point but lost the game.

Presentation

In addition to these structural points, I encourage my students to:
- Use tone and language appropriate for the audience.
- Write in a style that is direct, assertive, energetic, and concise (prefer active, personal voice over passive voice; prefer action verbs over weak verbs linked to general nouns; avoid wordiness).
- Use highlighting (bullets, boldface, italics, underlining) to engage the reader and reinforce your main points.
- Proofread to eliminate errors in spelling, usage, grammar, and punctuation.

The attributes of effective writing—persuasive or otherwise—cannot be entirely accounted for by measuring them against items on a checklist. But a checklist can be useful. It's good for clarifying expectations, removing some of the guesswork from writing, and identifying relative strengths and weaknesses in a writer's style and approach.

Concentrate on Beginnings and Endings

As I discussed in Chapter 4, the first and last words in your sentences count more than the words in the middle. The same principle applies to paragraphs and entire documents. Beginning and endings count more than middles.

Write a good introduction.

Your most important paragraph is your first one. It introduces the subject, sometimes directly ("The purpose of this manual is to explain our company's procedures for responding to complaints from customers"), sometimes indirectly ("It was a bright cold day in April, and the clocks were striking thirteen"). The introductory paragraph typically ends with a statement of thesis or purpose. For more complex documents, the introductory paragraph also includes an organizational statement, typically appearing after the thesis statement.

In narrative and certain types of expressive writing, the opening paragraph (or paragraphs) introduces not only the subject (the theme or central concern), but also the setting (the time and place), and one or more of the central characters. For more expressive types of writing (including articles, stories, and novels), the introductory paragraph usually opens with a lead intended to engage the interest of the reader.

Use your lead to engage your reader.

In expository writing, a good lead provides the information and context needed by the reader to understand the subject or purpose. In persuasive writing, a good lead prepares the reader intellectually and emotionally to accept the writer's point of view. In sales letters and sales proposals, for example, a lead might offer dramatic savings for a purchase or appeal to the customer's needs or desires. In narrative writing, a good lead invites the reader into the story by offering an intriguing scene or introducing an interesting character. The purpose of your lead is to convince your reader that the text that follows is worth the time it will take to read it.

As an illustration of the importance of a good lead, consider the following examples. Which lead arouses your curiosity in a way that makes you want to read the story?

> Merchandising tasks are important. The appearance of your department, the accuracy and timeliness of your markdowns, the display of new merchandise—our customers expect these to be in order. But the work can't be done at the expense of serving our customers. Your most important job is to put our customers first!

> Pumpkins in the pool? It sounds like a Halloween prank, but in reality it's our third annual Pumpkin Relays Swim Meet.

My guess is you chose the second example, the lead to a brochure providing information about programs at the YWCA. Its sharp visual image and playful tone make it engaging. The first example, from a company newsletter, opens with a nondescript statement. Note that it would be improved if the first sentence were simply omitted.

Consider two more examples, both from *Update*, a newsletter of the University of Minnesota:

> The basement dance studio in Norris Hall is a long, narrow room with a bank of mirrors along one wall and thick black mats, marked off in lanes, on the floor. This morning the lawn-level windows are open to catch any breeze, and a gleaming studio upright stands in a corner.
>
> Three barefoot students—two women, one man—watch closely as their teacher, Maria Cheng, demonstrates a dance sequence. In a silky black tunic and loose pants, Cheng looks like an elegant martial arts master, sure and fluid in her moves.

> Joanne Leslie doesn't skip classes anymore, and she makes sure to sit in front. Scott Burstein studies standing up. These ideas—and

a sharpened focus on what they want to accomplish as students—they acquired in a course called Becoming a Master Student.

"If you're a student, you're choosing to be a learner, and there are things to be known about what that really means," says Joyce Weinsheimer. She directs the Learning and Academic Study Skills Center, which offers the master student course. "Wanting to learn more about how you learn should not be seen as something remedial," she stresses.

The first, which uses a scene-setting technique, is evocative because the description appeals effectively to the senses. (The scene is described in a way that makes you want to be there.) The second is engaging because it focuses on individual characters.

Use the first sentence of your paragraph to announce your topic or create a transition.

As I pointed out above, paragraphs come in all shapes and sizes. It is common practice, however, to open a paragraph with a topic or transitional sentence. If you think of your paragraphs as units of development or stages in your argument, think of the first sentence of each paragraph as an opportunity to signal your reader that a new stage has been reached. Note, for example, that I began this paragraph with a transitional sentence (one that points backward), followed by a topic sentence (one that points forward).

Transitions may be announced by phrases, such as *As I pointed out above,* or by connecting words, such as *nevertheless, therefore, consequently, indeed, then, accordingly, however, moreover,* and *also.* Your choice of a phrase or a word is based on a number of factors, including how fast or slow you want your pace to be (long transitions set a slower pace; short transitions set a faster pace), distance traveled (if you are referring to a thought expressed in a previous chapter, you are more likely to use a phrase; if you are referring to a thought expressed in the previous paragraph, you are more likely to use a word), complexity of material (longer transitions give your reader a false sense of security), and sophistication of your reader (knowledgeable readers require less assistance and are less prone to anxiety attacks).

As I discuss in Chapter 10, the key to creating coherence is using transitional language to connect your sentences and paragraphs. Writers who make these connections tend to be easy to follow; writers who fail to make them tend to leave their readers feeling momentarily lost or confused by the direction their discussion has taken. To avoid losing your reader as you progress through the stages of your development, connect your paragraphs.

Use the last sentence of a paragraph for special effect.

Because the last sentence in a paragraph is followed by a pause created by a break in the text, it has particular emphasis. Use that sentence to resolve the point you have developed in the paragraph. A short, punchy sentence works especially well in this position. For particular emphasis, you can break this sentence from the paragraph and present it as a one-sentence paragraph.

Likewise, a witty comment or a lighthearted statement will seem funnier if it is delivered as the last sentence rather than buried somewhere in the middle of a paragraph. In *On Writing Well*, William Zinsser describes the opportunity offered at the end of a paragraph:

> Take special care with the last sentence of each paragraph—it is the crucial springboard to the next paragraph. Try to give that sentence an extra twist of humor or surprise, like the periodic "snapper" in the routine of a stand-up comic. Make the reader smile and you've got him for at least one paragraph more.

To illustrate skillful use of concluding sentences, I once read aloud the first few paragraphs of Bart Sutter's article "The Next Best Thing to Nobody" (which appeared in the winter 1996 issue of *The Boundary Waters Journal*) to students in an essay-writing class. Each time the students laughed, I noted, was in response to the final sentence of a paragraph. Note the structure of Sutter's lead paragraph:

> A couple years back, when I checked the calendar for my annual lake trout trip, my eyes bugged out. The fourth week in May was completely free. Instead of nibbling at the edge of the Boundary

Waters on a long weekend, I could really go somewhere. I decided on a route with lots of options and the provisional goal of reaching a body of water at the heart of the BWCAW, which, for purposes of public communication, I'm going to call Eagle Lake. I believe that honesty is the best policy for everything except blueberry patches and fishing spots.

A few paragraphs later Sutter explains how a friend at first declined, then accepted Sutter's invitation to be his canoeing partner:

When I called him with my proposal, Tom turned me down with a groan of regret; he was already committed to a trip that week. But the next day he called to ask if he could still come along. He had decided to back out of the other trip and rearrange his schedule in order to go with me. Was I flattered. Why had he changed his mind? Well, he said he couldn't resist the chance to see this new country on the route I'd mapped out. Besides, he thought I'd make a fine partner. He been out with plenty of guys over the years, but way too many of them just couldn't seem to stop talking. That wasn't why he went into the woods, to listen to somebody's monologue. He'd thought about this a lot. He felt he knew me fairly well, and he figured I was the next best thing to nobody.

With the concluding sentence of that paragraph, the author offers not only a funny line but an explanation of the title. Later, in a paragraph in which he describes the silence of the Boundary Waters, Sutter presents us with the most carefully crafted sentence of the piece—and, again, it comes at the end of a paragraph:

Since we both have a high regard for silence, we traveled in a kind of luxurious quiet. Such peace is hard to come by these days. The noise of our infernal machinery is nearly omnipresent; clocks and refrigerators hum in our sleep. But the silence of canoe country is more than lack of racket. Silence is not the absence of sound. True silence is spacious and easily includes the splatter of waves, the song of the wind, the jabber of warblers in the high treetops. Out of deep silence, it has always seemed to me, comes the best of what we know—poetry, music, the most moving conversations.

Note, too, how Sutter inverts the structure of the last sentence, a technique I discussed in Chapter 4.

Conclude conclusively.

Your last paragraph should leave the reader with a sense of completion or resolution, particularly in narration and persuasion. In narration, your story can end at any point in the chronology of events as long as the last paragraph seems appropriate to the theme or characters. A good ending to a story is simply one that feels right. Although it may not resolve all issues, it invites the audience to consider the significance of what has transpired by placing everything that preceded it in a new light. The questions "Why did it end here?" and "What does it mean?" are closely linked.

In persuasion, your concluding paragraph is a restatement of your argument. Often it includes a call to action. The wording is usually similar—but should not be identical—to the language in the introduction and the presentation of the argument. In all types of writing your conclusion carries special emphasis, but in persuasion it is the most important paragraph of the text. It represents your best opportunity to drive home your point and to make it memorable to your audience. As a conclusion to an essay on school funding, for example, a student in one of my classes wrote, "Because of the shift in funding, the city schools received less money for children's education. And we wonder why Johnny or Sally can't read."

As this student did so successfully, conclude conclusively. Conclude with flourish. Conclude with style.

CHAPTER 9: SUPPORT

Support Your Assertions
OFFER SPECIFIC, CONCRETE, RELEVANT DETAILS.

OFFER ENOUGH—BUT NOT TOO MUCH—DETAIL.

APPEAL TO THE SENSES WITH SPECIFIC, CONCRETE, COLORFUL DETAIL.

APPEAL TO LOGIC WITH FACTS AND STATISTICS.

USE ANECDOTES TO MAKE YOUR POINT.

USE ANALOGY AND METAPHOR TO EXPLAIN YOUR THINKING.

QUOTE OTHERS TO ENHANCE YOUR CREDIBILITY.

DOCUMENT YOUR SOURCES.

For Persuasive Writing, Determine a Rhetorical Strategy
USE A COMBINATION OF RHETORICAL APPEALS.

AVOID COMMON FALLACIES IN PERSUASIVE WRITING.

FOLLOW STANDARD RULES OF EVIDENCE.

DON'T FORGET YOUR READER.

{Support}

Support Your Assertions

Minneapolis is a lovely city. Through its heart runs the Mississippi River, cascading over the muffled beat of St. Anthony falls. The downtown, a mix of high-rise office buildings, classy retail centers, restored brick warehouses, and a few old theaters, gives way to neighborhoods of tree-lined boulevards and corner shops. Near its western border a chain of lakes is surrounded by park land and walking paths, on the south a parkway meanders beside Minnehaha Creek past another set of lakes and Minnehaha Falls, and on the southeast a great river gorge slices through layered sandstone and limestone bluffs. A center of commerce, education, culture, and recreation, Minneapolis achieves a pleasing balance between urban appeal and natural beauty.

In that paragraph I follow a fundamental two-step pattern in writing: I make an assertion, then I support it with examples and detail. Without that second step, I would be asking you, my reader, to accept on blind faith my opinion ("Minneapolis is a lovely city").

There are many ways to support your assertions. In this chapter, I discuss some of the more common ones.

Offer specific, concrete, relevant details.

As I discussed in Chapter 2, Joseph Conrad advised writers not to tell their readers, but to show them. Don't just tell your readers, "Susan works hard." Show them: "Last month Susan came in at 6:00 A.M. every day to help complete the internal audit on time." Don't just tell your readers, "Morale is declining." Show them: "This year grievances increased by 14 percent, and employee turnover by 8 percent."

In *Handbook for Writers,* Lynn Quitman Troyka offers a handy memory device called "RENNS," which stands for *R*easons, *E*xamples, *N*ames, *N*umbers, and *S*enses (sight, sound, smell, taste, and touch). Thinking of RENNS will help you determine whether you have provided sufficient detail. It will also suggest ideas for different types of detail you might use in developing your thought. As Troyka points out, most paragraphs do not make use of every category of details, but a fully developed paragraph will usually make use of more than one.

A common mistake on the part of beginning writers is to offer insufficient evidence to support or explain their assertions. Don't make the reader guess at your meaning. Illustrate your points with specific, concrete details. Support your points with evidence that is specific, detailed, colorful, relevant, and adequate. Use anecdotes, analogy, metaphor, and direct quotes to illustrate your points.

Offer enough—but not too much—detail.

One of your most important decisions as a writer is how much detail to offer in support of your arguments. How much is enough? How much is too much? The answer, of course, depends on the three things you must keep in mind whenever you write: your purpose, your audience, and your subject.

Your thesis or statement of purpose (which I discussed in Chapter 6) will help you determine which details are relevant and which are extraneous. In addition to purpose, consider your audience. What does your reader need to know to understand your message? What does your reader already know? What needs to be pointed out or made explicit? A good assessment of your audience requires insight and imagination. Finally, consider your subject. How much explanation or development is required to achieve your purpose with a particular audience?

As a general approach, err on the side of including too much detail when you draft, then cut back as you edit. "Cut what does not contribute to the whole," as Donald Hall points out in *Writing Well.* "But first, you must have a whole." To help you decide what to retain and what to cut, keep in mind this simple guideline: If a detail does not contribute in some significant way to achieving your purpose, delete it.

In descriptive writing, make sure every detail is relevant, whether you are describing a scene for the purpose of creating a certain mood or describing "a mechanism and the function of its parts"—to use Judith VanAlstyne's words in *Professional and Technical Writing Strategies*—so that the reader can "judge the efficiency, reliability, and practicality of the mechanism." In narrative writing, every detail—as Kurt Vonnegut points out—should remark on a character or advance the action. In expository writing, every detail should help explain or illuminate the subject. And in persuasive writing, every detail should serve a particular strategic purpose.

Appeal to the senses with specific, concrete, colorful detail.

As I discussed in Chapter 2, language that refers to things that can be seen, heard, smelled, tasted, or touched generally makes a more vivid impression than abstract language. Rather than write about how clear-cutting a forest "changes the landscape," describe "a field of ruts and stubble." Rather than describe a happy occasion by writing "We celebrated our victory," write "Within minutes of the announcement the champagne corks were popping and project team members were hugging."

Appeal to logic with facts and statistics.

Your reader wants to know not only what you think but why you think it. Provide the factual evidence that led you to your conclusion. Back up an assertion such as "Starting a small business is risky" with a fact such as "Twenty-five percent of them fail within the first five years."

Use anecdotes to make your point.

As I discussed in Chapters 6 and 7, one of the most effective ways to illustrate your thinking is to tell a story. Anecdotes, like parables, use the narrative appeal of character and action to reinforce a point or to teach a lesson. I've noticed, for example, that whenever I tell a story in my writing workshops, the participants momentarily open their half-closed eyes and lift their nodding heads.

Use analogy and metaphor to explain your thinking.

If you are writing without making comparisons, you are neglecting one of the most powerful tools of communication. Figurative language makes your writing vivid. It not only draws on your own creativity but appeals to your reader's imagination, thereby evoking an active response. After an assertion such as "The first time you get up on water skis is exhilarating," offer a comparison such as "You feel as though you are a plane skimming across a runway and about to take off." As I discussed in Chapter 5, the quality of your metaphors can be evaluated according to three criteria: aptness (your metaphor seems right, even though you may be finding similarity between two very dissimilar things), simplicity (it isn't overly elaborate, forced, or contrived), and novelty (it is unexpected or offers an element of surprise).

Quote others to enhance your credibility.

Use testimony from credible sources. Direct quotes bring a fresh perspective, create a sense of immediacy, and add emphasis to your writing. (As I'm sure you've noticed by now, I like to quote other writers to support my points.) Rather than say "Writing is hard work," quote a writer like Red Smith, who once said, "There's nothing to writing. All you do is sit down at a typewriter and open a vein."

Document your sources.

For more formal types of research and academic writing, you need to cite the sources of quotations, summaries, paraphrases, and any facts or ideas that are not common knowledge, and your citations must follow standard documentation styles. The three most commonly used styles are those of the Modern Language Association (MLA), used in English and the humanities; the American Psychological Association (APA), used in psychology, the social sciences, and business; and *The Chicago Manual of Style*, used in history and book publishing generally. In addition, there are a number of style manuals specific to particular fields or disciplines, such as *The Associated Press Stylebook and Libel Manual* in journalism; *Scientific Style and Format: The CBE Manual for Authors, Editors, and Publishers* in biology; and *The Style Manual for Political Science.*

MLA and APA styles are similar, but they differ on certain key points. In fact, they are just similar enough to be confusing. Both styles use the same three components of documentation: signal phrases (or phrases of attribution), parenthetical references for in-text citations (rather than footnotes or endnotes, as required by *The Chicago Manual of Style*), and lists of sources following the text.

For Persuasive Writing, Determine a Rhetorical Strategy

In Chapter 8, I discussed how rhetorical strategy influences the arrangement and organization of your arguments. Here, I return to rhetorical strategy as it determines the type of support you use in developing your arguments.

There are three basic types of appeals: appeals to reason *(logos)*, appeals to emotion *(pathos)*, and appeals to ethics *(ethos)*. Generally, the most effective persuasive writing makes use of all three types.

Logical appeals rely on evidence, research, examples, and data to convince the reader of the truth or validity of an argument. They invite a reasoned response and are usually most effective when the reader is expected to disagree with what is being asserted.

According to Arthur Biddle in *Writer to Writer*, "The logical method is directed to the rational faculty of the audience through the reasonableness of the piece. It employs facts, data, and evidence that the mind can weigh in assessing the truth or validity of the assertion. This is the classical mode of argumentation."

Emotional appeals attempt to arouse the feelings, instincts, or biases of your reader. As professional fund-raisers know, the most effective way to motivate a sympathetic audience to shell out the money is to follow the formula of "feelings first; facts follow." Common in advertising and fund-raising letters, emotional appeals often rely on what Herschell Gordon Lewis in *How to Write Powerful Fund Raising Letters* calls the "five great motivators": fear, exclusivity, guilt, greed, and anger. Emotional appeals are generally most effective when the reader is expected to agree with the argument.

Despite their usefulness, emotional appeals are sometimes neglected by writers who think them inappropriate in carefully reasoned writing. According to Arthur Biddle:

> Perhaps because [emotional appeal] has been so often abused . . . this approach has acquired a bad name. Yet rhetoricians from the time of Aristotle have known that men and women are emotional beings as well as rational. A responsible appeal to the feelings of the audience, far from being reprehensible, is often necessary to create a frame of mind receptive to your logical arguments.

Ethical appeals rely on the reader's sense of right and wrong. As Biddle points out, they also depend on the writer's credibility and reputation "as a reliable, qualified, experienced, well-informed, and knowledgeable person whose opinions . . . are believable because they are ethically sound." In other words, with ethical appeals, "the audience is moved not only by *what* is said but by *who* said it."

Use a combination of rhetorical appeals.

People are complex. They are rational, emotional, spiritual beings. If you want to change their opinion about something or get them to accept your point of view, you need to appeal to them on more than one level.

Consider, for example, the following illustration of how to combine all three rhetorical modes. Imagine you are the chair of the Department of Philosophy and your university's central administration has proposed cutting your department's supply budget. "None of the other philosophers has new computers," they have told you, "so why should you?" What would you do?

You could protest on the grounds that a new computer could be purchased (with an educational discount) for only $1,500, and that a new computer would increase your department's productivity by 5 percent, and that 5 percent of your department's operating and expense budget of $60,000 is $3,000, which amounts to a net gain of $1,500 *(logos)*. Or you could argue that a cut in your supply budget would so thoroughly demoralize the faculty in your department that they might resign and seek positions at competing institutions *(pathos)*. Or you could appeal to central administration's sense of fairness by pointing out that every faculty member in the school of business got a new computer last year and that the humanities faculty always seems to come last in appropriations *(ethos)*. But your most persuasive argument would combine all three appeals.

As a rule, when writing to a sympathetic audience, appeal first to feelings and emotions; when writing to an unsympathetic or hostile audience, appeal first to reasons and logic. And for most persuasive writing situations, follow Aristotle's advice. Appeal to the whole person: the head *(logos)*, the heart *(pathos)*, and the soul *(ethos)*.

Avoid common fallacies in persuasive writing.

As you gather your evidence to support your arguments, avoid these six common errors:

1. Presenting a false premise
2. Wrongly assuming that a premise is accepted by the audience
3. Providing too few examples to support an assertion
4. Offering irrelevant evidence or examples
5. Making *ad hominem* (or "to the man") attacks on the person advancing the argument rather than challenging the argument itself (a variation of which is name-calling)
6. Overgeneralizing the conclusion (especially making faulty assumptions regarding an entire group, race, class, or sex on the basis of a few examples) or seeking to derive a broader conclusion than the evidence warrants

Follow standard rules of evidence.

To be persuasive, your evidence must meet five criteria. It must be:

1. Accurate
2. Specific and detailed
3. Sufficient and complete

4. Relevant and connected to the argument
5. Meaningful and appropriate to the audience

"Everyone loves Jesse Ventura!" might serve to arouse a crowd at a campaign rally, but it cannot be said that the statement is accurate. "Because everyone loves Jesse Ventura and thinks he's doing a fantastic job as governor of Minnesota, he should run for President" compounds the error because it offers a conclusion based on a false premise and insufficient evidence.

Remember: The best way to support your argument is to offer evidence that is specific, concrete, relevant, accurate, and colorful. And as I have said before, to make your evidence colorful, use detail that appeals to the senses.

Don't forget your reader.

For all types of writing—from sales proposals to personal essays and appellate court briefs—the pattern is the same: First you assert, then you support. The two steps lead in opposing directions. When you make an assertion, you look inward. You concentrate on your own thoughts and how to express them. When you support your assertion, you look outward. You turn your attention to information that will help your reader comprehend your meaning and appreciate your point of view. To acknowledge your reader is to acknowledge that all communication involves relationship. For this reason, supporting your arguments is one of the most powerful—and empowering—things you can do as a writer.

CHAPTER 10: COHERENCE

Connect Your Thoughts

Connect Your Sentences and Paragraphs
TELL YOUR READER WHERE YOU'RE GOING.
USE TRANSITIONAL WORDS AND PHRASES.
REPEAT KEY WORDS AND PHRASES.
USE PARALLEL STRUCTURE TO BIND WITH RHYTHM.
MAINTAIN A CONSISTENT STRING OF TOPICS.

Use Sentence Beginnings and Endings to Create Flow
START WITH OLD INFORMATION.
END WITH NEW INFORMATION.
END WITH WHAT YOU INTEND TO DEVELOP NEXT.
USE "IT SHIFTS" AND INVERSIONS TO MOVE
   NEW INFORMATION TO THE RIGHT.
USE THE PASSIVE VOICE TO MOVE OLD
   INFORMATION TO THE LEFT.

Maintain Continuity and Flow Within Sentences

KEEP ADJECTIVE PHRASES TOGETHER.

HELP YOUR READER KEEP TRACK OF SUBJECTS AND VERBS.

AVOID UNNECESSARY SHIFTS IN SUBJECT, MODIFIED SUBJECT, PERSON, VOICE, AND TENSE.

1. Shifts in person
2. Shifts in subject
3. Shifts in modified subject.
4. Shifts in voice.
5. Shifts in tense.

ARRANGE YOUR MATERIAL ACCORDING TO NATURAL PROGRESSIONS.

1. Increasing specificity.
2. Chronology or sequence.
3. Increasing complexity.
4. Increasing length.
5. Increasing importance.
6. Increasing intensity.

MAINTAIN UNITY AND COHERENCE.

CHAPTER TEN

{Coherence}

Connect Your Thoughts

In well-written text, one thought is connected to another. The words and sentences are arranged logically and coherently. As a result, the reader moves easily from one point to the next and understands how the individual points relate to the whole. A well-written text seems unified and conveys a singleness of purpose.

In a poorly written text, on the other hand, the connections are not apparent and the development seems disjointed. As a result, the reader is often surprised or unprepared for the next thought and doesn't understand how the various points relate to one another. A poorly written text contains elements that seem irrelevant or unrelated to the central argument.

Just as you should arrange your sentences into logically developed, coherent paragraphs, you should arrange your paragraphs into a coherent whole. In this chapter you will learn techniques of making your text hold together so that the reader sees the connections.

Connect Your Sentences and Paragraphs

The process of reading is, by nature, linear and sequential. In other words, every sentence operates in the context of what precedes it. Conversely, the thought of every sentence is developed, elaborated, limited, or in some way modified by what comes after it. The coherence of your text depends on how carefully you make connections, not only within your sentences, but also between your sentences and between your paragraphs.

Tell your reader where you're going.

Perhaps the most obvious way to make your text hold together is simply to tell the reader where you're going. The more you can help your reader anticipate what comes next, the more your text will seem to cohere. As I noted earlier, an organizational statement would be out of place in narrative writing (where the reader prefers to be surprised by the events of an unfolding plot), but such a device is particularly useful in expository and persuasive writing (as when an attorney introduces a claim by writing "The plaintiff seeks to establish beyond a reasonable doubt the following points: That the defendant . . ."). If your report has three components, tell your reader "this report has three components" and list them. As a rule, your organizational statement should appear as the last sentence of your introduction.

If your memo addresses two issues, for example, tell the reader in your opening what to expect. Don't surprise the reader with your second point. Compare, for example, the following openings:

> The Planning Council is amending the Development Guide to reflect 1996 legislative actions. The primary purpose is to remove all outdated or legislatively repealed information. Another purpose is to update text and graphics to reflect recent planning activities.

> To reflect 1996 legislative actions, the Planning Council is amending the Development Guide in two ways: First, we are removing all . . .

Use transitional words and phrases.

Use connecting words and phrases to establish relationships between your sentences and paragraphs. Demonstrative pronouns and demonstrative adjectives (*this, that, these,* and *those*), for example, are good for indicating connections. As their name implies, they "demonstrate," "show," or "point," and the direction they point is backward. Another type of connecting word, a conjunction, comes in two varieties: coordinating and subordinating. Coordinating conjunctions (*and, but, or, nor, for, yet,* and *so*) join elements of equal value (as in *She wrote the memo and sent it*); subordinating conjunctions (words such as *although, because, if,* and *when*) subordinate or diminish the importance of the phrases or clauses they introduce (as in *Although she wrote the memo, she didn't send it*).

Here are some commonly used transitional expressions, presented according to their functions:

Amplification or addition

also	in addition	equally important
and	many	in other words
besides	moreover	similarly
first, . . .	too	likewise
second, . . .	finally	furthermore
third, . . .	next	another reason

Cause/effect; consequence or result

and so	so	due to
accordingly	if	thus
as a result	then	it follows
because	since	hence
consequently	therefore	

Comparison or analogy

in the same way	equally	again
likewise	similarly	also
analogously		

Contrast or alternative

but	conversely	on the other hand
however	in contrast	although
in spite of	nevertheless	though
on the contrary	contrary to	alternatively
still	yet	despite

Condition or concession

although	if	unless
even though	provided that	no doubt

| of course | to be sure | it is true |
| granted that | | |

Conclusion

finally	in short	as a result
at last	in summary	consequently
in conclusion	to conclude	accordingly
therefore	thus	to summarize

Emphasis

of course	after all	to repeat
obviously	above all	unquestionably
again	in fact	indeed

Illustration or example

for example	specifically	as an illustration
for instance	that is	in effect
particularly	in particular	namely
in other words	to illustrate	

Relationship in time

next	then	at times
as soon as	until	beforehand
last	later	earlier
before	afterward	after
when	recently	eventually
subsequently	simultaneously	at the same time
thereafter	since	currently
during	from now on	meanwhile
now	at present	once
soon	while	

Repeat key words and phrases.

Your reader remembers. (Or at least an attentive reader does.) Once you present a word or an idea, that word or idea takes on special meaning. From that moment on, you and your reader are speaking a private language. A gerund is no longer just a part of speech, but a verbal noun, one that can serve as a subject or an object in a sentence. A crayfish is no longer any crayfish, but a particular crayfish, the one you caught at the end of the dock with a ball of bread and dropped into the boiling pot of water but then couldn't bring yourself to eat. When you repeat that special word or refer to that particular experience, it reminds your reader of the world you have created or the context in which you are operating.

You might link the paragraphs in an essay about your last summer days at the lake before leaving for college, for example, by repeating words such as *red pine seedlings, sandbar, sunfish, dock, crayfish, childhood, adulthood,* and *memories.* You might give coherence to a story about moving your mother or father to a nursing home by referring to feelings and concepts such as *love, support, abandonment, loss, memory,* and *security.* You might end one paragraph, for example, with "It was a decision based on love" and begin the next with "Even decisions based on love, however, can feel like abandonment."

Use parallel structure to bind with rhythm.

In addition to making connections by using words that point and by repeating key words and phrases, you can bind individual parts of a piece into a more coherent whole by using rhythm. As I discussed in Chapter 4, one of the most powerful and commonly used methods of establishing rhythm is parallel structure. When you use parallel structure, you create a pattern, and the pattern serves to increase coherence.

As an example of how parallel structure can be used as a coherence device, look again at the opening paragraphs of this chapter (the parallel elements are marked by italics):

> *In well-written text,* one thought is connected to another. The words and sentences are arranged logically and coherently. *As a result,* the reader moves easily from one point to the next and understands how the individual points relate to the whole. *A well-written text* seems unified and conveys a singleness of purpose.
>
> *In a poorly written text,* on the other hand, the connections are

not apparent. The development seems disjointed. *As a result,* the reader is often surprised or unprepared for the next thought and doesn't understand how the various points relate to each other. *A poorly written text* contains elements that seem irrelevant or unrelated to the central argument.

Note how the parallel structure—*In well-written text, As a result, A well-written text*—in the first paragraph establishes a pattern that helps the reader anticipate what comes in the second paragraph: *In a poorly written text, As a result, A poorly written text.*

Maintain a consistent string of topics.

Another method of achieving flow is to begin successive sentences with the same topic. Although this method will create monotony if carried too far, it can enhance continuity by linking one sentence to the next. Consider, for example, two versions of a paragraph from Susan Sontag's *AIDS and Its Metaphors.* The first version (which I have altered from the original) lacks continuity because each sentence takes a different topic as its subject. The second version maintains continuity because each sentence takes the same topic (with one slight variation) as its subject. (Topics are underlined.)

Strictly speaking, <u>AIDS</u>—acquired immune deficiency syndrome-is not the name of an illness at all. <u>A spectrum of illnesses</u> causes AIDS, which is the name of a medical condition. <u>Other illnesses</u>, so-called opportunistic infections and malignancies, must be present for the condition to meet the definition of AIDS, in contrast to syphilis and cancer, which provide prototypes for most of the images and metaphors attached to AIDS. But though AIDS is not in *that* sense a single disease, <u>doctors</u> find it convenient to regard it as one—in part because, unlike cancer and like syphilis, <u>it</u> is thought to have a single cause.

Strictly speaking, <u>AIDS</u>—acquired immune deficiency syndrome—is not the name of an illness at all. <u>It</u> is the name of a medical condition, whose consequences are a spectrum of illnesses. In contrast to syphilis and cancer, which provide prototypes for most of the images and metaphors attached to AIDS, the very definition of AIDS requires the presence of other illnesses, so-called opportunistic infections and malignancies. But though not in *that* sense a single disease, AIDS lends itself to being regarded as one—in part because, unlike cancer and like syphilis, it is thought to have a single cause.

The reason the second paragraph is easier to follow is that continuity was maintained by the unbroken string of topics.

Use Sentence Beginnings and Endings to Create Flow

Coherence between sentences also can be achieved by following a simple principle: Begin your sentences with information familiar to your readers, and end your sentences with information unfamiliar to your readers. In other words, to create a natural progression and flow in your writing, look back before you look ahead. Williams calls this strategy the principle of "something old, something new."

Start with old information.

Use the principle of "something old, something new" to check the ordering of your information when you are revising for continuity and flow. Consider, for example, the placement of the phrase *during this time* in these sentences: "Frostproof, Inc., has been selling its line of super-insulated long underwear for more than ten years. We have improved our product substantially *during this time.*"

After its first mention, the reference to time *(more than ten years)* represents old information. Note how moving what is now a familiar idea to the beginning of the second sentence improves continuity between the two sentences: "Frostproof, Inc., has been selling its line of super-insulated long underwear for more than ten years. *During this time* we have improved our product substantially."

Likewise, consider the sequence of ideas in these two sentences: "As I mentioned in the unit meeting, we plan to merge our marketing and research departments. We must resolve a number of issues, however, *before this happens*." Now reverse the order of the main clause and the prepositional phrase in the second sentence: "*Before this happens,* however, we must resolve a number of issues." Note how this more logical sequence helps the reader look back before looking ahead.

Here's a passage for you to reorder according to the principle of something old, something new (old information is in italics): "Temporary employment is easier to find during the late summer. Demographics have shifted *as a result:* Thousands of Hispanics have moved to Minnesota to find work."

(If you moved *as a result* to the beginning of the second sentence, you improved the coherence of the passage. It now reads: "Temporary employment is easier to find during the late summer. *As a result,* demographics have shifted: Thousands of Hispanics have moved here to find work.")

End with new information.

The something old, something new principle also applies to the placement of technical terms in your sentences. As Williams points out, your readers will more readily grasp a technical term, particularly an unfamiliar one being used for the first time, if they encounter it at the end, rather than the beginning, of a sentence. For example, rather than "*Metadiscourse* is the language writers use to indicate what they are thinking," write "Language used by writers to indicate what they are thinking is called *metadiscourse.*"

End with what you intend to develop next.

Logic suggests that the best place for information that will be developed in subsequent sentences is at the end. For example, if you mention two or more items but intend to discuss only one, present that one last. Rather than "We attribute our phenomenal success to many factors, including hard work, *careful planning,* and effective communication. *Our planning* got off to a good start when . . . ," write "We attribute our phenomenal success to many factors, including hard work, effective communication, and *careful planning. Our planning...*"

Many writers end on the wrong note when they use two common sentence structures: sentences beginning with *there are* or *there is,* and sentences with colons. For example, rather than "To prevent burnout, there are several practices that one can employ," write "Burnout can be prevented by several practices." Rather than "There are three errors that writers frequently commit," write "Writers frequently commit three errors."

Sentences with colons often follow the same pattern. Rather than "Our demands include: . . . ," write "We have three demands: . . ." Rather than "Mae West once said she found two kinds of men attractive: the kind with muscles and the kind without," write "Mae West once said she liked two kinds of men: the kind with muscles and the kind without." Again, coherent writing is a matter of keeping related elements near each other.

Use "it shifts" and inversions to move new information to the right.

Although *there are* constructions can result in discontinuity, *it is* constructions can help you keep things in the right order. For example, in a legal brief discussing the requirements for establishing fraud, rather than "Establishing the requisite intent to mislead would be equally difficult," use an "it shift" to create a smooth transition: "It would be equally difficult to establish the requisite intent to mislead." (Note that when used in this construction, *it* is not a pronoun. It has no meaning in itself but is merely a place-holding word. As I discussed in Chapter 1, place-holding words such as *it, there,* and *what* are called expletives. Although expletives often result in wordiness, they can be used to increase emphasis as well as to improve continuity and flow.)

Similarly, a subject-complement inversion (which I discussed in Chapter 4 as a technique for adding variety to your sentence structure) is a handy technique for ordering information according to the something old, something new principle. For example, consider how both rhythm and continuity of thought are improved when this sentence, "Maintaining quality control is *another challenge,*" is rewritten as "*Another challenge* is maintaining quality control."

As another example, consider the sentence you are reading now as well as the sentence that comes after this colon: "The little links are equally important." Note that in the first sentence, the old information *(As another example)* comes first and the new information *(consider the sentence)* comes last, as it should. In the second sentence, however, the connection to old information *(equally important)* comes not at the beginning but at the end of the sentence. For a more natural, coherent order, reverse the sentence parts so that they follow the something old, something new principle: "Equally important are the little links." You can see how the order of the revised sentence leads the reader—logically, coherently, and efficiently—from what has been developed (something old) to what will be developed (something new). As illustrated by the first sentence in this paragraph (the paragraph you are reading), the something old, something new principle is particularly useful when creating a transitional sentence whose function is to connect the thought of one paragraph to the next.

Here's a sentence for you to revise according to the something old, something new principle. "Establishing the requisite intent to mislead would be equally difficult." *(Hint:* Move the old information from the last part of the sentence to the first part.)

Use the passive voice to move old information to the left.

In addition to "it shift" constructions and inversions, another method for moving old information to the left and new information to the right is the passive voice. For example, note the momentary discontinuity in the relative clause or dependent clause that follows the main clause of this sentence: "We are studying advertisement strategies *that other companies use* to recruit minorities." Compare that discontinuity with the smoother connection in "We are studying advertisement strategies *used by other companies* to recruit minorities." The problem with using the active voice in the relative clause *(that other companies use)* is that it introduces a second subject *(companies)* before indicating how that subject relates to *advertisement strategies.* In contrast, the passive voice *(used by other companies)* moves the modifying word *used* forward so that it is adjacent to, and links with, the phrase it modifies. The result is that the momentary "hitch" (discussed below) is eliminated and the wording flows more naturally.

Here's another example of using the passive voice to create the appropriate sequence of information. Note the break in continuity between these two sentences: "Our apparatus indicates whether a remote party has attempted to initiate a three-way call by using a 'hook flash' signal. Depressing and releasing a telephone hook switch generates a 'hook flash' signal." Once mentioned in the first sentence, *"hook flash" signal* becomes old information and, as such, it should be placed at the beginning, rather than at the end, of the second sentence. The passive voice enables you to arrange the information in this something old, something new order: "Our apparatus indicates whether a remote party has attempted to initiate a three-way call by using a 'hook flash' signal. A 'hook flash' signal is generated by depressing . . ."

For practice, see if you can use passive constructions to eliminate the "hitches" in these sentences:

- Information our engineers *provide* to our marketing staff must be accurate.
- The plan our marketing staff *unveiled* is ambitious.
- A goal all writers *share* is clarity.

(*Hint:* Move the italicized words toward the beginning of the sentence.)

Maintain Continuity and Flow Within Sentences

Have you ever thought about how golf courses are laid out?

Not far from the green of one hole is the tee for the next. Because one hole is linked to another in this logical fashion, you save walking distance and time.

Makes sense, doesn't it? There's a reason golf courses are laid out this way. Who would want to finish playing one hole and then have to walk the distance of a fairway to get to the next tee?

Well-constructed, coherently arranged sentences work the same way. They maintain the links between the various units of composition, both large and small. Here are some techniques to help you maintain those links in green-to-tee order.

Keep adjective phrases together.

When you make comparisons using phrases such as *such as, different from, similar to,* and *other than,* be careful not to split the adjective phrase (write "phrases *such as*" rather than "*such* phrases *as*"). If you divide the phrase, you create what Williams calls a "hitch in the rhythm of a sentence." To avoid this hitch or minor break in continuity, avoid dividing the phrase and placing one part before the noun and one part after. Instead, place both words of the phrase after the noun. For example, rather than "a *different* style *from* mine," write "a style *different from* mine." Rather than "a *similar* strategy *to* hers," write "a strategy *similar to* hers." Rather than "*other* reasons *than* greed," write "reasons *other than* greed." And rather than "The pro used *as creative* a design *as* anything of Arnold Palmer's in laying out this golf course," write "The pro used a design *as creative as* anything of Arnold Palmer's . . ."

For practice, revise these sentences to reconnect the split adjective phrases:

- She offered a *different proposal* from mine.
- I offered a *similar proposal* to John's.
- We acted for *other reasons* than those you cited.

(*Hint:* Reverse the order of the italicized words.)

Help your reader keep track of subjects and verbs.

Sentences with long gaps between subjects and verbs are disorienting. Reducing those gaps helps the reader see how the subjects and verbs relate. You can accomplish this by rearranging the sentence to avoid the interruption, or by clearly marking the interruption.

Compare the following sentences:

> This statement of need and reasonableness, reflecting the requirements of Minnesota Statutes, sections 14.23 and 14.131, and summarizing the need and reasonableness for each proposed amendment, is required by the Administrative Procedure Act.

> As required by the Administrative Procedure Act, this statement of need and reasonableness reflects . . . and summarizes . . .

If you prefer an order that maintains the long gap between subject and verb, you can make it easier for your reader to follow your meaning by marking the intervening phrase or clause with dashes. For example, consider the following sentence with and without dashes:

> The current requirement that the person who supervises physician assistants be present and available on the premises more than 50 percent of the time when the supervisee is providing health services is inconsistent with federal regulations.

> The current requirement—that the person who supervises physician assistants be present and available on the premises more than 50 percent of the time when the supervisee is providing health services—is inconsistent with federal regulations.

Perhaps the easiest revision, however, is simply to divide an unwieldy sentence into two shorter sentences:

> The current requirement is inconsistent with federal regulations. It stipulates that the person who supervises physician assistants be present and available on the premises more than 50 percent of the time when the supervisee is providing health services.

Avoid unnecessary shifts in subject, modified subject, person, voice, and tense.

Coherence comes from connectedness, continuity, and consistency. (Think of these attributes as the four Cs of writing.) Coherence also is a matter of creating an expectation in your reader's mind and meeting that expectation. You can maintain coherence by avoiding unexpected departures from established patterns. Those departures frequently take the form of unnecessary shifts in subject, modified subject, person, voice, and tense.

Avoid these common errors:

1. Shifts in person

Change "If writers proofread carefully, you will avoid making embarrassing errors" to "If writers proofread carefully, they will avoid making embarrassing errors."

Here's a sentence for you to revise: "If managers want to succeed, you must communicate effectively."

2. Shifts in subject

Change "Although some people consistently arrive on time, there are others who do not" to "Although some people consistently arrive on time, others do not." (In the first sentence, the subject of the introductory dependent clause, *people*, is continued in the main clause with the word *others*, but only after it is needlessly delayed by *there are*.)

Change "Please let me know if there are any problems" to "Please let me know if you have any problems." (Because the first part of the sentence is in the imperative, the implied subject is *you*.)

Here's one for you to revise: "Although these products have good price values, uniqueness is lacking in all of them."

3. Shifts in modified subject

Change "When pickled, I think herring tastes like caviar" to "When pickled, herring tastes like caviar to me." (The shift in the first sentence is called a "misplaced modifier" because the modifying phrase, *When pickled*, is not properly placed near the word it modifies. Since correcting the problem involves changing the word order in the main clause, however, it might more logically be called a "misplaced modifiee.")

Change "Working twelve-hour days, the project was completed on time" to "Working twelve-hour days, we completed the project on time." (This sort of shift is called a "dangling modifier" because the implied subject fails to appear, which leaves the modifying phrase, *Working twelve-hour days*, dangling.)

Here's one for you to revise: "When plastered, you are ready to paint your walls."

4. Shifts in voice

Change "We secretaries take pride in our work, and our assignments are completed on time" to "We secretaries take pride in our work, and we complete our assignments on time." (In the first sentence, the voice shifts from the active in the first clause to the passive in the second clause.)

Here's one for you to revise: "If standard programming information is needed, refer to the Project Implementation Manual." (Note the shift from the passive voice in the first clause to the imperative or command mode in the second clause. Try using the active voice in the first clause. The active voices seems less incongruous when coupled with the imperative mode because *you* serves as the subject in both clauses.)

5. Shifts in tense

Change "The team members worked on the project for three months, and they do a first-rate job" to "The team members worked on the project for three months, and they did a first-rate job."

Here's one for you to revise: "Your coverage would terminate and will not convert to an individual plan."

Here's how you might have corrected the sentences I asked you to revise:

Change this	To this
If managers want to succeed, you must communicate effectively.	If managers want to succeed, they must communicate effectively.
Although these products have good price values, uniqueness is lacking in all of them.	Although these products have good price values, they all lack uniqueness.
When plastered, you are ready to paint your walls.	When plastered, the walls are ready to be painted.
If standard programming information is needed, refer to the Project Implementation Manual.	If you need standard programming information, refer to the Project Implementation Manual.
Your coverage would terminate and will not convert to an individual plan.	Your coverage would terminate and would not convert to an individual plan.

Or this
Your coverage will terminate and
will not convert to an individual
plan.

Arrange your material according to natural progressions.

One of the best, and most obvious, ways of maintaining coherence is to go
with the flow. In other words, respect the natural order of things, which, for
our purposes here, we might define as any progression that seems logical and
reasonable to your reader. You can create a natural progression in any number
of ways: by moving from general to specific, from less recent to more recent
(or from more recent to less recent), from simpler to more complex, from
shorter to longer, from less important to more important, and from less vivid
to more vivid.

1. Increasing specificity

Your reader naturally prefers to move from the general to the specific. As an
illustration of this preference, consider the "number-age-nationality rule."
Few native speakers of English are consciously aware that they know this rule,
but virtually every native speaker follows it. For example, I'll give you three
adjectives and one noun, and I'll ask you to place the four words in what you
consider their most natural order. The adjectives are *French*, *three*, and *young*,
and the noun is *explorers.*

How did you arrange them? Chances are you placed them in this order:
three young French explorers. In fact, no other order—*young three French explor-*
ers or *French three young explorers,* for example—seems right. Although you
weren't told to arrange the adjectives in a progression from general to specific,
you did so naturally.

Your reader expects the same type of progression in your writing, so meet
that expectation by arranging your words and thoughts—within sentences,
paragraphs, and documents—so that you progress from the general to the
specific. Rather than "little nice house," write "nice little house." Before
describing and illustrating seventy-five ways to make a million dollars, identify
the general categories into which the specific methods fall (such as making

money honestly, making money dishonestly, helping others, and helping yourself).

2. Chronology or sequence

Rather than "She hired a lawyer, filed a complaint, and gathered her evidence," write "She gathered her evidence, hired a lawyer, and filed a complaint," which reflects the order of occurrence. Rather than "Writing with style involves imitating the techniques of good writers and reading their work," write "Writing with style involves reading good writers and imitating their techniques," which again reflects chronology. Rather than "Connect your paragraphs and sentences," write "Connect your sentences and paragraphs," which reflects the order in which they are created.

3. Increasing complexity

Just as a child learning mathematics is better able to grasp the subject if the teacher begins with basic concepts and progresses to more complex ones, your reader will follow your development more easily if you progress from the simple to the complex. Before explaining the intricacies of how a mechanism works, for example, explain its purpose. Before describing a comma splice (two complete sentences linked with a comma rather than separated with a period or other closing punctuation mark), explain what constitutes a complete sentence (a group of words that contains a subject and a verb and expresses a complete thought).

4. Increasing length

The same principle of natural order applies to length. When you are working with successive phrases and clauses of unequal length, arrange them so that they progress from shorter to longer. This arrangement is especially important in parallel structures, where beginning with shorter clauses and moving to longer ones establishes the pattern earlier in the sentence. The sooner the rhythm of the sentence is made apparent to the reader, the more coherent the sentence will seem.

For example, compare "My primary responsibilities are to create a new database of economic reporting techniques, to reorganize the branch offices, and to manage staff" with "My primary responsibilities are to manage staff, to reorganize the branch offices, and to create a new database of economic reporting techniques." Read both versions out loud. Can you hear how the order of the second version creates a more natural rhythm? Likewise, compare "He had fine manners, was a hard worker who never wasted time, and was literate" with the way Pauli Murray actually wrote the sentence in *Proud Shoes: The Story of an American Family:* "He was literate, had fine manners, and was a hard worker who never wasted time."

Here's another example. Compare "We can meet these professional development goals with surveys, on-site assessments, purchase of necessary equipment and software, and training" with "We can meet these professional development goals with training, surveys, on-site assessments, and purchase of necessary equipment and software." In this example, however, there is a problem with the revised version. Although following the order of increasing length produces a more pleasing rhythm, it also creates an illogical chronology or sequence (assuming assessment of needs and purchase of equipment precede training). In examples like this, you must choose between better sounding prose and more logical development.

5. Increasing importance

If your intent is to emphasize priority, you should follow a descending order. In other words, present your more important information first and your less important information last, regardless of the relative length of the successive words or phrases. Compare, for example, "He was dismissed for insubordination, carelessness, and tardiness" with "He was dismissed for tardiness, carelessness, and insubordination." As reflected by the first version of this sentence, content should take precedence over style.

6. Increasing intensity

The principle of increasing intensity applies broadly, from narration to description. In narration, your plot should move toward climax. In description, your most vivid and memorable detail should be your last. Compare, for example, "I was desperate for the company of someone who cared for me, eager to become part of the family, willing to do my share" with "I was willing to do my share, eager to become part of the family, desperate for the company of someone who cared for me."

In well-written periodic sentences—whether constructed with narrative or descriptive elements—the successive clauses are usually arranged in order of increasing importance, intensity, or vividness, or some other climactic scheme. Consider, for example, George Orwell's periodic sentence, that I quoted in Chapter 4. His sentence loses some of its effectiveness if the most striking detail is presented first rather than last:

> The scarred buttocks of the men who had been flogged with bamboos, the wretched prisoners huddling in the stinking cages of the lock-ups, the grey, cowed faces of the long-term convicts— all these oppressed me with an intolerable sense of guilt.

Compare that version with the way Orwell wrote the sentence:

> The wretched prisoners huddling in the stinking cages of the lock-ups, the grey, cowed faces of the long-term convicts, the scarred buttocks of the men who had been flogged with bamboos—all these oppressed me with an intolerable sense of guilt.

There are, of course, times when considerations of priority, chronology, diplomacy, or persuasive strategy override arrangements based on rhythm and technique. In those cases, once again, content takes precedence over style. Otherwise, arrange your material according to the natural order of things.

Maintain unity and coherence.

To maintain unity is to make sure everything fits together. Remember: A coherent piece of writing never leaves the reader wondering why a particular point is significant or how a particular piece of information is relevant. Every part relates to the whole. Well-constructed sentences and paragraphs connect with the thoughts of what preceded them the way a green is linked to the next tee in golf. They maintain both little links (within sentences) and large links (between sentences and paragraphs) in green-to-tee order.

As the nineteenth-century English author Thomas De Quincey once wrote, "All fluent and effective composition depends on the connections." I wonder if De Quincey ever played golf.

{PART THREE}

Drafting and Revising

CHAPTER 11: THE WRITING PROCESS

Write in Stages

APPROACH WRITING AS A FOUR-STAGE PROCESS.

1. Prewriting: Prepare to write.
2. Drafting: Get it down.
3. Revising: Fix it up.
4. Proofreading: Make it presentable.

FIRST BE THE ARTIST, THEN THE CRITIC.

ALLOW TIME BETWEEN DRAFTS.

PROOFREAD BY MAKING MULTIPLE PASSES THROUGH YOUR FINAL COPY.

Overcome Writer's Block and Get Started

THINK POSITIVELY—ABOUT YOURSELF AND YOUR ABILITY TO WRITE.

COMPOSE YOURSELF.

WARM UP BY WRITING QUICKLY AND FREELY, WITHOUT STOPPING.

MAKE A PLAN.

ALLOW YOURSELF THE FREEDOM OF AN IMPERFECT FIRST DRAFT.

BE A BULLDOZER RATHER THAN A BRICKLAYER.

ESTABLISH A WRITING ROUTINE.

KNOW THE TRICKS OF THE TRADE.

Overcome the Challenges of Long Writing Projects

REJECT THE "I NEED A BLOCK OF TIME" MYTH.

COMMIT YOURSELF TO "SEAT TIME."

GIVE YOURSELF CREDIT FOR STARTING.

TAKE IT "BIRD BY BIRD."

DIVIDE A LONG PROJECT INTO SMALLER TASKS.

USE THE SLASH-AND-BRACKET METHOD OF DRAFTING.

LEAVE SOME THINGS FOR LATER.

DON'T MEASURE YOUR PROGRESS TOO CLOSELY.

FINISH YOUR FIRST BAD DRAFT.

EXPECT TO GET BORED.

LOOK FORWARD TO THE DOWNHILL SIDE.

Apply Principles of Time Management to Writing

PLAN YOUR TIME.

CONCENTRATE ON THE TASK AT HAND.

TAKE BREAKS.

AVOID CLUTTER.

ACCEPT IMPERFECTION.

LEARN HOW TO SAY NO.

DON'T PROCRASTINATE.

Develop Good Writing Habits

WRITE (AND READ) WITH A DICTIONARY WITHIN REACH.

USE A THESAURUS WHEN YOU CAN'T THINK OF THE RIGHT WORD.

WRITE WITH A STYLE MANUAL WITHIN REACH.

WRITE AT THE SAME TIME EVERY DAY.

START EARLY.

TAKE TIME TO REVISE YOUR WRITING.

DON'T LET THE NEGATIVE VOICES GET YOU DOWN.

WORK WITH AN EDITING PARTNER OR MENTOR.

Make a Lifetime Commitment

READ.

LEARN THE RULES OF LANGUAGE SO THAT YOU CAN WRITE WITH CONFIDENCE.

PRACTICE.

STUDY GOOD WRITERS AND IMITATE THEIR STYLE.

{The Writing Process}

To read advice about how to improve your writing is one thing; to put that advice into practice is another. With the five keys to great writing and the five elements of composition in hand, I now turn to actually getting the job done: how to get started, how to finish, and how to use the process of writing to your advantage. I've discussed the theory. Now for the practice.

Write in Stages

Most writing takes place over time, not in a single moment or in a flash of inspiration—despite what we might have gotten away with on an occasional late night in high school or college. The process of writing includes four stages and at least ten steps:

Writing is problem-solving. It helps to think of writing as a series of decisions and choices that generally should be made in a certain order. If you take it one step at a time, you're more likely to make the best choices.

Approach writing as a four-stage process.

The four major stages of writing are prewriting, drafting, revising, and proofreading. In practice, these stages often overlap, but each stage calls for a particular kind of attention and a particular set of skills.

1. Prewriting: Prepare to write.

You begin writing by thinking—by considering your purpose, your audience, and your subject, and by contemplating how you can best accomplish your

{ Stages and Steps in the Process of Writing }

Prewriting

1. Determine your topic and your purpose.
2. Consider your audience's expectations.
3. Know your subject.
4. Decide on your point of view (or your relationship as an author to your material) and, if appropriate, your persuasive strategy.
5. Organize your thoughts (jot down notes or make an outline).

Drafting

6. Write your first draft.

Revising

7. Edit and revise your draft.
8. When possible, set your writing aside to let it "go cold."
9. Read it again (preferably aloud) and make final revisions.

Proofreading

10. Proofread your final copy.

goals. In the prewriting stage, you gather information, conduct research, take notes, outline your thoughts, and perhaps do some warmup writing exercises to loosen up and get in the mood to write. It is also at this stage—not later—that you overcome writer's block. One of your main goals in prewriting is to make yourself want to write and to get excited about your purpose and subject.

2. Drafting: Get it down.

Drafting is the stage when you begin to produce copy. The most important point to keep in mind when drafting is to keep moving. Rather than stopping to edit and revise as you go, focus on purpose, audience, and subject. Don't compose or sound out everything in your mind. Write it down. Try out a word, phrase, sentence, or idea on paper or on screen. Later, in the revising phase, when you have a fresh look at it and see it in a broader context, you will know if it works.

For most writers, drafting is the most difficult stage. Don't make it more difficult than it needs to be by trying to draft and revise simultaneously.

When drafting, don't try to create perfect text. Keep your revising and editing to a minimum. The secret is to write your first draft as quickly and freely as you can, knowing you will come back later and revise.

3. Revising: Fix it up.

Revising is the stage when you make it good. The word *re-vise* comes from the Latin word *viser*, which means "to see" and serves as the root for a number of English words, including *vision, envision,* and *visor.* It is at the stage of revising that you have another look, you view your text again, and you do so on two levels: deep and surface. First go back and reconsider broad issues such as your approach, point of view, organization, and persuasive strategy. Concentrate on *what* you are saying and *how* you are saying it, and revisit underlying questions relating to purpose, audience, and subject. After that, check your copy for surface issues: word choice, clarity, sentence structure, and the mechanics of language (spelling, grammar, and punctuation).

4. Proofreading: Make it presentable.

Proofreading is the stage when you worry about accuracy. Have you misspelled or mistyped any words? Have you omitted a number in an enumerated list, or have you copied and pasted text when you intended to cut and paste it? If you are writing on the job, review your text to see if you have made it visually attractive by highlighting key points with boldface font, italics, and perhaps bulleted lists. Check for typographical errors. As I discuss below, proofreading should be accomplished in distinct stages.

First be the artist, then the critic.

These four stages of writing can be grouped into two broader phases: the creative and the critical. In the first, you produce. In the second, you edit and revise.

First be the artist. Permit yourself to be as creative and spontaneous as possible. Turn off your critical mind and let the words flow. As the poet Michael Dennis Browne advises, think of your first draft as an open audition: Anyone is welcome to come and try out.

Allow yourself the luxury of the first draft. Keep reminding yourself that you don't have to produce perfect copy on your first try. Know when to say, "That's good enough for now." (This advice sounds so easy to follow, but it can be one of the hardest lessons for a writer to learn and practice.) To accept the imperfection of the first draft is a wonderful freedom. It releases you from the censorship of self-criticism.

In the second phase, be the critic. Go back to your draft and revise it with a critical eye and ear. As I advised when discussing organization in Chapter 8, after you have captured your thoughts in sentences, think more deliberately in paragraphs. And as I advised when discussing coherence in Chapter 10, check your connections. Make sure your thought flows from sentence to sentence and from paragraph to paragraph.

Both phases, the creative and the critical, are necessary and valuable, but think of them as fundamentally distinct activities. Try not to let the critical intrude on the creative. If you attempt to correct as you create, you risk stifling your natural expression. Peter Elbow makes the point convincingly in *Writing Without Teachers:*

> The habit of compulsive, premature editing doesn't just make writing hard. It also makes writing dead. Your voice is damped out by all the interruptions, changes, and hesitations between the consciousness and the page. In your natural way of producing words there is a sound, a texture, a rhythm—a voice—which is the main source of power in your writing. I don't know how it works, but this voice is the force that will make a reader listen to you.

Allow time between drafts.

The problem with trying to edit and revise as you go is that it is difficult to distinguish between the words as you hear them in your head and the words as they actually appear on the screen or the page. If you allow time to pass between the act of writing and the act of revising, you will be a better reader, which in turn will make you a better editor.

The naturalist writer Aldo Leopold had a wonderful method of letting his text go cold. He had a drawer in his desk he called his "freezer." Whenever he finished drafting something, he would put it in his "freezer" to let it cool off. Then he would take it out and give it a final reading. Leopold found that letting time pass between drafting and editing helped him be less preoccupied with what he had *meant* to say and better able to judge what he had *actually* written.

If you can manage it, give your writing at least a day to "go cold." If not a day, an hour. During that time, it helps to think about what you have written without looking at it. When you return to your text, you will find that you are more likely to see your words as they will be perceived by your reader.

Proofread by making multiple passes through your final copy.

To eliminate those distracting and embarrassing errors that undermine your credibility and diminish the effectiveness of your writing, proofread your copy carefully. It is difficult to check for different types of errors in a single pass through your document, so make four distinct passes. Each time through, look for a different type of error, progressing from more general errors, such as missing pages of text, to more particular errors, such as missing commas.

Here's the four-part approach, in the format of a checklist:

{ Proofreading Checklist }

First Check: Does it look right?

☑ Text is appropriately highlighted (bullets, paragraphing, boldface, underlining, etc.) to engage reader and reinforce main points.

☑ Common word-processing errors (copy/cut miscues, sequence errors, editing scraps, template tipoffs, page-numbering peccadillos, and hidden headers) have been eliminated.

Second Check: Is it effective and complete?

☑ Central idea or purpose is clearly stated and developed.

☑ Main points are limited in number and receive appropriate emphasis.

☑ All subordinate ideas are clearly related to the central idea.

☑ Material is arranged in a logical and coherent sequence.

☑ Reader is given the information needed to take the desired action.

Third Check: Does it sound right?

☑ Word choice is clear, specific, accurate, unassuming, and free of clichés and misused jargon.

☑ Sentences are free of wordiness, ambiguity, and unnecessarily involved constructions.

☑ Tone is appropriate to the audience.

Fourth Check: Is it correct?

☑ Spelling, including technical terms and proper names, is correct.

☑ Correct words are used to convey the intended meaning.

☑ Generally accepted rules of grammar and syntax are followed, including parallel construction, subject/verb agreement, pronoun/noun agreement, appropriate verb tense, pronoun case, possessive forms, etc.

☑ Punctuation, particularly placement of commas and apostrophes, reflects standard usage.

For easy reference, this proofreading checklist also appears in Appendix IV.

Overcome Writer's Block and Get Started

Being too critical too early often results in the dreaded phenomenon called "writer's block," "pencil paralysis," "cerebral constipation"—and other things too colorful to report here. As I mentioned above, a chief cause of writer's block is the self-imposed expectation that you will write perfect copy in a single draft. If you approach writing as a process that has various distinct stages, however, you will be more likely to overcome the obstacles that prevent you from writing.

Think positively—about yourself and your ability to write.

At the 1976 St. Lawrence Writer's Conference, I heard the novelist Gail Godwin describe a trick she uses to silence that inner critical voice all writers hear from time to time. Godwin explained that she thinks of this self-censoring tendency in terms of Freud's notion of the Watcher at the Gate, a little creature that sits perched on the edge of your subconscious mind. Even as your thoughts are first taking shape, this creature says things like, "Stupid. Unoriginal. Doesn't sound right. Don't let it out." When Godwin hears this inner voice, she looks the Watcher at the Gate right in the eye and says, "Be quiet. I know you're there. You have a legitimate role to play, but you're too early. First I create. Then I revise."

Think positively—about yourself and your ability to write. Writing is a mind game, and you can talk yourself out of success even before you begin.

Compose yourself.

Writing requires concentration, and concentration involves focusing on the task at hand. It involves putting out of your mind the myriad thoughts and concerns that may distract you from that task. Unfortunately, the home or workplace environment often is not conducive to mustering the mental concentration you need to write.

As you begin to write, you might find that your thoughts are disjointed and chaotic, as though you are speeding down the freeway in your car, weaving in and out of multiple lanes of traffic, worried that you might not arrive at your destination in time. You might be annoyed about something someone said to you earlier in the day or preoccupied with all the things you need to get done this week.

The next time you sit down to write—and you find your mind awhirl from the competing demands on your time—take a moment to relax. Take a deep breath. Hold it. Count slowly to ten. Exhale.

Imagine pulling off the freeway and sitting quietly by yourself in the woods. Or on a beach. Or in the mountains. Or in your office early in the morning before anyone else has arrived. Or in a musty library reading room with the late afternoon sun slanting through the windows. Anywhere you feel comfortable.

If you feel the urge to daydream, give in to it. Psychologists tell us that daydreaming is a necessary and useful mental process. When your mind says it needs to do some housecleaning, let it clean house. Allow yourself that luxury. In a few moments you'll feel yourself coming to a point of rest.

This is the frame of mind—one of concentration and focus—required for writing.

Warm up by writing quickly and freely, without stopping.

"Write clearly and with great honesty. . . . Write. Trust yourself. Learn your own needs."

A good way to put yourself in the mood to write is to read—or if you have already read it, to review and browse—Natalie Goldberg's *Writing Down the Bones*. Goldberg offers various stratagems for getting started, and more than any other author I know, she captures and conveys a sense of empowerment.

Like Dorothea Brande, Peter Elbow, and others before her, Goldberg suggests that you begin with a freewriting exercise. The exercise is simple: Simply start writing and don't stop. You can start anywhere you like, with a thesis statement ("The purpose of this piece is . . .") or a description of your mood. Just write whatever comes into your head.

The idea is to relax. Don't work hard. Just write. Don't worry about what it sounds like. Don't worry about spelling, grammar, or punctuation. Don't worry about anything at all. There are only three rules: You can't stop writing. You can't go back and read what you've written. And you can't change anything. Try to keep your thoughts flowing until you reach your conclusion, or until you run out of ideas. Only then should you go back and start shaping and editing.

And as Goldberg advises, write honestly. Begin by saying exactly what you are thinking, as clearly as you can say it. Don't worry about impressing your reader, your boss, your mother, your father, your seventh-grade English teacher—don't worry about impressing anyone, not even yourself.

Just write.

Don't stop to choose your words. Don't pause to revise or to organize your text. Don't even look at your screen as you type. Just keep hitting the keys, trying to keep up with your thoughts as they tumble out of your head.

When you do this exercise, you might produce text that is disjointed, or you might write something that doesn't sound too bad, but the quality of the text is not what matters. What matters is whether the warm-up exercise puts you in the mood to write. If it does, you have achieved your goal.

Make a plan.

After you have warmed up, take the next step: Make a plan. You might begin by jotting down your thoughts—do it by hand if writing on paper helps you think. If your assignment is complex, make an outline. At the top of your outline write your purpose in a short, simple declarative sentence. List your main points. Think of specific details, examples, and illustrations that will support your argument. Consider your audience. Ask yourself which points of evidence will be most compelling to your reader. As I discussed in Chapter 8, use an outline to help you think.

Allow yourself the freedom of an imperfect first draft.

Hemingway—never one to follow his own advice—was fond of saying, "The only thing that matters about your first draft is that you finish it." In other words, just do it. Give yourself the benefit of sketching out a draft that is nothing more than a beginning. This approach frees you from the tyranny of perfectionism. It's a wonderful freedom. Once you have created a text, you can always go back and rewrite and polish and fuss over it. Remember: Your first draft is only "sloppy copy." The idea is to get it written, not right.

Be a bulldozer rather than a bricklayer.

There are essentially two kinds of writers: bricklayers and bulldozers. Bricklayers are writers who are incapable of going on to the second paragraph until they are completely satisfied with the first. They find it impossible to write sentence two until sentence one is absolutely perfect. For them, writing tends to be tedious, exhausting, and time-consuming.

Bulldozers, on the other hand, charge right through the first draft. They just keep plowing ahead until they get to the end. They don't care what their text sounds like along the way because they know that once they've got the words down, they can go back and revise. For them, writing is enjoyable, energizing, and rewarding.

To overcome writer's block, think of yourself not as a bricklayer but as a bulldozer. Just keep moving forward until you have completed your draft.

Establish a writing routine.

Many writers find that writing comes more easily if they write at the same time every day. Some prefer to write in the morning, the time of day Henry David Thoreau called "the awakening hour," before they become preoccupied with the incidentals of their daily routines.

Some writers make appointments with themselves to protect their writing time. They believe that keeping a regular writing schedule helps their minds and bodies develop a kind of rhythm, so that when the time comes to write, they are more likely to have the energy and concentration that writing demands. Some even reserve a certain place in their home or office where they do nothing but write. They don't balance their checkbooks there, and they don't talk on the phone there. When they sit in that certain place, it's time to write.

By playing to their natural rhythms and cycles, they find that their minds and bodies are ready for the difficult task of writing.

On the other hand, many on-the-job writers find it difficult or impossible to reserve a particular time of the day for writing. Whatever your situation, be as regular and disciplined as possible. The point is not to wait for "inspiration."

Know the tricks of the trade.

In addition to the self-imposed expectation that you will write perfect copy in a single draft, there may be other obstacles that prevent you from getting started, and these obstacles may be related to deeply personal issues. To some extent, you must figure out the causes for these obstacles and discover your own methods for overcoming them.

Nevertheless, you can learn from the experience of other writers. Simply reminding yourself that writer's block is a problem not just for you but for most writers is consoling. In addition to the approach I have advocated above, in which you begin creatively and you end critically, you might find the following specific tricks of the trade helpful:

- Forget about logical development and sequence. Start writing the easiest part of your document first, whether that be the opening, the middle, or the closing.
- Change the location of where you are writing. Go outside or downstairs to the lounge or to a crowded cafeteria. Try a new environment.
- Stand up from your writing desk, throw up your arms, and turn around three times. Jump up and down. Run in place. Get your heart pumping and your blood circulating.
- Make a list of key words you'll use when you're ready to begin writing.
- Write the opposite of what you're trying to express, both in content and tone.
- Talk it out, either to yourself or to a friend, explaining what it is you're trying to get down in writing.
- Make a list of all the things that prevent you from writing. Then, having made your list, either do the things you simply must do before you start writing, or make up your mind that they can wait until later and set your list aside.
- Compose yourself. Gather your thoughts. Make an outline, but don't hesitate to change it along the way.
- Make certain you know your purpose, audience, and subject. Don't let the unknown obstruct you.
- Write with honesty. Be direct, simple, straightforward in your expression. Concentrate on your meaning and how best to convey it. Worry about tone and style later when you revise.
- Write something every day—or at least regularly. When you write infrequently, you always start cold.
- Ignore that inner voice that says, "You can't write." Talk back to it. Say, "I *can* write. I *am* a good writer. This is only a draft." Say it out loud if that helps. Shout it if you need to.
- Imagine you have only one minute to tell your reader why you are writing. Start talking. Don't stop for sixty seconds. Now, write for sixty seconds, again without stopping.

- Think of your reader as your best friend. Picture a kind face, a warm, friendly smile. Imagine this friend saying with great concern and sincerity, "Tell me. What's on your mind?"
- Give in to it. Sometimes the best way to overcome writer's block is to accept it. Don't fight it. If your mind is swirling with thoughts and anxieties when you sit down to write, maybe your mind is trying to tell you something. Maybe it needs a little time to do some sorting. Don't feel guilty about wasting time. The time you spend daydreaming and collecting your thoughts may turn out to be the most productive and creative part of your day.

Overcome the Challenges of Long Writing Projects

If you have ever tried to complete a long report or book-length document by a certain date, you know how it feels to write under pressure. Here are some of the lessons I have learned—or relearned—from my experience in writing this book, lessons that relate to how to find time in a busy life to complete a long-term writing project:

Reject the "I need a block of time" myth.

If you wait for a block of time, you may never get started. I have a friend, a history professor, who tells his students that, rather than spend ten minutes worrying about a paper that is due next week, spend ten minutes making an outline or writing the first paragraph.

If you want to write, write. Do as the poet-doctor William Carlos Williams did: Write a few lines every day, no matter how tired you are from making your rounds.

Commit yourself to "seat time."

There's only one way to complete a long writing project, and that's with seat time. Some days the words will come easily. Most days they won't. But if you're not in your seat, they won't come at all. So get your rear in gear and your derriere in the chair.

Give yourself credit for starting.

Measure your success not by the number of pages you write each day, but by the consistency with which you bring yourself to the task. A good day is any day in which you devote some time to writing. Like a baseball batter on a hitting streak, see how many days you can go without breaking your string.

When your goal is simply to write every day, you feel good the moment you begin, and the question shifts from "*Will* I write?" to "*When?*"

Take it "bird by bird."

In her book by that title, Anne Lamott tells a story about her brother when he was ten. He had been given three months to write a report on birds. On the last day of summer vacation, her brother was "at the kitchen table close to tears, surrounded by binder paper and pencils and unopened books on birds, immobilized by the hugeness of the task ahead" when, Lamott tells us, "my father sat down beside him, put his arms around my brother's shoulder, and said, 'Bird by bird, buddy. Just take it bird by bird.'"

Take it one step at a time. Before you know it, you're making progress, and once you're making progress, you start feeling better about the prospects for completing your task.

Divide a long project into smaller tasks.

Writing a book is a matter of accomplishing a number of specific tasks, such as thinking about your purpose, organizing your text, listing examples to use in supporting a particular point, and writing a particular paragraph. As the novelist Annie Dillard once said, "When you think about writing a book, you think it is overwhelming. But, actually, you break it down into tiny little tasks any moron could do."

Use the slash-and-bracket method of drafting.

Every writer develops his or her own tricks for making the process of writing as efficient as possible—or at least less inefficient than it otherwise would be.

One practice I have found helpful is to mark alternative wording with slashes when I find myself unable to determine which version is better. This method allows me to continue drafting, knowing I have marked a choice / to be made at a later time / I will make later. Not only does this method enable me to maintain momentum, but I find it easier to make the choice when I come back to it.

Square brackets also provide a convenient way to mark problems or points that need further development. *[Give an example here?]* If a word, sentence, or paragraph doesn't sound right, mark the problem with brackets—*[Revise this?]*—and come back to it later. Well, you get the idea. Don't let a problem or unresolved question hang you up. Keep moving.

Leave some things for later.

As I discussed above—and as I continually remind myself—writing is a process. It goes better if you think in terms of writing in stages. The main thing is to keep moving. Save certain types of editing for later. Know when to say, "That's good enough for now"—words that don't come easily if you are the compulsive type. Just keep reminding yourself that you will come back later. Remember, your goal is to get it written, not right.

Don't measure your progress too closely.

Once you've started, keep going. Don't look up too often. Pretty soon all those little bits of writing add up to something significant.

Finish your first bad draft.

Don't quit because you don't like what you've written. You have to complete your first bad draft before you can start making it good. Remember: Editing is the easy part.

Expect to get bored.

No matter how excited you are about your topic when you begin, expect your enthusiasm to ebb. Just keep going.

Look forward to the downhill side

To use my agent's analogy, "Writing a book is like pushing a grocery cart up a hill. It's slow going for the first half, but eventually you reach the top, and you can jump in and ride down." That's the part I look forward to.

Apply Principles of Time Management to Writing

The process of writing and the principles of time management share common ground. Both writing and managing your time make three demands of you: They require planning, organization, and discipline.

In *Getting Things Done: The ABC's of Time Management*, internationally known expert Edwin Bliss offers ten basic techniques of time management. Here's how you can apply those techniques to your writing:

Plan your time.

"You need a game plan for your day," Bliss contends. "Otherwise, you'll allocate your time according to whatever happens to land on your desk." Likewise, when writing anything more complicated than a brief memo or a routine document, you need an outline. Without one, you'll tend to write whatever random thoughts occur to you. With one, you'll write more logically and systematically.

Concentrate on the task at hand.

Bliss's notion that "people who have serious time-management problems invariably are trying to do too many things at once" explains two common causes of writer's block: being too distracted to settle down to the assignment at hand, and trying to draft and edit at the same time.

As I suggested earlier, to increase your concentration, write down your purpose in a simple declarative sentence. Then write your first draft as freely and quickly as you can, knowing you'll come back and edit later.

Take breaks.

As Bliss points out, if you work for long periods without taking breaks, "energy decreases, boredom sets in, and physical stress and tension accumulate." The same applies to writing. Even if you become engrossed in your topic, take periodic breaks. Stand up, move around, keep your blood flowing—but avoid distractions that might draw your attention completely away from what you are writing.

Avoid clutter.

Because, as Bliss contends, "you can think of only one thing at a time," and because "you can work on only one task at a time," you will work—and write—more efficiently if you organize your papers, clear your desk regularly, and maintain an orderly, comfortable environment.

Accept imperfection.

Don't be a perfectionist. Striving for excellence is "attainable, gratifying, and healthy," but striving for perfection is "often unattainable, frustrating, and neurotic." Being a perfectionist is not only a "terrible waste of time," it's also an impediment to timely communication. Besides, given the complexity of English grammar and syntax, not even the experts agree on what constitutes "perfect" writing.

Learn how to say no.

Bliss considers the "frequent use of the word *no*" to be "perhaps the most effective . . . of all the time-saving techniques ever developed."

The same applies to editing. Avoid falling in love with your prose. Learn to say no to any word, phrase, sentence, or paragraph that "does not contribute to your goals." Also, have the discipline to say no to less demanding, more enjoyable, perhaps more immediately gratifying activities that will prevent you from writing.

Don't procrastinate.

Bliss quotes William James, who in his 1890 book, *Principles of Psychology*, offers two points of advice on how to overcome procrastination: "Decide to start changing as soon as you finish reading this article, while you are motivated" and "Don't try to do too much too quickly."

The important thing is to get started. If at first your progress seems insignificant, remember the words of E. L. Doctorow, who once compared writing a novel to driving a car at night: "You can see only as far as your headlights, but you can make the whole trip that way."

Develop Good Writing Habits

Writing for most people does not come easily. As with any challenging task, however, you can learn to overcome the obstacles by developing good habits.

Write (and read) with a dictionary within reach.

You're more likely to use your dictionary if you keep it handy. If you put off looking up a word until later, you might forget to check it. A good dictionary is an essential tool for a writer. Use it to look up words whose meanings are only vaguely familiar to you. Check their root meanings for information that will help you remember them. Learn how to spell and pronounce them. Move them from your larger comprehensive vocabulary, which you depend on as a listener and reader, into your smaller expressive vocabulary, which you depend on as a speaker and writer.

Use a thesaurus when you can't think of the right word.

As I discussed in Chapter 2, whether printed or programmed, a thesaurus is an indispensable tool for the writer—when used properly. Use the thesaurus to remind yourself of words you have some experience with and feeling for. As a rule, however, don't use a synonym if you are encountering it for the first time.

Write with a style manual within reach.

Don't guess at the conventions of language, punctuation, and numbers usage. If you are uncertain whether a comma should go before or after the closing quotation marks or whether you should spell a number as a word or write it as a figure, look it up in a style manual such as William Sabin's *The Gregg Reference Manual.* (See Appendix V for a list of recommended resources.)

Write at the same time every day.

As I discussed above, try to write at the same time, and in the same place, every day. The point is not to wait for inspiration.

Be pragmatic about getting the job done. As the poet Carolyn Forché told a creative writing class at the University of Minnesota, it's important to write at the same time and at the same place every day, even if only for half an hour, "so the Muse will know where to find you. Otherwise, she goes to the next house."

Start early.

Start writing as soon as possible after you have your assignment. The sooner you begin to write (or to "compose" your thoughts), the sooner your subconscious mind can start working on the material. Even if you don't have time to make a substantial start on your assignment, it's still a good idea to take a few moments to jot down some notes or outline your main points. You may be surprised at how much easier it is to write your first draft when you have begun in this way.

Whenever possible, let time be on your side.

Take time to revise your writing.

Remember, good writing is revised writing. Except for the most routine and straightforward writing assignments, don't expect your first draft to be your final draft. It almost always takes more than one try to get it right. And as I discussed above, after you have written your first draft, set your piece aside to let it "rest" or "go cold" before giving it a final reading. Allowing some time to pass will help you see what you have written from the reader's perspective.

Don't let the negative voices get you down.

Critics have been putting down writers—sometimes with great wit and scathing cruelty—for as long as writers have been writing. Two hundred years ago Samuel Johnson (as I noted earlier) offered this devastatingly clever appraisal to an aspiring author: "Your manuscript is both good and original; but the part that is good is not original, and the part that is original is not good." Even Groucho Marx got into the act when he stung S. J. Perelman with this unforgettable zinger: "From the moment I picked your book up until I laid it down I was convulsed with laughter. Someday I intend reading it."

A participant in one of my writing workshops once told me, "Before I started this job, I used to enjoy writing, but now I hate it. No matter what I write, my boss tears it to pieces." A colleague who heads the writing assessment program at a California university told me about one of her professors in graduate school who would comment on each paper as he handed it back to its author. Once, to emphasize his displeasure, the professor said, "And here's what I think of Ms. Smith's paper." Then he pulled a lighter from his pocket, lit the paper, and dropped it burning into a metal wastebasket. Mortified, the student burst into tears and left the classroom.

In *Writing to Learn,* William Zinsser describes a "fear of writing" that "is planted in countless people at an early age—often, ironically, by English teachers, who make science-minded kids feel stupid for not being 'good at words,' just as science teachers make people like me feel stupid for not being good at science." According to Zinsser, "Whichever our type, the loss of confidence stays with us for the rest of our lives."

No wonder so many people hate to write. For them, writing is less an opportunity for expression than an invitation for humiliation and ridicule. The problem, of course, is that much of what is written *does* need correction. Even the most accomplished writers can profit from the suggestions of a good editor.

Work with an editing partner or mentor.

Every writer needs a good editor. Ask for suggestions and criticisms from a colleague, friend, or editor. If something is wrong with your writing or if something could be improved, it's better to find out before you send or submit your final copy.

Find a colleague, friend, or mentor—someone you know will be positive and constructive in his or her criticism (preferably someone more skilled and experienced than you)—and work together proofreading and editing. Make a deal: They read your stuff; you read theirs. In committing yourself to help another writer improve, you might find that you are helping yourself.

Make a Lifetime Commitment

Your relationship with language is dynamic. No matter how skilled and accomplished you are as a writer, there is always something else you can learn, always another insight you can acquire, always a new trick or technique you can add to your repertoire. One of the most exciting and exasperating things about being a writer is that your work is never done. You can never completely develop your skills, and you will never solve all the mysteries of language.

Here are four things you can do to improve your writing over time.

Read.

Read for pleasure. Read for fun. Read every day, if possible. Read authors you find especially engaging, including some who challenge you, and read everything they have published.

Spend time in the company of good writers. If all you ever read is mediocre writing, your chances of writing anything better are slim. If all you ever read is bad writing—well, you get the idea.

Reading develops your ear. It gives you a feeling for the rhythm and cadence and flow of language. It suggests the range of possible sentence structures and patterns. It helps you realize the possibilities for imaginative use of figurative language and various figures of speech. Perhaps most important, reading expands your vocabulary.

Just as you wouldn't try to be a musician without listening to music, don't try to be a writer without reading.

Learn the rules of language so that you can write with confidence.

Be intentional about improving your writing. Identify your weaknesses and deficiencies. If there are gaps in your writing background, fill them. Learning the rules and conventions of language isn't rocket science, but it does require some effort, attention, and time. As a matter of practice, whenever you have a question about correct grammar, punctuation, or usage, don't guess. Look it up. As I suggest above, keep a style manual within reach when you write.

Learn the rules so that you can put them behind you. Learn the rules so that you will know when you must follow them and when you may break them.

Practice.

If you want to be a good pianist, you have to practice playing the piano. If you want to be a good writer, you have to practice writing.

Write frequently. Better yet, write frequently and write in a variety of styles and genres, from journal entries and informal letters to executive summaries and long reports.

Some fiction writers like to write poetry on the side to keep their ears sharp, just as some jazz musicians like to play classical music to work on their techniques. Whether you are a musician, a writer, or a surgeon, you'll perform with more precision if you stay in practice.

Study good writers and imitate their style.

Keep a file of writing samples that impressed you in some way. Go back to them from time to time and remind yourself of what you liked about them. Then try to create the same effects in your own writing.

I remember the time the critic and editor Malcolm Cowley visited our creative writing class at Vanderbilt. After entertaining us with stories about Fitzgerald, Wolfe, and Hemingway, he offered this advice: The next time you read something that you find compelling, a passage whose language seems extraordinarily well crafted, mark the passage, come back to it, and study it. Read it out loud. Copy or type it over word for word. Do whatever you can to get close to the language that moved you. In other words approximate as nearly as possible the author's experience in choosing those particular words, to see how they feel in sequence and in relationship with one another, and to experience how the sentence structures unfold. Then write something like it.

In this way, he told us, you discover a writer's secrets and you make them your own.

Years later, when reading Toni Morrison's *Beloved*, I came across a passage that sent chills down my spine. It began, "The stove didn't shudder as it adjusted to its heat." Before I realized what was happening, Seth's haunted house was trembling and pitching, a table came rushing across the floor, and Paul D had grabbed it by its leg and was bashing it about, "wrecking every-thing, screaming back at the screaming house."

I marvelled at Morrison's uncanny ability to glide effortlessly between the natural and the supernatural worlds. How did she do it? I wanted to know.

I took Cowley's advice and copied and studied the passage. I took it apart and wrote another passage like it. Although I will never write like Toni Morrison, I learned something from her about writing with conviction and about using sudden, unexpected movement as a narrative technique.

I hope you will do the same.

APPENDIX I

{A Glossary of Grammatical Terms}

active verb (or **active voice**) A verb form that indicates the subject is the *performer* of the action, as in "Everyone in our department read the book." In contrast, a **passive verb** indicates the subject is the *receiver* of the action, as in "The book was read by everyone in our department."

adjective A word that modifies a noun or a pronoun, as in "The book was *wonderful*" and "It was a *complex* problem."

adverb A word that modifies a verb, an adjective, another adverb, or a whole phrase, clause, or sentence, as in "I read the book *quickly*" and "It was a *very* complex problem."

article A type of adjective. *The* is the definite article. *A* and *an* are indefinite articles.

clause A group of words that has a subject and a verb. *See* **phrase, independent clause,** and **dependent clause**.

comma splice The incorrect joining of two complete sentences or main clauses with a comma alone, as in "I don't mean to insult you, however, I do want to make a suggestion."

conjunction A word that connects and shows the relation between words, phrases, and clauses, as in "A word that connects *and* shows the relation between words, phrases, *and* clauses." A **subordinating conjunction** (such as *when, while, if, although,* and *because*) introduces dependent clauses and connects them to main clauses, as in "*Although* you missed your plane, you can still make it in time for the opening of the conference."

dangling modifier A modifying phrase or clause that does not sensibly connect to any word in a sentence, as in "After reading your reports, it is recommended that you take a writing class." *See* **misplaced modifier**.

dependent clause (also called a **subordinate clause**) A clause that is not a sentence, does not stand alone, and must be joined to a main clause to form a grammatically complete sentence, as in "*Although I wrote an angry response,* I decided not to send it." *See* **independent clause** or **main clause**.

independent clause (also called a **main clause**) A grammatically complete sentence, one that contains a subject and a verb and that expresses a complete thought. *See* **dependent clause** or **subordinate clause**.

misplaced modifier A modifier positioned incorrectly in a sentence, as in "When well stewed, you add the tomatoes to the pot." *See* **dangling modifier**.

noun A word that names a person, place, thing, or idea. A **proper noun** names a particular person, place, or thing, as in "the *Lincoln Center*" and "the Department of Human Resources."

parallelism (or **parallel structure** or **parallel construction**; sentences with parallel construction are sometimes called **balanced sentences**). The principle that words, phrases, or clauses presented in a pair or in a series must be of the same kind or formation, as in "Our government is of the people, by the people, and for the people" and "Ask not what your country can do for you; ask what you can do for your country." An example of nonparallel structure is, "Our guidelines were found to be inaccurate, inconsistent, and not complete."

passive verb (or **passive voice**) The verb form that indicates the subject is the *receiver* of the action, as in "The book was read by everyone in our department." In contrast, an **active verb** indicates the subject is the *performer* of the action, as in "Everyone in our department read the book."

phrase A group of words that lacks a subject and a verb, as in "We found the report *in the top drawer*." *See* **clause**.

predicate The verb part of a sentence. It tells what the subject did or how it was acted upon, as in "He *stomped out of the meeting*" and "She *sought his advice*."

preposition A connecting word such as *in, on, of,* and *with*. **Prepositional phrases** are prepositions and their objects, as in "in the drawer," "on the floor," and "with malice."

pronoun A word that takes the place of a noun, as in "*She* wrote the proposal" and "*It* was excellent."

sentence fragment A dependent clause (one that does not stand alone) that is incorrectly punctuated as though it were a main clause (or a complete sentence), as in "Although I disagree."

verb A word that expresses action or a state of being, as in "She *questioned* the logic behind the proposal."

APPENDIX II

{Checklist: Keys to Great Writing}

The purpose of this appendix and Appendix III is to help you pull it together, to gather the various tips and techniques presented throughout this book so that you can see them at a glance, continue to work with them over time, and incorporate them into your writing.

I compiled these appendices with the thought that they would be useful to you both now and in the future. If you return to this book for a review six months—or six years—from now, or if you simply want the lessons to stay fresh in your mind as you continue to develop your writing skills, Appendix II and III are the sections to turn to.

{1. ECONOMY: Eliminating Patterns of Wordiness }
Make every word count.

- ☑ **Delete unnecessary modifiers** (rather than *true fact*, write *fact*; rather than *free gift*, write *gift*).
- ☑ **Eliminate redundant categories and word pairs** (rather than *pink in color*, write *pink*; rather than *first and foremost*, write *first*).
- ☑ **Replace wordy expressions with single words** (rather than *during the course of*, write *during*; rather than *until such time as*, write *until*).
- ☑ **Watch for wordiness in sentence beginnings and endings** (rather than *What I want to say next is*, write *Next*; rather than *Does it stink like rotten meat would smell to you?* write *Does it stink like rotten meat?*).
- ☑ **Take the most direct route** (rather than *The first point that needs to be made is*, write *First*; rather than *not significant*, write *insignificant*).

{2. PRECISION: Diction, Word Choice }
Use the right word.

- ☑ **Draw on a broad vocabulary** to use the most precise, appropriate words for your meaning and audience (often the simplest, not the fanciest, word).
- ☑ **Choose words for their sound, mood, and feeling** (their connotation) as well as their **literal meaning** (their denotation).
- ☑ **Use words that convey definite meaning** (rather than *We were affected*

by the news, write *We were relieved by the news* or *We were devastated by the news*).

☑ **Use words that appeal to the five senses** (rather than *The room smelled good,* write *The room smelled of freshly cut oranges;* rather than *My bicycle is dirty,* write *My bicycle is coated with red mud*).

☑ **Use natural language** as opposed to needlessly formal, fancy, or awkward language (rather than *As per our discussion,* write *As we discussed;* rather than *It is imperative that we commence in a timely fashion,* write *We need to start on time*).

{ 3. ACTION: Movement, Verbs }
Use action verbs to animate your writing.

☑ **Make your sentences tell stories** (rather than *An investigation was conducted concerning our accounting procedures,* write *The IRS investigated our accounting procedures;* rather than *There was a crash in the stock market,* write *The stock market crashed*).

☑ **Use verbs to animate your descriptions** (rather than *The tree was big,* write *The tree rose one hundred feet into the air;* rather than *The lawn was expansive,* write, as Fitzgerald did, *The lawn started at the beach and ran toward the front door for a quarter of a mile*).

☑ **Prefer the active voice over the passive voice** (rather than *The Frisbee was thrown to my son,* write *I threw the Frisbee to my son;* rather than *An attempt was made to determine the cause for the system failure,* write *We tried to determine why the system failed*).

☑ **Prefer action verbs over nominalizations** (rather than *make a recommendation,* write *recommend;* rather than *take under consideration,* write *consider*).

☑ **Avoid noun stacks** (rather than *an acquisition candidate identification process,* write *a process for identifying candidates for acquisition;* rather than *quality control improvement recommendations,* write *recommendations for improving quality control*).

{ 4. MUSIC: Variety in Sentence Length, Structure, Rhythm, and Type }

Listen to the sound of your language.

☑ **Use punctuation** to create pauses and emphasis:

—**Use colons** to create pauses and anticipation.

—**Use semicolons** to suggest a close relationship between two statements.

—**Use dashes** to create abrupt pauses and emphasis.

☑ **Vary your sentence structure** to create emphasis and energy.

☑ **Use subordinate elements** to indicate relationships, control emphasis, and create variety.

☑ **Place important words at sentence endings** for closing emphasis.

☑ **Use elliptical constructions** for economy and cadence.

☑ **Use sentence inversions** (anastrophe) for variety and emphasis.

☑ **Use repetition** for emphasis and rhythm:

—**Repeat words in sentence beginnings.**

—**Create a succession of short sentences.**

☑ **Place a short, punchy sentence after a longer, more complex sentence** for variety and emphasis.

☑ **Use sentence fragments** for a conversational style and for emphasis.

☑ **Use rhetorical sentence types for effect:**

—**Use loose sentences** (those in which subordinate elements follow the main clause) for a relaxed structure.

—**Use periodic sentences** (those in which subordinate elements precede the main clause) for emphasis, expectancy, and flourish.

—**Use balanced sentences** (those that contain parallel elements—also called **coordinated** and **parallel sentences**) for emphasis and rhythm.

—**Use antithetical sentences** (those with contrasting elements, often in parallel structure) for emphasis and contrast.

{ 5. PERSONALITY: Liveliness, Unpredictability, Humor, Sincerity }

Write with creativity and imagination.

☑ **Use figurative (or nonliteral) language** to appeal to your reader's creativity and imagination.

☑ **Use comparisons and analogies** to clarify or reinforce your meaning.

☑ **Use metaphors** to point out similarity between dissimilar things.

☑ **Use similes** (comparisons using *like* or *as*) for intentional effect (*He works like a horse*); **use metaphors** (comparisons not using *like* or *as*) for insistent, surprising effect (*He is a horse*).

☑ **Make unlikely comparisons** to surprise your reader and convey your originality.

☑ **Evaluate your similes and metaphors** on the basis of their aptness, novelty, and simplicity.

☑ **Use personification** to add life to your writing.

☑ **Be playful** or use a lighthearted tone to appeal to your reader's sense of humor and intelligence.

—**Use wit** (from the Old English *witan*, "to know") to create a comic twist or surprise, as Peter De Vries did when he said, "I love being a writer. What I can't stand is the paperwork."

—**Use puns** (plays on words) advisedly—not everyone appreciates them.

—**Use situational irony** to convey the disparity between perception and reality.

—**Use verbal irony** (Socratic irony)—which often involves saying the opposite of what you mean—to convey the disparity between literal and implied meaning.

—**Use understatement** (meiosis) for a more subtle style of humor.

—**Use overstatement** (exaggeration or hyperbole) for a more outlandish style of humor.

—**Use self-deprecating humor** to poke fun at yourself.

☑ **Use language that reflects your personality and values.**

APPENDIX III

{Checklist: Elements of Composition}

{1. PURPOSE: Central Idea, Thesis}

State your purpose clearly.

☑ **Choose a subject you care about.**

☑ **Provide sufficient background and context to make your subject understandable.**

☑ **Connect subordinate ideas or secondary arguments to your main purpose or central idea.**

☑ **Select a mode of discourse that suits your purpose and audience:**

—Use **description** to provide information about a person, setting, scene, or object.

—Use **narration** (including anecdote) to tell a story.

—Use **exposition** to inform your reader.

—Use **persuasion** to induce your reader to think, act, or feel a certain way.

☑ **Analyze your audience, using four questions from Munter:**

—**Who** are they?

—What do they **know**?

—What do they **feel**?

—How can you **motivate** them?

{2. POINT OF VIEW: Tone, Attitude, and Humor}

Establish your relationship with your material and your reader.

☑ **Maintain a consistent point of view.**

☑ **Maintain a consistent level of formality.**

☑ **Use a personal tone in most correspondence.**

☑ **In narrative writing:**

—Use a **limited** point of view to create **intrigue**.

—Use a **subjective** point of view to heighten **drama**.

—Use a **limited** point of view to create **humor and irony**.

—Use **contrasting** points of view to add **interest**.

—Use a **persona** for effect.

☑️ **For persuasive writing:**
—Adopt a **reasonable tone**.
—Know when to **hedge** and when to **insist**.
—Use the **you viewpoint** to involve your reader.
—Use **anecdotes** to create **sympathy for your perspective**.
☑️ **Use disparity to create humor and irony.**

{ 3. ORGANIZATION: Arrangement }

Plan and organize your material.
☑️ **Use an outline to help you think and plan.**
☑️ **Use the three-part paragraph to help you organize your thoughts.**
☑️ **For persuasive writing:**
—Take a **direct approach** when writing to a **sympathetic audience**.
—Take an **indirect approach** when writing to an **unsympathetic or hostile audience**.
—Take an **indirect approach** when delivering **bad news**.
—Adapt the standard **five-part argument** to your purpose and audience.
—**Acknowledge the opposition** to strengthen your argument.
—**Recognize your reader** and offer to take the **next step** in correspondence.
☑️ **Pay particular attention to introductions and conclusions.**
☑️ **Make the first and last sentences the strongest parts of your paragraph.**
☑️ **Use your lead to engage your reader.**
☑️ **Conclude conclusively.**

{ 4. SUPPORT: Selection of Detail }

Support your assertions.
☑️ **Offer specific, relevant details.**
☑️ **Offer enough—but not too much—detail.**
☑️ **Appeal to the senses with concrete, colorful detail.**
☑️ **Appeal to logic with facts and statistics.**
☑️ **Use anecdotes to make your point.**

☑ **Use analogy and metaphor to explain your thinking.**

☑ **Quote others to enhance your credibility.**

☑ **Document your sources.**

☑ **For persuasive writing:**

—Use a **combination of rhetorical appeals**.

—Avoid **common fallacies** in persuasive writing.

—Follow standard **rules of evidence**.

{ 5. COHERENCE: Connections, Flow }

Connect your thoughts.

☑ **Use an organizational statement to tell your reader where you're going.**

☑ **Use transitional words and phrases.**

☑ **Repeat key words and phrases.**

☑ **Use parallel structure to bind with rhythm.**

☑ **Maintain a consistent string of topics.**

☑ **For continuity from one sentence to another:**

—**Start** with **new information**.

—**End** with **old information**.

—**End** with what you intend to **develop next**.

—Use "**it-shifts**" and **inversions** to move new information **to the right**.

—Use the **passive voice** to move old information **to the left**.

☑ **For continuity within sentences:**

—Keep **adjective phrases together**.

—Help your reader **keep track of subjects and verbs**.

—**Avoid unnecessary shifts** in subject, modified subject, person, voice, and tense.

—Arrange your material according to **natural progressions**.

APPENDIX IV
{Checklist for Proofreading}

Because it is difficult to check for different types of errors in a single reading, make four passes through your text. Each time through, look for a different type of error, progressing from the general to the particular.

Begin not by reading your text but by looking it over. Make sure you haven't omitted anything or accidentally repeated something. Check for other common word-processing errors (copy/cut miscues, sequence errors, editing scraps, template tipoffs, page-numbering peccadillos, and hidden headers).

In your second pass, read for content (clarity, coherence, organization, and logical development). In your third pass, check for word choice and tone. In your fourth pass, check for correctness (rules of grammar, punctuation, and usage).

{Proofreading Checklist}
First Check: Does it look right?

☑ Text is appropriately highlighted (bullets, paragraphing, boldface, underlining, etc.) to engage reader and reinforce main points.

☑ Common word-processing errors (copy/cut miscues, sequence errors, editing scraps, template tipoffs, page-numbering peccadillos, and hidden headers) have been eliminated.

Second Check: Is it effective and complete?

☑ Central idea or purpose is clearly stated and developed.

☑ Main points are limited in number and receive appropriate emphasis.

☑ All subordinate ideas are clearly related to the central idea.

☑ Material is arranged in a logical and coherent sequence.

☑ Reader is given the information needed to take the desired action.

Third Check: Does it sound right?

☑ Word choice is clear, specific, accurate, unassuming, and free of clichés and misused jargon.

☑ Sentences are free of wordiness, ambiguity, and unnecessarily involved constructions.

☑ Tone is appropriate to the audience.

Fourth Check: Is it correct?

☑ Spelling, including technical terms and proper names, is correct.

☑ Correct words are used to convey the intended meaning.

☑ Generally accepted rules of grammar and syntax are followed, including parallel construction, subject/verb agreement, pronoun/noun agreement, appropriate verb tense, pronoun case, possessive forms, etc.

☑ Punctuation, particularly placement of commas and apostrophes, reflects standard usage.

APPENDIX V

{Recommended Resources and Reading}

Works Cited

Abrams, M. H. *A Glossary of Literary Terms.* 7th ed. Harcourt Brace College Publishers, 1999.

Biddle, Arthur. *Writer to Writer.* McGraw-Hill, 1985.

Bliss, Edwin. *Getting Things Done: The ABC's of Time Management.* Scribner's, 1976; updated and reissued 1991.

Britton, James, et al. *The Development of Writing Abilities.* Macmillan Education, 1975.

Bryson, Bill. *The Mother Tongue: English and How It Got That Way.* W. Morrow, 1990.

Corbett, Edward, and Robert Connors. *Style and Statement.* Oxford University Press, 1998.

Elbow, Peter. *Writing Without Teachers.* 2nd ed. Oxford University Press, 1998.

Flachmann, Kim, and Michael Flachmann. *The Prose Reader: Essays for Thinking, Reading, and Writing.* 5th ed. Prentice-Hall, 1998.

Goldberg, Natalie. *Writing Down the Bones: Freeing the Writer Within.* Shambhala, 1998.

Hacker, Diana. *A Writer's Reference.* 4th ed. Bedford Books of St. Martin's Press, 1999.

Hall, Donald, and Sven Birkerts. *Writing Well.* 9th ed. Addison Wesley Longman, Inc., 1997.

Kinneavy, James. *A Theory of Discourse: The Aims of Discourse.* Norton, 1980.

Lamott, Anne. *Bird by Bird: Some Instructions on Writing and Life.* Pantheon Books, 1994.

Lewis, Herschell Gordon. *How to Write Powerful Fund Raising Letters.* Pluribus Press, 1989.

Mellinkoff, David. *Mellinkoff's Dictionary of American Legal Usage.* West Publishing Company, 1992.

Miller, Casey, and Kate Swift. *The Handbook of Nonsexist Writing for Writers, Editors, and Speakers.* 2nd ed. Harper and Row, 1992.

Minot, Stephen. *Three Genres: The Writing of Poetry, Fiction, and Drama*. 4th ed. Prentice-Hall, 1988.

Munter, Mary. *Guide to Managerial Communication: Effective Business Writing and Speaking*. 5th ed. Prentice-Hall, 1999.

O'Conner, Patricia. *Woe Is I: The Grammarphobe's Guide to Better English in Plain English*. Grosset/Putman, 1996.

Orwell, George. "Politics and the English Language," *A Collection of Essays*. Harcourt Brace Jovanovich, 1946.

Stilman, Anne. *Grammatically Correct: The Writer's Essential Guide to Punctuation, Spelling, Style, Usage, and Grammar*. Writer's Digest Books, 1997.

Strunk, Jr., William, and E. B. White. *The Elements of Style*. 4th ed. (with index). Allyn and Bacon, 1999.

Sweetnam, Sherry. *The Executive Memo: A Guide to Persuasive Business Communications*. John Wiley & Sons, 1992.

Troyka, Lynn Quitman. *Simon and Schuster Handbook for Writers*. 5th ed. Prentice-Hall, 1998.

VanAlstyne, Judith. *Professional and Technical Writing Strategies*. 4th ed. Prentice-Hall, 1998.

Vonnegut, Jr., Kurt. *Palm Sunday: An Autobiographical Collage*. Delacorte Press/Seymour Lawrence, 1981.

Westheimer, Patricia, with Jacqueline Senteney. *The Executive Style Book*. Scott, Foresman, 1988.

Williams, Joseph. *Style: Ten Lessons in Clarity and Grace*. 6th ed. Addison Wesley Longman, Inc., 1999.

Wydick, Richard. *Plain English for Lawyers*. 4th ed. Carolina Academic Press, 1998.

Zinsser, William. *On Writing Well: An Informal Guide to Writing Nonfiction*. 6th ed. Harper & Row, 1998.

———. *Writing to Learn: How to Write and Think Clearly About Any Subject at All*. Harper & Row, 1989.

———. *Writing With a Word Processor*. Harper & Row, 1983.

Reference Manuals, Style Guides, and Dictionaries

The American Heritage Dictionary of the English Language. 3rd ed. Houghton Mifflin, 1992.

The Associated Press Stylebook and Libel Manual. Norm Goldstein, ed. 6th ed. Addison-Wesley, 1996.

The Chicago Manual of Style: The Essential Guide for Authors, Editors, and Publishers. 14th ed. The University of Chicago Press, 1993.

Gibaldi, Joseph. *MLA Handbook for Writers of Research Papers.* 5th ed. Modern Language Association of America, 1999.

Hacker, Diana. *A Writer's Reference.* 4th ed. Bedford Books of St. Martin's Press, 1999.

Merriam-Webster's Collegiate Dictionary. 10th ed. Merriam-Webster, 1996.

Publication Manual of the American Psychological Association. 4th ed. American Psychological Association, 1994.

Sabin, William. *The Gregg Reference Manual.* 9th ed. Glencoe/Macmillan McGraw Hill, 2000.

{ Index }